Sexual Politics

For Caroline Gonda and Alison Hennegan
Jamie Kinniburgh
Steve Mathewson
and Grahame Miller

Sexual Politics

An Introduction

Richard Dunphy

Edinburgh University Press

© Richard Dunphy, 2000

Edinburgh University Press Ltd
22 George Square, Edinburgh

Typeset in 10 on 12½ Stone Serif
by Hewer Text Ltd, Edinburgh, and
printed and bound in Great Britain by
MPG Books Ltd, Bodmin

A CIP record for this book is
available from the British Library

ISBN 0 7486 1247 5 (paperback)✔

Contents

Contents

Preface

This book has its origins in an Honours undergraduate course, *Gender, Power and Sexuality*, which I teach at Dundee University. Over the years of teaching this course, and talking to the several hundred students who have taken it since its inception in 1991, I have been struck by the fact that most books on the subject of gender and sexuality tend to fall within one of three discrete areas: feminist theory, critical studies of masculinity (mostly from the viewpoint of heterosexual masculinity), and lesbian and gay studies. Despite obvious convergences and over-laps, as well as divergences on occasion, between these discrete litera-tures, it is rare that approaches and insights from all three are drawn upon in a single text. I have tried to integrate these fields of study in this book and to span the division between theory and practice, focusing specifically on contemporary sexual politics in the UK.

The book is divided into three sections. Part I attempts to lay some theoretical and historical foundations. Differing theoretical approaches to the study of gender and sexuality are explored through a discussion of debates between various schools of social constructionism and sociobiology or biological determinism. The theoretical importance of the work of Michel Foucault is examined, as well as criticisms of the limitations of his work which have been offered by feminists and others. And the impact and limitations of queer theory are explored, suggesting that there are important lacunae in queer theory (and other forms of postmodernist theory) which undermine its usefulness as a theoretical tool. There is also comment on debates over the meaning of some key terms which are used throughout the book – sex, sexuality, gender, power.

Part II comments on the complexity of sexuality and of sexual identities (and of identity politics in general). Recent research work on the emergence of modern sexualities is analysed. A further chapter introduces the study of gender, analyses ideologies of gender, and then explores how these ideologies of masculinity and femininity affect both intimate behaviour and social relations through two case studies.

One of these studies is drawn from an aspect of the so-called public sphere (paid work) and the other from the so-called private sphere (emotion work). Finally, there is an analysis of how ideologies of gender are reproduced and gender boundaries policed.

Part III provides an overview of some contemporary debates within sexual politics – between feminists and postfeminists, within lesbian, gay, bisexual and queer politics, and within so-called men's politics. This exploration of debates and issues within contemporary sexual politics continues by focusing on the commercialisation and commodification of sex – discussing the power of advertising and the media, and considering the political, social and cultural issues raised by prostitution and pornography. Finally, the discussion is expanded to include an examination of the role of the state in maintaining patriarchal and heterosexist power relations in the UK. This is done through a number of case studies – of state promotion of heterosexual privilege and of the ideology of the patriarchal family under the Conservative administrations of the 1980s and 1990s, considering whether there have been significant changes to family policy since the election of a Labour government in 1997, and of the inadequacies of state responses to sexual violence.

In writing this book, I owe a debt of gratitude to a number of people. Nicola Carr of Edinburgh University Press first suggested to me that I ought to consider writing a book on sexual politics in Spring 1998. She has since been wonderfully supportive and encouraging. Susan Malloch, secretary of the Department of Politics at Dundee University, gave invaluable back-up assistance and raised my spirits on more than one occasion. Above all, I am indebted to the five close friends to whom this book is dedicated and who have helped to shape my views on sexual politics. Caroline Gonda and Alison Hennegan lavished hospitality on me in Cambridge and shared their thoughts on queer theory with me over cups of peppermint tea and the music of Louis Gottschalk. Jamie Kinniburgh took my undergraduate course at Dundee, *Gender, Power and Sexuality*, and went on to become a trusted friend and my essential guide on visits to London. Steve Mathewson has taught me the truth of Oscar Wilde's maxim, 'true friendship is worse than love, it lasts longer'. Grahame Miller corrected my grammar, raised my motivation and reaffirmed my faith in the strength of friendship between men.

Richard Dunphy
Dundee
February 2000

Part I

Foundations

Chapter 1

Theoretical and historical foundations

Introduction

The habit of thinking in terms of opposing categories – of dualities, or binaries – has become central to Western cultures. For example, we tend to think and speak in terms of dualities between black and white, weak and strong, healthy and sick, normal and abnormal (or pathological), right and wrong. We inhabit a culture which seems to revolve around fixed categories, opposites, and which seems much less comfortable with ambiguity, change, blurs, transmogrifications. It is arguably a culture which is more comfortable with certainty than with uncertainty – even if, or when, certainties are shown to be false.

Ever since modern science has sought to control and regulate gender behaviour and sexual behaviour, sexual dualities have been used to label and categorise people.

On the issue of gender and sexual binaries, a great deal of cultural, political and emotional effort and energy has been vested in constructing, reproducing and sustaining certain opposing categories. This has happened despite the huge changes which have taken place in Western societies over the past few centuries, and which have transformed the context and meanings of such categories. For example, much effort has been vested in articulating and reproducing alleged differences between men and women. Different strengths, weaknesses, thought patterns, emotions, modes of social and personal behaviour, dress codes, tastes, aptitude for social, political and occupational roles and so on, have been attributed to the opposing categories of 'man' and 'woman'. Ever since the European Enlightenment, this tendency to view 'men' and 'women' as opposites has intensified. We have become accustomed to speaking in terms of 'the opposite sex'. Very often reason and rationality have been attributed to men, and emotions and feeling to women, invoking these myths in an effort to exclude women from positions of political and social leadership – or even having the right to vote – and to exclude men from the responsibilities and joys of child-rearing and nurturing. In our culture, the categories of masculinity and femininity exercise a powerful hold even on those who regard them as problematic and unsatisfactory. We can truthfully speak of ideologies of masculinity and femininity as amongst the most dominant or pervasive ideologies in our society.

Likewise, at least since the late nineteenth century when the primary role in categorising sexual behaviour and naming what is 'normal' and what is 'perverse' passed, in most industrial societies, from the religious to the medical and scientific professions, we have lived with the notion of distinct categories of people labelled 'homosexual' and 'heterosexual'. (The category 'homosexual' was coined by the Viennese writer Karol Benkert in 1869, 'heterosexual' emerging somewhat later.) Since that time, new discourses have tried to establish the male 'homosexual' as a distinct type of person – as opposed to same-sex attraction or same-sex acts being seen as a potential in everyone. As Peter Tatchell (1996: 37) puts it, 'prior to that time . . . there were only homosexual acts, not homosexual people . . . [For] the medieval Catholic Church . . . homosexuality was not . . . the special sin of a unique class of people but a dangerous temptation to which any mortal might succumb. This doctrine implicitly conceded the attractiveness of same-sex desire, and unwittingly acknowledged its pervasive, universal potential'.

With the invention of the modern male homosexual as a specific category of person, he is endowed by the controllers of the emerging new discourses on sexuality – doctors, scientists, politicians, judges and moralists – with distinct thought patterns, physical and mental characteristics, ways of walking, talking and dressing, moral weaknesses, and modes of social and personal behaviour. All of which are held to mark his difference, to set him apart from and to define his nature in opposition to the 'normal', 'healthy' man. It is some time before the word heterosexual is even adopted, and it never gains such wide dissemination as the category 'homosexual'. Heterosexuality remains one half of an opposition which defines itself largely (when it feels the need to define itself at all) by the difference it attributes to homosexuality; just as masculinity is defined largely (in so far as it feels the need to define itself at all) by reference to what it is not – effeminate, the feminine Other, the Second Sex.

It was some time later before the existence of lesbian desire could even be admitted, and the category of the lesbian as a distinct type of person constructed. This was not, as the story goes, because Queen Victoria did not wish to believe that lesbianism could possibly occur. It is related to the long denial of the sexual desire of women in general, and the construction of female sexuality as passive, dependent upon the male, 'kissed into life' or existence only by the male. A dominant discourse on human sexuality which denied that 'normal' women were capable of strong sexual desires at all, branded sexually confident women as 'hysterical', and condemned millions of women – right up to the 1970s and 1980s – to the futile and self-destructive search for the 'vaginal orgasm' (dismissing clitoral pleasure as infantile) would always have great difficulty in conceding the possibility of lesbian desire. Whilst the male homosexual, from his invention in the late nineteenth century, became someone on to whom all society's anxieties and hang-ups about sexual behaviour and gender demarcation would be projected, the lesbian remained for many decades a shadow. And even today, when confident and self-affirmative lesbian identities have emerged and are available to women, images of 'lesbianism' are still regularly appropriated by a male heterosexual pornographic imagination which cannot accept that this is one party to which men are not invited and at which their presence is not necessary.

Once we start to theorise about sexual difference we begin to understand why sexuality and gender are such a fought-over political battleground. Sexuality and gender have become part of the agenda of the Right in particular, in Europe and North America in recent decades, as seldom if ever before. The Left, for all its espousal of equality and change and sympathy in many (but by no means all) cases with the demands of the feminist and lesbian and gay movements, has been much slower to appreciate the importance of sexual politics.

The past two decades have seen fierce battles – still continuing – over, for example: gender equality in the workplace; family policy – including the question of whether single parents and non-heterosexual couples, should receive state recognition as families; the 'crisis of marriage'; divorce; abortion, contraception and reproductive rights; gay and lesbian sexuality; bisexuality; children's sexuality; rape and sexual abuse; privacy; domestic and sexualised violence; sex education; pornography and censorship; issues of sexual consent; AIDS and issues of sexual health, sexual morality, and rights – including the right to live and die without stigma; even dress and hair length. Through it all, the state and its institutions – police, judiciary, education system, legislature, executive and in some countries the state or established church – have intervened actively, seeking to define the limits of what David Evans (1993) calls 'sexual citizenship'. Gender and sexuality appear everywhere. The issues fought over appear sometimes as a metaphor for the wider moral decay of society and sometimes as wider hopes and aspirations of humanity for a better society, depending on where you stand politically. Here is the spectre of sexual anarchy versus the utopia of sexual democracy.

At the core of all of this has been an ongoing battle over difference.

Are we fundamentally different (men, women, gay, straight, bisexual, queer) at all? If fundamental differences do exist, are they rooted in 'nature' or in social conditioning? Or in a combination of both? If the latter is the case, then how do biology and social conditioning interact? How mutable are our differences?

In the 1990s, so-called queer theory (for a discussion of which, see below) helped accentuate debate within both feminism (see Chapter 3) and lesbian and gay studies as to just how different people are. Do our similarities and our aspirations towards a universal humanness – beyond male, female, gay, straight – of which we are all as yet incomplete manifestations (but with the potential to develop), outweigh our differences and call into question our whole way of viewing reality through the categories of difference? Are there certain fundamental biological and genetic differences between men and women, and gay and straight, which explain most differences in gender and sexual behaviour and which undermine equal rights agendas or attempts to move society in the direction of greater sexual democracy? Or is it possible to distinguish between biological categories and socially constructed meanings and significances which have been placed upon those categories but do not stem logically and inevitably from them; and thus to mobilise against gendered and sexualised oppression by seeking change?

Social constructionism versus biology

This battle is being fought out against the background of the old clash between biology and society, 'nature' versus 'nurture'. On the one hand are the schools of thought variously referred to as biological determinism, or biological theories about gender and sexuality or sociobiological theories of difference; on the other hand, various forms of what is usually known as social constructionism. The former tend to emphasise the allegedly natural basis – that is, basis in nature – of gender and sexual divisions, although they differ profoundly in their emphasis and political project. The latter argue for the primary, or sometimes exclusive, role of upbringing, social conditioning, social relations of power, or personal choice. They differ profoundly in emphasis, degree and political intent. Of course, many positions acknowledge both the biological and social aspects of gender and sexual differences.

Biological determinism, at its most extreme, would have us believe that masculinity and femininity are fixed for all time, rooted in nature, the object of dispassionate scientific enquiry. A similar approach may be adopted towards sexual desire, where a particular type of heterosexual behaviour – predatory or dominant sexual behaviour on the part of men directed towards women, and passive or receptive behaviour on the part of women directed towards men – is deemed natural. Patterns of heterosexual behaviour which do not conform to the dominant man/passive woman dichotomy may well be branded pathological. There has certainly been a long tradition of so describing homosexual desire. For example, the penal codes of many countries in the contemporary world – from Kenya to India to Afghanistan – still brand any same-sex relationship as 'carnal knowledge contrary to the laws of nature' and impose penalties ranging from a fine in India to fifteen years imprisonment and flogging in Kenya to death by stoning or beheading in Afghanistan. (All three countries cited are former British colonies and the concept of 'carnal knowledge contrary to the laws of nature' is part of the colonial legacy.)

From an extreme position of biological determinism, two logical conclusions would seem to flow: that attempts to alter allegedly natural behaviour – such as violence or aggression in men, or passivity in women – are at best doomed to fail and are at worst an interference with the natural order of things; and that those who deviate from what is deemed natural 'masculine' or 'feminine' behaviour are acting contrary to nature.

This attempt which biological determinists have made to identify an unchanging male and female essence, rooted in 'nature', means that such theories might also be referred to as a form of essentialism. (However, while biological determinists might be thought of as essentialists, not all essentialists base their arguments on science; some base their arguments on religious dogmas.)

At its most extreme, biological determinism clearly exhibits a marked conservative bias. There is little room for advocacy of social engineering or progressive social change within a paradigm which sees human sexuality and gender behaviour as determined by the adaptationist requirements of human biological evolution. Biological theories of gender and sexuality have been used to justify resistance to progressive social policies in all sorts of ways – including many which have been largely discredited. These include, for example:

- the notion that women are simply unfit for certain types of work – or for any work outside the home and the notion that men's 'natural' strength and aggression accounts for wage differentials. For example, the conservative US writer George Gilder, a leading advocate of the policies of the Reagan administration, once famously declared that 'the difference between the sexes fully accounts for all gaps in earnings' (quoted in Fausto-Sterling 1992: 6);
- the idea that, as Charles Darwin put it, men are at a higher stage of

evolution than women, possessing greater intellectual and rational abilities – and are thus born leaders, and the claim that male violence is a natural and healthy expression of masculinity;

- the belief that childbirth is a relatively painless procedure, as was sometimes claimed by male scientists well into this century (either because women were said to have a higher capacity for pain endurance than men, or because they have the 'maternal instinct' to outweigh any residual pain); or the alternative belief that labour pains are actually 'beneficial' in that they protect a woman's 'modesty' by ensuring that she derives no sexual pleasure from the process of childbirth. Poovey (1987: 143) quotes a 1847 lecture by W. Tyler Smith, a founder of the Obstetrical Society, in which he opposed interventions to ease the pain of childbirth and asked rhetorically, 'may it not be, that in woman the physical pain neutralizes the sexual emotions, which would otherwise probably be present, but which would tend very much to alter our estimation of the modesty and retiredness proper to the sex, and which are never more prominent or more admirable than on these occasions?';

- and, perhaps most famously of all, the dogma, derived from Sigmund Freud, that 'clitoral orgasm cannot be the natural way of a mature female'. As Stephen Jay Gould puts it, this 'shibboleth of pop culture during the heady days of pervasive Freudianism' caused untold frustration and misery to millions of women who were told by a brigade of psychoanalysts and by hundreds of articles in magazines and 'marriage manuals' that they must make this biologically impossible transition [from clitoral to vaginal orgasm] as a definition of maturity. (Gould 1995: 52–3)

A biologically driven essentialism also influences the work of the English conservative philosopher Roger Scruton. In his book, *Sexual Desire* (1987), he formulates the argument that female passivity and domesticity work in the context of the monogamous heterosexual relationship (marriage) to tame and control a natural male sexual instinct which might otherwise lead men to destroy society by copulating with everyone in sight. From this premise, Scruton seems to believe that he has derived a justification for discrimination against homosexuals – seen as the embodiment of untamed male sexual promiscuity and thus subversive of civilisation. Lesbians tend to be overlooked.

Not all biological or socio-biological theorists subscribe to such extreme positions. Many recognise that the balance between the respective influences of nature and nurture on gender and sexual behaviour is neither settled nor perhaps capable of being settled. Many would agree with Michael Gazzaniga who argues that natural selection affects human behaviour in a vast and complex array of ways, but concedes that the influence of culture upon sexual behaviour – at least in what he terms its 'extreme forms' – is a view 'well founded and one for which there is abundant support' (Gazzaniga 1992: 151). Other biologists or socio-biologists, including Anne Fausto-Sterling and Stephen Jay Gould, have taken the lead in demolishing the pretensions of biological determinism or essentialism and in arguing for the importance of environment, culture and human choice.

Neither can all biological theorists be accused of being conservative reactionaries, sexists and homophobes, deploying science in the cause of defending traditional power relations (although some of them are certainly open to such charges). The gay scientist Simon Le Vay (1993) claims to have found evidence in the section of the brain known as the hypothalamus which may provide a clue as to why some people are attracted to their own sex and others to the other sex. (Note the 'either/ or' approach to sexual attraction implicit in looking at the issue in this way; bisexuality tends to be ignored.) Other scientists attempting to discover a biological explanation for homosexuality have also argued that if they can establish homosexuality as just another natural variant of human behaviour – like left-handedness – then they will undermine anti-gay prejudice. They can scarcely be accused, then, of being motivated by sexism or homophobia. Le Vay would agree with the claim made by another scientist working on the search for a so-called gay gene, Dean Hamer (1995: 218) that 'biology is neutral'. Yet it is precisely such a claim that is likely to be scrutinised critically by social scientists, as we will see. Nor is it the case that all social constructionists would deny the existence of biological limits altogether. The picture is much more complex.

Deborah Rhode (1990: 1–9) points out that reactions to this debate from within feminisms – and one might add from within lesbian and gay studies – have been diverse, but fall into broadly three groups.

First, there are those who accept the existence of fundamental difference, rooted in biology, and even celebrate it or attempt to harness it to a feminist or a gay or lesbian agenda; for example, by extolling allegedly female virtues – peace, love, nurturing – over allegedly male attributes – aggression, war-mongering, planet-destroying. (Such efforts also find echoes in parts of 'New Age' culture, such as the 'mother earth' or 'earth goddess' themes of neo-Paganism.) Some writers have even sought to turn Darwin on his head by arguing for the natural superiority of women over men – as did the feminist Darwinian Eliza Gamble, writing in the late nineteenth century (quoted in Fausto-Sterling 1992: 4); or by extolling – as some gay writers have – the allegedly natural superiority of gay men in terms of greater sensitivity, greater artistic creativity, and more advanced emotional development over heterosexual men. Or again, as Le Vay has attempted to do, by countering homophobia with an attempt to establish that homosexuality is rooted in biology. (A profoundly naive endeavour, it may be argued: since when has the discovery of genes or chromosomes shaken the foundations of racism or sexism?)

The majority of feminist writers dismiss biological determinism and regard 'mother earth' or 'earth goddess' themes as politically naive. It is also the case, as Stevi Jackson (1996a) has argued, that the revival of biological arguments to explain sexual difference within some gay male political discourses has caused renewed tensions between feminism and such gay theorists.

Most feminist writers would belong to the second group identified by Rhode, those who deny the extent or the essential nature of gender and sexual difference and emphasise the cultural construction of difference. They focus on how physiological differences between men and women and differences in the life span are related to differences in diet, occupation, roles in the sexual division of labour, and so on. Or they emphasise the cultural reproduction of ideologies of mothering and maternity and the ways in which men until very recently have been shut out of the emotional world of child-rearing, and they deny the existence of an essential difference between the 'maternal' and 'paternal' instincts. The argument here is that men are potentially just as caring and nurturing as women but the social and cultural construction of masculinity in our society has until recently (and may still) forced many men to hide in shame or embarrassment feelings which might be branded 'weak'.

Again, from a gay and/or lesbian perspective, some take the view that there is no essential difference between those attracted to their own sex or gender, and those attracted to the other, or those attracted to both. They see that the potential for homosexual and heterosexual attraction is present in everyone but that cultural and social factors condition what is expressed and what repressed.

A third broad group regards attempts to oppose social and cultural factors to biological factors in this stark way as misconstrued and doomed to failure. Whilst in general leaning towards a social constructionist view of gender and sexuality, not least in the attention paid to the meanings and significances attached to gender, gender relations and sexual definitions in our society, these writers prefer to emphasise two things: (1) that the centrality given to difference, also within the debates over gender and sexuality in which feminists are engaged, is mistaken and diverts attention from how much we all have in common

biologically as well as emotionally, intellectually, morally, and politically; and (2) that we should, as Anne Fausto-Sterling says:

> reject the search for unique 'root causes', arguing instead for a
> complex analysis in which an individual's capacities emerge from
> a web of interactions between the biological being and the social
> environment. Within this web, connecting threads move in both
> directions. Biology may in some manner condition behaviour, but
> behaviour in turn can alter one's physiology. Furthermore any
> particular behaviour can have many different causes. (Fausto-Ster-
> ling 1992: 7–8)

The distinction between those who believe in cultural or social
determinism and those who believe in 'a web of interactions between
the biological being and the social environment' has been summarised
by Carole Vance (1992) as follows: social determinists tend to deny that
there is any such thing as a natural sex drive or lust or undifferentiated
sexual impulse which resides in the body due to physiology. The sexual
impulse itself is constructed by history and culture. Moreover, the
direction of desire – for example homo- or hetero- sexuality – is seen
as neither intrinsic nor inherent but constructed by social forces. Most
recently, such a perspective has informed much of what has become
known as 'queer theory'.

On the other hand, what Vance calls 'middle-ground' social constructionists – approximating to what Fausto-Sterling has in mind
when she talks of interactions between biology and social environment
– accept an inherent sexual impulse and argue that we should concern
ourselves with how that impulse is constructed in terms of sexual acts,
identity, community, choice, morality, ideology. In other words, we
focus upon meanings, significances and metaphors and what these tell
us about power relations and power structures in our society. This
approach is consistent with what Jeffrey Weeks (1995) has called the
historical approach to sexuality, and this introduction to sexual politics
will adopt such an approach. It does not mean that we have to close our
minds dogmatically to the possibilities that the natural sciences may
yet reveal important new insights into human sexual differentiation. It
does focus our critical faculties on both the social and political processes that influence the types of research which are carried out and
publicised, and what society chooses to make of the results of that
research, and on the speculative and biased nature of what often passes
for research within the natural (as, indeed, within the social) sciences.

It seems somewhat diversionary to consider questions which, even if
we will be able to answer them some day, do not furnish us with any

greater understanding of why society is organised in the ways that it is. Knowing what causes differentiation in human skin pigmentation, fascinating though that is, does not furnish a satisfactory explanation for the phenomenon of racism. Similarly, the biological explanation for why one person is right-handed whilst another is left-handed, is of less interest than why, even recently, being left-handed was considered such a stigma that one friend was forced by both parents and teachers to write with his right hand – which he still claims caused him great childhood trauma and damaged his education. It is also interesting to understand why the Christian church taught for centuries that writing with the left hand was a sign of demonic possession, and why forced exorcisms upon left-handed people were still performed in Mediterranean Catholic countries into the twentieth century.

Do we need to know what 'causes' homosexuality or heterosexuality? It seems more important to know what causes such intense and neurotic homophobia as we have witnessed over the past century, and what that tells us about our society. If we ever establish that there is any genetic factor which might partially explain a greater disposition towards one expression of sexual desire rather than another in some people – and we are very far from this – then the important questions about what we do with such a discovery will be moral, political, and ideological. Would the discovery of a genetic basis to sexual attraction finally undermine discrimination against non-heterosexual people by establishing that variations of sexual orientation are all equally rooted in nature? Or would it furnish powerful homophobic forces with a new weapon in their drive to undermine and remove the rights of non-heterosexual people, perhaps even the right to life itself? The infamous remarks of a senior religious leader (a former Chief Rabbi) in the UK a few years ago that, if a gay gene could be discovered, he would consider it morally acceptable to test pregnant women and offer them the option of aborting any foetus likely to develop into a non-heterosexual person – homophobic extermination in the womb – indicate that the huge moral and cultural debates around sexuality and human identity will not be solved either way by the biological sciences alone. (It might help, perhaps, if biologists turned their attention to the search for genes which cause bigotry, intolerance and religious fanaticism).

As indicated earlier, social constructionists would dispute Dean Hamer's claim that 'biology is neutral'. Indeed, social constructionists have raised a number of important methodological objections to the claim that the natural sciences are free from bias or that differences in gender and sexual behaviour and identity can be objectively explained by scientifically revealed truths about nature and biology. Here are four of those objections.

First, there are the numerous sampling and methodological errors which notoriously bedevil such experiments. To take the example of Le Vay (the scientist who has claimed to have discovered gay genes), there has been furious controversy over his methodology. For example, it has been argued that

- much of his original research involved operating on the brains of gay men who had died from AIDS-related illnesses and comparing them to the brains of straight men, most of whom had not. Thus Le Vay's original sample was scarcely wholly representative of gay men in general; AIDS-related illness can and often does involve brain damage. Moreover, he looked at only six straight men who had died from AIDS-related illness and in all cases they were intravenous drug users, which could make a difference;
- he based his claims upon a very small sampling;
- his entire research was based upon the assumption – never offering the slightest proof – that if you are a gay man you have more sexual partners than if you are a straight man. Even if he was right, at least where his sample is concerned, then it has been argued that the difference he found between hypothalami might relate to levels of sexual activity, not sexual preference;
- he ignored lesbians altogether and included the brains of only six straight women in his sample (Le Vay claimed to have found similarities between the hypothalami of gay men and straight women);
- his actual results – hyped up out of all proportion in the media – showed considerable overlap between his gay and straight male samples.

A separate research project on the same theme, involving Dean Hamer and his team of scientists, claimed a small break-through in July 1993. They did not claim to have discovered a gay gene, but rather that they thought they knew where it might be located – in a region of the X chromosome which boys inherit from their mothers. This research has been criticised for concentrating on self-identifying 'out' gay men – the research protocol meant that the findings can at most be claimed to apply to self-identified members of a modern, socially constructed community – the urban 'gay community' (Rosario 1997: 6). Rosario argues that different results might well have been obtained if the research had included sexually active 'homosexual' men who are closeted – men who have sex with other men but who would never identify themselves as 'gay' or 'homosexual' – or indeed had it excluded self-identified gay men who are either celibate or sexually active with women.

More recently the methodological and sampling problems associated with this kind of research have been underlined by new research carried out in Canada. In April 1999 the US journal *Science* reported that scientists at the University of Western Ontario had re-examined the findings of Hamer's team by carrying out research on a different sample. As with the 1993 research, they had concentrated on pairs of gay brothers but had actually based their research on a larger sample – fifty-two pairs of brothers as opposed to forty pairs in the case of Hamer's research. They concluded that they were unable to locate any genetic marker for homosexuality. This latest research cautions us against the foolishness of becoming over-excited about hasty claims of scientific break-throughs.

None of this, of course, means that such research is not legitimate or that it cannot increase our knowledge. It simply indicates that the natural sciences are not necessarily more free from methodological errors and value-judgements than the social sciences.

Second, such research has often – not always – neglected interactions between physiological and environmental factors. For example, we have already commented upon the fact that the influence of diet, nutrition, and the division of labour upon perceived physical differences between men and women is often overlooked. Many biologists increasingly recognise the complex interactions between environment, culture and society and biology – or nurture and nature. However not all do. Moreover, once the media get hold of their reported discoveries, journalistic simplification frequently distorts the more subtle of their arguments. Dean Hamer has both acknowledged the complexity of his subject, and the caution with which results need to be treated – a caution which is usually thrown to the wind by sensational newspaper headlines:

> We knew also that genes were only part of the answer. We assumed the environment also played a role in sexual orientation, as it does in most if not all behaviors. To most people, the environment means nonbiological factors, such as family upbringing, life experiences, and religion. To geneticists, however, the word 'environment' means anything and everything that is not inherited, including some factors that are purely biological. So, from our point of view, undergoing prenatal development in a womb swimming with male hormones is as much an environmental factor as growing up in a devoutly religious household.
>   . . . Such independent environmental factors would affect DNA studies in much the same way as multiple independent genes. Some individuals would be gay even if they didn't have the 'gay gene'. (Hamer and Copeland 1995: 82)

Third, scientists, far from being objective, frequently hold assumptions which reflect their social conditioning, value judgements and vested interests. Amongst these are the male medical scientists who claimed that childbirth is relatively painless because women have a 'natural' higher pain threshold. Could a female scientist, especially one who had given birth, have come out with such a statement? In the past, scientists have been much criticised for generalising that findings for men must also hold for women. There is a long, and thoroughly discredited, tradition of assuming that homosexuality is an illness and of searching for the most absurd and fantastic 'cures'. In the past, scientists have claimed to have 'discovered' that lesbians are taller than heterosexual women, and that the 'essence' of masculinity and femininity might be deduced from isolating active chemicals in bulls' testicles and pregnant women's urine (enabling them to diagnose the 'deviance' embodied in homosexuals). Even the discovery, in the 1930s, that oestrogens and androgens occur in both men and women led merely to a modification of this type of research (Vines 1993: 18–9).

Perhaps one of the most outrageous examples of prejudice and ignorance masquerading as 'scientific research' involves the work of the Viennese scientist Eugen Steinach in the period from 1917 to the mid-1920s. Steinach believed that the desire to have sex with women was due to the levels of male sex hormone circulating in the body. In 1917 he teamed up with a surgeon to begin experimenting on homosexual men. He decided that these men must be showing female type sex behaviour because of a lack of male sex hormone, and that he could 'correct' this by removing their testicles and transplanting the testicles of a 'normal' man – causing their homosexuality to disappear. He thus offered to 'cure' homosexual men who were unhappy with their sexuality. But surely no 'normal' man was going to volunteer to have his testicles removed and donated to a would-be homosexual recipient? So where could Steinach obtain these wondrous heterosexual balls, the guarantors of 'normal' and 'healthy' relationships with women? He came up with a perfect solution – the testicles of heterosexual rapists and other sex offenders who had been sentenced by the courts to undergo castration . . . By the 1920s, his experiments had been discredited. Such research should not be thought of as merely an historical curiosity. The sad fact is that many of the prejudices which informed it have continued into the contemporary era. In 1997 the Home Office released files which revealed that the UK government had funded 'research' in the 1950s which involved academics from London University's Birkbeck College administering electric shocks to homosexual prisoners in British prisons in a futile attempt to 'discover the causes of homosexuality' (*The Guardian*, 28 November 1997). And as late as the

1970s, US scientists were experimenting with the testicles of homo-sexual prisoners in US jails who had been sentenced to castration.

There are many other examples which could be cited in support of social constructionists' claim that the biological sciences are all too often influenced by prejudice and moral/cultural blindness which they turn to the study of gender and sexuality. To give one more example, Fausto-Sterling (1992: 248) cites the study of rhesus monkeys' sexual behaviour (by Slimp and co-workers) upon which Le Vay based his earlier work into the allegedly natural differences between homosexual and heterosexual men. This study noted that male monkeys often displayed their rumps to other males for inspection and sometimes for mounting. (Not uncommon behaviour in the animal world. Any marine biologist, for example, could quote chapter and verse about the research into sexual relationships between male dolphins.) It also noted that male monkeys sometimes were mounted in this way by female monkeys. The scientists concluded that this was evidence that the male monkeys in question were 'feminised'. As Fausto-Sterling puts it, '. . . the logic seems bizarre. Behaviors that occur in both sexes (mount-ing and presenting) are nevertheless defined as either male or female', and changes in behaviour are presented as evidence of pathological masculinisation or feminisation. Assumptions about 'real' masculine and 'real' feminine behaviour, derived from human society, are im-puted to behaviour common in both sexes of the animal species in question, and then the scientists decide that a male monkey mounting another male monkey is more masculine than the male monkey being mounted! Clearly, such a conceptual mess makes a mockery of any claim to scientific objectivity.

In fact, explanations offered by the biological sciences for gender and sexual behaviour have a pretty sorry history. At various times in the past century it has been claimed that masturbation causes homosexu-ality; that masturbation leads to madness or impotence; that women could not masturbate. It has been claimed that homosexuality was a disease which could be cured by electric shock treatment or by per-forming lobotomies; and that depression in women is caused by hormones (instead of asking whether trying to bring up several chil-dren, trapped in poor accommodation on a low income, might possibly have anything to do with it). We have been told that because men have bigger brains than women they must be more intelligent and more highly developed. And, of course, that hormones explain all sex differences.

The fourth main objection raised by social constructionists is that the selection of 'problem' to be 'solved', mode of experimentation, and classification of results is surely both normative and a highly political exercise. Why are certain types of research carried out and not others? Why are tens of millions of pounds being spent in an attempt to discover a gene which 'causes' homosexuality? Why not spend this money on research which attempts to discover a gene which 'causes' homophobia, or violence and aggression, or why not spend it on research into AIDS or cancer? It is important to look at the question of which companies, corporations, government agencies are paying for the research, and why. Since the choice of research is so obviously influenced by normative political factors, it seems naive to assume that this will have no bearing on the possible outcomes. After all, we know that both the tobacco companies and the anti-smoking lobby can roll out their sponsored scientists every time there is a debate on smoking to argue for completely contradictory findings. It is on such grounds that many social constructionists would call into question Hamer's contention that 'biology is neutral' (Hamer 1995: 218).

This objection would not, in itself, form a sufficient basis for challenging the claims of biologists and geneticists, who will immediately retort that there should be no limits to scientific enquiry. And of course there should not be. But, taken with all the other criticisms of 'scientific objectivity' which we have examined, the question of political and commercial influence on the types of research that are sponsored, funded, and therefore undertaken and publicised, is very important to bear in mind.

A related, if different, type of criticism might be raised in connection with some types of research carried out within the field of social psychology, such as that by McKnight (1997). In a interesting but highly speculative book, McKnight (a professor of psychology) justifies the search for a 'cause' of homosexuality on the grounds that a 'life-long preference for non-reproductive sex' challenges the central tenets of Darwinism, that 'great unifying force which social theory, particularly psychology, so desperately needs for internal coherence' (1997: x). His ultimate conclusion is that homosexuality can be explained as 'an evolutionary by-product, part of our variable sexual orientation and held in balance against its deleterious consequences by selecting for enhanced heterosexuality' (1997: 186). The criticism that can be raised here relates not so much to political and commercial influences on the selection of 'problem' to be 'solved' or explained, but rather to epistemological concerns.

How does McKnight arrive at his conclusion that homosexuality involves a 'life-long preference for non-reproductive sex'? Many homosexual men are fathers. (He ignores lesbians, claiming, without any strong evidence, that they are fewer in number than homosexual men and that in any case 'my suspicions are that lesbianism and male homosexuality have very little in common at an evolutionary level but this is simply a guess, no more'.) Why does he not investigate the case of heterosexuals who either cannot have children, or who express a 'life-long preference for non-reproductive sex' (through use of contraception, voluntary sterilisation, and so on) or who opt for celibacy? Do they not pose a challenge to his Darwinism? How does he arrive at his knowledge of what constitutes a 'homosexual' and what constitutes the frequency and nature of 'homosexual sex'? How can an hypothesis such as that which he offers be verified? McKnight admits that his book is 'speculative' and 'does not pretend to rigorous empiricism', and also that even many Darwinists 'see a large gap between everyday life and ultimate evolutionary explanation and are not fazed by what seems to be maladaptive (non-fitness enhancing) behaviours' (1997: xi-xii).

Ultimately, to collapse or reject the epistemological underpinnings is to open this type of research to the charge of functioning as a form of regulation and control rather than as wholly disinterested scientific enquiry.

The work of Michel Foucault: tensions between Foucault and feminism

The French philosopher Michel Foucault (1926–84) was a theorist who set himself the task of demystifying the categories of the sex professionals – the scientists, psychologists, sexologists and psychoanalysts – and of unmasking the centrality given to sex in our society. His work has had an enormous influence on subsequent attempts to sketch a history of sexuality, that is, to show how sexuality has been historically constructed in different epochs and cultures. In particular, the first volume of Foucault's *The History of Sexuality* (1981) offers a radical critique of the ways in which our understanding of sex and sexuality is shaped. That is, in relation to the power and influence of those who contribute to the debate. The work expresses what Bristow (1997: 167) has called Foucault's 'supreme scepticism towards sexuality as a matter of life and death'.

Foucault argued that, in the human species, there is no such thing as any fixed sexual impulse – that is to say a sexual impulse or lust or desire which can be reduced to an essence, an absolutely essential core which cannot be reduced further – present in human biology and surging forth to determine human behaviour throughout history. Rather, sexuality was seen by him as an historical construct. What we understand by sexuality (the term is itself a late nineteenth-century concept) at any given time, in any given society, is shaped by discourses about

sexuality. These discourses involve complex and contradictory relations of power. Foucault set out to study how these discourses shape our
perceptions about sex and sexuality and how they function to regulate,
control and govern our bodies – and to call into existence 'reverse'
discourses which challenge their dominance.

Foucault made what was at the time a startling claim. Why, he asked,
are we so obsessed with sex in the Christian West? Could it be that
discourses around and about sexuality have given it a central symbolic
place in our culture, and that the history of sexuality in the West is not
merely a continuous history of repression and denial, but a broken
history – full of ruptures and contradictions – by which sexuality has
come to be encouraged and regulated as a central element in the
operation of power? In other words, Foucault challenged us to consider
'how sexuality concentrated extremely potent transfers of power that
have exerted considerable influence on the regulation of the social
order' (Bristow 1997: 169). Foucault sought to establish that the history
of sexuality in the West over recent centuries demonstrates that
sexuality is not some force that Western culture has consistently sought
to repress and contain. Rather, an enormous amount of cultural energy
has been invested in producing and reproducing new ways of talking
and writing about sexuality – discourses; society has never been so
sexualised. Thus the Victorian era, often presented in terms of straightforward sexual repression and denial, actually saw a near-obsession
with the language and delineation of sexuality.

For Foucault, the discourses around and about sexuality which
emerged are contradictory and mean that sexuality embodies 'dense
transfer points for relations of power: between men and women, young
people and old people, parents and offspring, teachers and students,
priests and laity, an administration and a population' (Foucault 1981:
103). This is because the very act of naming and talking about forms of
sexuality in particular ways creates the possibility of challenging those
categories of thought and control. An example might be legal attempts
to repress homosexuality. Such attempts force the state – through its
legal and medical discourses – to open a dialogue (however 'distasteful'
this dialogue might be to those who occupy positions of power) about
the nature of what it is the state is trying to repress. This, in turn, creates
the possibility of a wider debate about the nature of homosexuality
than was previously possible. A similar line of argument might be
applied to the case of censorship. Following Foucault, one could argue
that censorship is ultimately doomed to failure as it is forced to name
and discuss – and create public interest in – the phenomenon which it
is trying to censor. It might be said that attempts at repression and
control call forth struggles through 'reverse' discourses. But this dia-

lectic cuts both ways: just as there is no straightforward history of repression, so, too, there is no straightforward path to liberation through sexuality. Foucault also shows that, behind the myth that through sexuality we can truly come to know ourselves and to be free, it may be that we are really being sold a 'product' which defines and regulates us in new ways.

The discourses Foucault identifies include, for example:

> medical discourses which seek to define what is healthy and un-healthy, biologically possible, natural and unnatural;
> moral and religious discourses which seek to define for us what is right and wrong, sinful and virtuous;
> political discourses which seek to define what is good and bad for society, for the polity;
> scientific and educational discourses which seek to define the level of knowledge we have attained about ourselves.

Knowledge, expressed through language, is power. Discourses embody power relations throughout society. So the forms and expressions which sexual desires, acts, behaviours, identities take – and the mean-ings attached to them – embody power relations. Foucault was really concerned with studying techniques and relations of power.

Foucault saw the emergence of the virtual cult of modern science in the nineteenth century as playing a key role in the sexualisation of modern societies. Sex and sexuality come to be regarded as central to who we are: through the discourses of modern science we become obsessed with sex and sexuality – reading and thinking about it, worrying about whether we can perform adequately, about how we look, about whether we are normal and healthy – and seeing sex and sexuality as containing deep secrets about our inner self if only we can unravel them. How many of us have never been swayed by the discourse – repeated endlessly in magazines, pulp fiction, films and television – that we have only to fall in love with the perfect partner and achieve sexual fulfilment, to transcend our darkest fears about life, death and loneliness, and discover who we really are? In an effort to do so, we turn to the experts: doctors, analysts, scientists, sexologists, agony aunts and uncles. Sexuality becomes central to social regulation. And of course, as we spend money on the search for sexual fulfilment, sexuality becomes central to the market economy.

The modern era sees the emergence of new mechanisms of knowl-edge and power centred on sex. Foucault coined the term 'biopower' to describe 'an explosion of numerous and diverse techniques for achiev-ing the subjugation of bodies and the control of populations' (1981:

140). He identified as central to modern sexuality four such new mechanisms of knowledge and power centred on sex: female sexuality is regulated in new ways with the 'invention' by modern science of the hysterical woman; children's sexuality is addressed by a discourse in the late nineteenth and early twentieth centuries obsessed with childhood masturbation and how to prevent it; procreative behaviour (in the shadow of Malthusian theories of the negative effects of population growth) is controlled in new ways – for example, artificial birth control; and sexuality in general is regulated by the invention of a new category, a new type of person – the homosexual, who is stigmatised and branded as a pervert. In other words, 'the hysterical woman, the masturbating child, the Malthusian couple, and the perverse adult' (Foucault 1981: 104–5) become the central aspects of new techniques of control. Biology and science, far from being neutral avenues of enquiry, are seen by Foucault as specifically ideological discourses, infused with power.

Foucault coined the term 'biopolitics' to explain the processes by which the professions compete with each other and cooperate with the state to regulate the functions of the human body. While the power to shape sexualities is spread throughout society, academics and professionals have participated in, and even pioneered, the production of regimes of knowledge – including discourses and classificatory schema, or ways of categorising people, labelling people and putting them in little boxes – that have constructed, destroyed and amended our bodies, sexualities and genders. So we can say that professionals, such as psychologists, teachers, doctors, priests, lawyers, social workers, counsellors, the police, journalists, judges, politicians, and civil servants, vie for new positions within these structures and relations of power and knowledge. Moreover, they can be seen as competing to direct attention to various sites in their struggles for power and knowledge. Thus, the 'discovery' of child abuse, marital rape, on-line computer porn, male rape, date rape, snuff movies, satanic sex, auto-erotic asphyxiation, as new subjects for the public agenda can be seen as examples of such sites recently in Britain. Likewise, the 'rediscovery' of discourses around the family and the ethics of abortion are recent examples of sites to be fought over, agonised over, and constructed in various ways by competing professionals.

Foucault's argument so far may be summarised as follows: (1) the history of sexuality is disjointed and varies across cultures; in a sense, there is no such thing as a history of sexuality – there are histories of sexualities; (2) the forms which sexuality takes and the meanings attached to these embody more general power relations in society. Foucault rejected the idea that sexuality is produced by some kind of rebellious biological energy which must have its way – the usual metaphor for the male orgasm.

He also rejected the idea that the history of sexuality is merely a history of repression or regulation by the state. He did not hold with the vulgar Marxist idea of a ruling class, holding state power, using that power to disseminate a dominant ideology which constructs sexuality through repression and regulation in ways that serve the interests of that ruling class. He regarded that as one-dimensional. (As do more subtle and dialectical Marxist analyses, such as those inspired by Antonio Gramsci.) Nor did Foucault hold with the feminist theory of patriarchy, or with the idea that one group – men – uses state power to repress and control another group – women. Instead he argued that power is all-pervasive rather than having a single centre. This means that the discursive construction of sexuality cannot be reduced to ways in which one group regulates or represses another, although it does include that, often centrally. He argues that we are all enmeshed in relations of power and affected by discourses about sexuality in complex ways.

Foucault's notion of power has proven troublesome for many socialists, feminists and liberals. One of his arch-defenders, David Halperin, concedes that many have found it 'so sinister, so repellent, and even so reactionary' (Halperin 1995: 16). This is because, in Foucault's view, power is not something which one person or group possesses and another group or person lacks; it is a relationship. People cannot be classified into those who have power and those who don't, allowing us to mobilise the powerless to fight against the powerful. Rather, power characterises the 'complex relations among the parts of a particular society . . . as relations of ongoing struggle' (Halperin 1995: 17). Political struggles are about altering relations of power and are ongoing. Foucault doesn't deny the reality of domination but he denies that 'domination is the whole story'; power can come from below and can be positive and liberating as well as negative – if we empower ourselves to exercise choice in the face of attempts to prevent us from doing so.

Three conclusions seem to stem from this: (1) within any power relationship, we are never powerless; we can always alter the nature of the power relationship – even if we can never escape from it – through defiance and mobilisation; (2) it is not possible to identify a group (a class or gender, for example) that straightforwardly holds and enjoys power, and a group that is straightforwardly exploited or repressed; consequently, it is illusionary to think that the latter can be mobilised against the former; (3) freedom does not involve liberation from power relations – the traditional message of Marxism and feminism – but rather resistance to the dominant discourses from within ever-changing power relations.

The first point is compatible with a Marxist or a feminist perspective on politics and on history, even if Foucault's formulation is open to criticism. It is the other two points that cause most problems for socialists, feminists and others who have been influenced by the traditional precepts of the Left. They are problematic for liberals, too, who share the Left's belief in the Enlightenment notion of progress and the forward march of human history. Here 'modernists' and 'post-modernists' part company most clearly. Foucauldian post-modernists are apt to accuse their Marxist, liberal and feminist critics of taking refuge in a politics of illusions, and the latter are inclined to reply that Foucauldians and their soul-mates (queer theorists, post-feminists) are in danger of contributing to a climate of pessimism and fragmentation in an era dominated by the spectre of the 'end of history' and the alleged triumph of capitalist consumer culture.

Certainly those most influenced by Foucault have on occasion mounted an assault on the whole idea of a progressive politics rooted in shared identities (such those based on sexuality, gender, class, race) which leaves one wondering if there is any basis on which a collective challenge to the status quo might be mounted. This can perhaps be illustrated by examining one of Foucault's central arguments – that concerning the nature of 'reverse' discourses.

Following Foucault, it can be argued that as soon as we fight back by formulating 'reverse' discourses – for example, a feminist discourse which challenges assumptions about the inferiority of women to men, or a lesbian and gay discourse which challenges the medical definition of same-sex attraction as a perversion – we engage with the dominant discourses. And as soon as we do so, we invent new labels and identities for ourselves to challenge the labels and identities which have been forced upon us. But those new labels and identities – for example, identifying oneself as gay or lesbian, or a feminist, or an anti-sexist man – in turn limit us and can be used to regulate us in new ways. Examples might include: (1) entrapping us in an identity which empowers us in one sense but with which we are only partly at ease; (2) forcing us to conform to the norms of the groups or communities in which we seek a sense of belonging; (3) constructing our thought patterns in new ways by telling us what it means to have a gay lifestyle, or what a feminist or a non-sexist man in the twenty-first century ought to think, or how they ought to behave. The 'sexperts' seek to monopolise knowledge here through magazine articles, television programmes and so on; (4) selling us a consumer package to suit our new identities.

In other words, Foucault seems to be saying that we participate in the system of regulation as soon as we try to change it. Although power relations and discourses change, we never escape from them; resistance is an ongoing affair. Certainly the notion that the path to human liberation lies through sexual liberation is dismissed. For example, Foucault would not idealise the 1960s as an era of sexual revolution but instead would look at how new discourses and techniques of power from the invention of the pill to partial decriminalisation of homo-sexuality served to regulate and control people's sexuality in new ways – through redefining the limits of the possible/permissable. More profoundly, though, the very possibility of such a thing as 'human liberation' seems to be undermined.

Foucault's work on sexuality is certainly open to criticism on a number of grounds. First, it would appear from reading Foucault that the history of sexuality is synonymous with a 'history of discourses about sexuality – a history which seems to be only traceable through internal links between discourses' (Sonja Ruehl, quoted in McIntosh 1993: 45). Foucault may then be taken to task for failing to explain adequately where his discourses come from in the first place, how they relate to the 'real lives' of ordinary people, and how changes in the dominant discourses come about. Foucault's anxiety to debunk any kind of functionalism means that ultimately he shies away from offering clear explanations. As McIntosh (1993: 45–6) points out, it has been left to others – for example, Jeffrey Weeks (1997) – to identify economic processes and changes in the class and industrial structure of society that point us in the direction of such explanations. Such lacunae in Foucault's work have allowed some of his Marxist critics to accuse him of contributing to a 'reductionist and functionalist account of processes of social control' (McNay 1994: 105). As McNay comments, 'there is a certain irony to these criticisms in so far as Foucault elaborated his theory of power in contradistinction to the economic reductionism that, in his view, hampered Marxist analyses'.

Moreover, depending on interpretation, his way of viewing history could suggest to some that it is not worth while opposing the status quo since we can never escape. He never went this far in his own life, supporting lesbian and gay rights and the feminist movement in France on the question of abortion rights, for example, and arguing that some repressive regimes, such as Nazi Germany, were more morally repug-nant than others. Nor did he succumb to pessimism in his theoretical work. In The History of Sexuality he is quite clear that 'a multiplicity of points of resistance', a 'plurality of resistances', not only exists but is neither always passive nor 'doomed to perpetual defeat' (1981: 96). But somewhat vague references to a 'plurality of resistances' do not add up to a convincing theory of historical change; indeed, the central thrust of post-modernism would appear to be precisely against any such 'grand historical narrative'. And Foucault explicitly rejected the idea that it was the business of the intellectual to point the way forward by delineating political strategies.

If Foucault is open to the criticism of offering us an inadequate explanation of historical change, perhaps an even more serious criticism of his work is that it contains a flawed understanding of power. Class, gender and race are largely absent from his thought as categories of power relations. He fails to acknowledge the existence of patriarchy, since in his schema of things it would seem that both men and women are discursive constructions and it becomes pointless to ask who has the greater power. Sandra Lee Bartky (quoted in Bristow 1997: 189) has pointed out that Foucault treats the human body as ungendered, assuming that the same processes of discipline, regulation and control which have applied to men have also applied to women. The specific ways in which women's bodies have been rendered 'more docile than the bodies of men' are ignored. Foucault may thus be accused of reproducing women's invisibility through a sexist account of Western history. Bristow concedes that '. . . on occasions he [Foucault] makes it almost impossible to see the structural inequalities the West has persistently created between men and women' (1997: 190).

Finally, on the question of agency Foucault has also faced critical interrogation. Many questions about why men and women might want to embrace or reject certain types of discourses and identities are left unanswered. Foucault's vehement rejection of both Marxism and psychoanalysis – he dismissed the work of Freud and others as a new system of regulation and control – means that his work 'has little or no interest in the subject's inner life. Such is Foucault's anti-humanism that he denies the subject any depth or psychological complexity. In this spirit, he firmly repudiates the realm of conflict between conscious and unconscious processes that fascinated Freud' (Bristow 1997: 196). Lois McNay has argued that the end result of this narrow-minded reaction against such humanistic enquiry is a flawed understanding of human subjectivity: Foucault 'provides no way of going beyond the minimal notion of the subject as a purely determined category to a fuller understanding of the subject as a thinking, willing, responsible agent of choice' (McNay 1994: 103–4).

It can be argued that there is an ever-present temptation in Foucault, especially given his celebration of the 'body and its dark pleasures' and his controversial celebration of (consensual) sado-masochism as an act of rebellion and self-definition, paradoxically to reduce the complexity of human sexuality and human subjectivity to a one-dimensional image. Transgressive sexual pleasure comes to be seen as somehow constituting, in and of itself, an act of resistance. Such a view is but a short step from what Linda Grant refers to as libertinage, and which she contrasts with the liberationist or millenarian tradition (Grant 1993: 38–9). Whereas the latter turns outwards, towards challenging material inequalities and seeking to change the world, the libertines 'turned their attention away from society, inwards, to the body, which they regarded as a pleasure machine or unmapped territory whose erotic geography they wanted to explore, discovering every conceivable site of sensation'. Such a turning away from the possibilities of progress in human affairs towards transgressive sex as the only 'authentic' experience can become, for Grant (and here she quotes Angela Carter's critique of de Sade), a form of infantile regression.

Whilst feminists and other theorists of gender and sexuality influenced by humanist thought have, perhaps, the greatest difficulties with these very considerable lacunae in Foucault's thought, some radical pluralist writers (whether feminist, post-feminist or 'queer') who have rejected the main ideologies of modernism have found Foucault stimulating, challenging and often inspirational. His work is undoubtedly the single most important influence upon those writers on sex and sexuality who might be described as 'post-modernist'. Perhaps, in large part, this attraction has to do with the general distrust of the grand ideologies of liberation which is characteristic of our time. Certainly, Foucault's emphasis on the contradictory and paradoxical nature of identities and discourses has proven attractive to those who see themselves engaged in a self-critical politics of resistance.

Jana Sawicki, for example, believes that feminism can usefully draw upon Foucault's thought and speaks of a Foucauldian feminism as one which recognises 'the double bind characteristic of every situation of oppression. Identity formation is both strategically necessary and dangerous. And, as feminists we must live within the tension and uncertainty produced by our oppressive situations'. Foucault's work, in other words, reminds us of the need to be ever vigilant and self-critical about identities and discourses, including those we adopt as part of our struggles. As she puts it, '. . . it would be a mistake to assume uncritically feminist political theories and practices developed in the context of patriarchal capitalism' and feminism needs to constantly question itself and 'dislocate' itself. Equally, it needs to 'use Foucault against himself, and [struggle] against the use of his work to undermine the very struggles he claimed to support' (Sawicki 1991: 108).

Sawicki's argument can be illustrated by considering what Biddy Martin (quoted in Bristow 1997: 198) calls the tendency of some American radical feminists to eulogise feminine virtue and to 'ontologize[s] woman in terms of an essential superiority and a privileged relationship to nature and truth. The tendency in such polemics is to counter what are considered to be male distortions of reality with what are held to be authentic female representations . . .'. Such a lapse into essentialism ultimately reproduces the woman=nature=truth v. man= culture=distortion dichotomy in ways that undermine the project of gender equality. For Martin and others, the significance of Foucault's work is that it challenges feminists to recognise that feminism cannot hope to 'recover an authentic and untainted ideal of femininity from patriarchal domination' (Bristow 1997: 198), or to sustain a convincing critique of patriarchy which rests on essential simplicities. Moreover, Foucault's emphasis on discourses forces us to consider ways in which both masculinity and femininity are understood and re-shaped over time and amongst cultures. It explodes myths of homogenous masculinity and femininity and challenges us to grapple with differences between, for example, black women and white women, women in the 'first world' and women in the 'third world', and so on.

Jeffrey Weeks is among the leading social scientists and historians who have taken Foucault's work as a valuable contribution to our understanding of how gender and sexuality are constructed by power and knowledge, but who reject any tendency to draw pessimistic conclusions from it. Indeed, Weeks (1991) points out that towards the end of his life, Foucault acknowledged that his work was moving in the direction of a celebration of sexual diversity and choice which could only mean an embrace of the possibilities and potentialities of change. Importantly, Weeks points out that we don't have to accept or reject Foucault as a package, any more than he did those theorists who went before him. We can, and should, select whatever we find useful and seek to build upon it.

In such a spirit, the present work recognises the huge contribution Foucault's analysis of power-laden discourses has made to the study of sexuality. In particular, it retains his emphasis on historical and cultural diversity and on the necessity to interrogate critically gender and sexual identities (along with others). But it departs from the thrust of Foucault's thought in at least three ways.

First, it regards Foucault's uncompromising rejection of both psychoanalysis and of any notion of an innate sexual drive or instinct or impulse as too extreme and unscientific. Such a rejection was motivated by the entirely understandable fear of the simplicities of biological determinism, for example, the tendency of Freud, Reich and others to reduce manifestations of human 'neurosis' to a 'blocked' or 'repressed' sex drive. Many examples could be produced to illustrate how biological theories of sex and sexuality have in fact functioned at the level of social control and regulation. And, once we take into consideration the social constructionist critique of the language in which we discuss matters sexual, it can be argued that 'no theory –

biological or physical . . . is socially unconstructed or "natural" ' (Assiter 1993: 89). However, it would make more sense to argue that culture conditions the terms in which biologists, psychoanalysts and others formulate and test their hypotheses and argue their findings – a fact of which many biological scientists are very much aware. The danger of an extreme social determinist position is that, as Assiter puts it, 'human bodies . . . are in danger of slipping altogether out of the picture'; human nature comes to be seen as 'plastic and mouldable' and sexual identities and desire becomes a matter simply of free will. Not only can we end up denying the existence of any important or significant material differences between human beings rooted in their biological make-up, but the assertion that all 'differences in gender and sexual orientation are . . . due to culture and conditioning, and are thought to be eliminable by changing the force of present social conditioning' (Assiter 1993: 96) becomes a matter of faith. It is one thing to recognise the cultural and historical diversity of meanings and significances attributed to forms of human sexual desire and gender behaviour, and to muster what is, after all, a considerable body of anthropological, historical and sociological evidence to challenge essentialist myths of unchanging masculinity, femininity, homosexuality or heterosexuality. It is quite another thing to assert, without any convincing evidence, that the direction of sexual desire (for example) is itself a matter of free will, 'lifestyle choice', or social conditioning and that human beings are 'blank slates or pieces of putty' (Assiter 1993: 96) upon which biology has inscribed nothing of fundamental importance.

Second, the present study agrees with Stevi Jackson (1996: 18–19) that there is a real problem in linking Foucault's 'conception of socially diffuse power to structural analyses of inequality'. In particular, there is a persistent temptation in Foucault to concentrate on historical disjunctions and ruptures and to underplay the extent to which patriarchal domination and power has displayed considerable resilience, surviving and being reproduced in new forms. This, in turn, leads Foucault to dismiss the concept of a dominant (patriarchal, capitalist) ideology in Western society. Jackson is worth quoting at length on this question:

> While I find Foucauldian analyses interesting in the way that they sensitize us to the multiplicity of often contradictory ways in which sexuality has been constructed and regulated, their inability to deal with the regularity and pervasiveness of patriarchal power, with the ways in which what counts as sexual has been constructed in terms of gender hierarchy is problematic. The idea that our sense of what is sexual, including our desires and practices, is discursively constituted

is potentially productive. But, whereas Foucault sees the concept of discourses as antithetical to ideology, I would argue that we need to retain a concept of discourses as ideological – in that they can serve to obscure or legitimate relations of domination and subordination. (Jackson 1996a: 19)

Finally, the present study tries to remedy Foucault's relative indifference to the extraordinary persistence of gender hierarchy and structural gender inequality by drawing upon feminist theories of patriarchy. Theories of patriarchy are numerous and diverse (for a useful brief summary see Acker 1989). The work of Sylvia Walby (1989, 1990), which is in terms of dual systems of patriarchy and capitalism, is particularly useful in redressing Foucault's gender blindness. Walby defines patriarchy as 'a system of social structures and practices in which men dominate, oppress and exploit women' (1989: 214). She cautions that the emphasis on *social structures* is important, 'since it clearly implies rejection of both biological determinism, and the notion that every individual man is in a dominant position and every individual woman in a subordinate one'. Her work challenges us to consider the complexity and historical diversity of patriarchy by focusing on six main structures 'which together constitute a structure of patriarchy' (1989: 220). These are: 'a patriarchal mode of production in which women's labour is exploited by their husbands; patriarchal relations within waged labour; the patriarchal state; male violence; patriarchal relations in sexuality; and patriarchal culture'.

The impact and limits of 'queer theory'

What became known in the 1990s as 'queer theory' is often rather vague, and perhaps deliberately so. In common with other manifestations of post-modernism, queer theory prides itself on challenging and subverting all existing categories of thought. 'All that is solid melts into air' might be its guiding slogan. As such, queer theorists can always deflect demands from critics for greater clarity and more rigorous analysis of their political and intellectual projects with the assertion that queer theory 'refutes any attempt at definition or categorization on the grounds that this reinforces the metanarrative it is trying to criticize' (Edwards 1998: 472). Of course, this also affords a smokescreen behind which all sorts of half-baked ideas and sloppy pseudo-theorising can take refuge, alongside genuinely innovative and challenging academic research. One queer writer recently acknowledged that queer theory faces criticism on grounds of 'its abstraction, its fetishising of discourse and apparent contempt for the mundane', but seeks to attribute its credibility problems to the fact that 'some of the arguments of queer theory have been diluted or misrepresented to the point of absurdity' (Spargo 1999: 66–7). Does this mean that there is a core of queer theory, from which deviations (in the form of dilutions or misrepresentations) can be detected? The problem with identifying such a canonical core is that several of its key texts (for example, Butler 1990) are written in language which almost seem to invite the sort of interpretations which can subsequently be dismissed as 'misrepresentations'.

The nebulous nature of queer theory means that trying to pin down its exact origins is sometimes difficult. What is clear is that queer theory is not to be confused with, although it might be said to have grown out of, lesbian and gay studies. In particular, the influence of Foucault has been paramount. According to Bristow (1997: 170), 'if [Foucault's] *The History of Sexuality* has been instrumental in shaping any field of inquiry, then its presence is assuredly most visible in queer theory, a field of study which has flourished since the early 1990s, and which takes Foucault's lead in resisting the naturalizing assumptions which undergird normative sexual behaviours'. In particular, Foucault's dissection of the ways in which sexual desire has been constructed through discourses in ways which seek to constrain it within a homo-/hetero- dualism has been inspirational to queer theorists (for example, Sedgwick 1991).

It has sometimes been argued that queer theory grew out of a new wave of political activism associated with the AIDS crisis in the 1980s and early 1990s. It might be more accurate to say that such activism contributed to the advent of what has become known as queer politics (discussed in greater detail in Chapter 4) – a phenomenon which itself has a sometimes problematic relationship with queer theory. Jackson (1996a: 4) has argued that queer politics can 'either as fashion accessory or mode of activism, become yet another subcultural or political "identity". This runs counter to queer theory's emphasis on deconstructing all identities, straight, gay or bisexual. From this perspective queer politics is often, as Teresa de Lauretis (1991) has commented, not queer enough to satisfy the theorists'.

Edwards (1998) points out that the real intellectual origins of queer theory lie in that branch of lesbian and gay studies associated with literary and cultural criticism. This is true of those leading queer theorists who have sought to bring a Foucauldian perspective to bear on their deconstruction of gender hierarchies and sexual identities through a re-reading of key cultural texts (such as Butler 1990, 1993; Dollimore 1991, Sedgwick 1991) and of popular journalism inspired by queer theory (for example, Simpson 1994, 1996). The purpose of such work has been to show that gender and sexual identities are 'increasingly open and confused or fragmented and difficult to categorize' (Edwards 1998: 472). This has involved not only a sustained assault on a language of sexual categorisation which constructs people's identities as either heterosexual or homosexual, but also an assault on the idea that human beings can be classified into two clear-cut groups, men and women.

Most famously, Judith Butler has argued that feminists made a mistake in assuming that either women or men are a group with common characteristics, interests and a shared identity. She dismisses the idea that masculinities and femininities are gender identities which are built by culture upon 'male' and 'female' bodies as too limiting and instead opts for a more voluntaristic interpretation of gender: gender becomes a cultural performance which floats free of any 'given' sex. Thus Butler argues that if sex and gender emerge from different sources – nature and culture – then gender does not necessarily proceed from sex. In other words, '. . . it does not follow that the construction of "men" will accrue exclusively to the bodies of males or that "women" will interpret only female bodies . . . When the constructed status of gender is theorized as radically independent of sex, gender itself becomes a free-floating artifice, with the consequence that *man* and *masculine* might just as easily signify a female body as a male one, and *woman* and *feminine* a male body as a female one'. (Butler 1990: 6) Later, she elaborates: 'there is no gender identity behind the expressions of gender . . . identity is performatively constituted by the very "expressions" that are said to be its results' (1990: 25). In such a view the transsexual or transvestite is no more enacting a performance of gender than are the rest of society; there is no such thing as a masculine or feminine identity that is not a cultural performance. The point of queer practice becomes to subvert what we understand as 'normal' or 'given' through unmasking and demystifying a wide diversity of gender 'performances', and through the enactment of a range of genders (which Butler calls 'gender trouble'). It thus becomes pointless to ask whether Dame Edna Everage or Germaine Greer is the more authentic expression of femininity, for example.

Butler offers us a real insight into the ways in which our understanding of masculinity and femininity are structured around society's acceptance of 'the concept of heterosexuality as the norm of human relationships. Compulsory heterosexuality is installed in gender through the production of taboos against homosexuality, resulting in a false coherence of apparently stable genders attached to appropriate biological sexes' (Spargo 1999: 54). In other words, if we simply

assume that 'masculinity' and 'femininity' are the stable gender identities which culture inscribes on male and female bodies, then we
overlook the many ways in which these gender identities in fact derive
their meanings from institutionalised heterosexuality. From a very
early age, we learn to relate to each other as 'boys' or 'girls' through
the assumption of normalised and naturalised heterosexuality, and a
particular type of heterosexuality at that: the boy is taller, stronger,
rougher, more aggressive and competitive and doesn't cry, the girl is the
opposite. Behaviour which doesn't fit this binary opposition is learned
(and punished) as gender inappropriate – sissiness in boys, or tomboy
behaviour in girls.

The fact is that we are not all heterosexual and not all men and
women who are heterosexual will experience their heterosexuality in
similar ways. Queer theory explores how gender identities police and
regulate us, and reflect assumptions of heterosexuality. For example, it
re-examines popular culture for evidence of heterosexual policing and
in doing so it encourages us to look at the seemingly familiar and taken-
for-granted with critical eyes. It also invites us to investigate the
possibilities of a plurality of masculinities and femininities, of a range
of ways of living our lives. In so far as this tends towards an implosion
of gender as a useful category of analysis, disentangling sex, gender and
desire, queer theory also encourages us to focus on the utopia of a
gender-free world.

However, Butler's writings are also highly problematic in a number of
ways. Her description of gender identities as 'free-floating' and her
choice of gay male drag as a prime example of gender performativity
have left her open to the charge of extreme subjectivism. If gender is a
cultural performance unrelated to any material or biological reality, and
if we can 'choose', resistance and subversion of existing sexual categorisations through altering our gender performance as we see fit, then
identities can be happily reinvented by their 'owners'. This may not be
what Butler intended, and in a later work she criticises the tendency to
attach too much importance to individual speech utterances at the
expense of collective action against underlying structures of sexism
(Butler 1997: 74); but some queer writers and activists have acted as if,
by a supreme act of individual will, one can simply refuse to be a man or
refuse to be a woman. Unfortunately, it is not easy to change the world
by opting out, and it is all too easy to become blind to structured gender
inequalities by simply insisting upon the 'unreality' of gender categories. It is one thing to highlight a range of possible masculinities and
femininities; it is another to suggest that these can be more or less
randomly distributed between men and women and bear no (more or
less) fixed relation to biologically sexed bodies. The criticism which

Assiter made of Foucault (cited earlier) – that material bodies are in danger of simply 'slipping away' – becomes relevant here. Butler (1993) acknowledges that a question her work frequently invites is 'what about the body, Judy', without however giving a clearly convincing answer.

The problem here is that it is not only identities which float free, dissolve or become fluid. The same can be said of solidarities between those who share an experience of oppression or marginalisation rooted in gender or sexuality, or class, race, or other; and perhaps even of the very material reality of that oppression or marginalisation. Queer theory is quite explicit on this point: gender and sexual identities will not serve as the basis for political solidarities. If 'men' are as able to 'perform' femininity as 'women', if 'straight queers' can be every bit as 'queer' as 'gay queers' or 'lesbian queers', then the very politics of solidarity and collective action which is necessary to fight back against inequality becomes undermined. To give an example, when a straight guy decides to 'play gay' by wearing his 'queer as fuck' tee-shirt and pink triangle badge, or when a man who has chosen to 'enact a performance of femininity' demands access to a women-only space, are these examples of radical, subversive acts which break down the walls of the ghetto and potentially liberate us from the tyranny of sexual categorisation? Or are they examples of individuals who belong to the dominant or privileged groups in society expropriating the identities and culture, forged through struggle, of the still marginalised and under-privileged groups?

To give another example, we may agree that men and women experience and live heterosexuality in a wide variety of ways (depending on age, class, wealth, race, sexual desire, levels of sexual activity and so on). But can it not be argued, as many recent feminist writings on heterosexuality have contended, that men (in general) and women (in general) relate differently to institutionalised heterosexuality, reflecting wider gender inequalities? And, if so, does the struggle to challenge and change institutionalised heterosexuality not presuppose a clear 'gender effect'?

It is precisely such political questions which bitterly divide queer theorists from their feminist and gay critics. Queer theorists may claim that they are opening up new possibilities for a politics of diversity, but their critics can argue that their 'dissolution' of identities and of identity politics and their extreme subjectivism reflects a bourgeois individualism which is more in tune with the right-wing ethos of affluent capitalist societies at the start of the twenty-first century than it is with the collectivist struggles of the feminist and lesbian and gay movements since the 1960s. What, exactly, is to be the basis of

collective resistance if not shared identities? Or is queer theory ultimately offering us a paraphrase of Mrs Thatcher's famous claim: that
there is no such thing as collective action, only individuals and their
theories?

In much the same way as we are apparently free to 'choose' to reshape
the confines of our gender identities through altering our cultural
performances, queer theorists argue that language can be reclaimed
and reinvented. The adoption of the term queer – once, and still, a
derogatory and abusive term for homosexual men – as a signifier for a
form of theory and politics which challenges all fixed identities is
significant. A queer political activist, Peter Tatchell, explained this as
follows:

> The New Queer Politics is about seizing the language of oppression
> and transforming it into a language of liberation; appropriating a
> traditional term of homophobic abuse and redefining it as an ex-
> pression of pride and defiance. By proclaiming ourselves queer, we
> subvert the derogatory meaning of the word and undermine its
> effectiveness as an insult. Responding to taunts with an unexpected
> 'yes, I am queer, so what!' deflates the power of the abuse, disarms the
> abuser, and empowers the intended victim. (Tatchell 1992)

Others have, however, questioned whether such a subjectivist approach to language really holds water. For example, Julia Parnaby has
argued that:

> Reclaiming 'queer' as a name is based on the assumption that merely
> to do so strips it of its homophobic power, that it turns the word
> against the queer-basher rather than the bashed. It is a direct con-
> sequence of post-structuralist arguments around language which
> claim that the meanings of words are constantly redefined each time
> they are used by the individuals who use them, and that we can
> therefore make words mean what we want them to mean. Clearly
> such arguments remove language from both its historical and social
> context. In heterosexist society 'queer' cannot be other than abusive,
> just as in white supremacist society racist statements are insults of
> hatred, and words like 'bitch' reflect patriarchy's misogyny. (Parnaby
> 1993)

The emphasis here on social context is important and should alert us
to the fact that terms may have different meanings depending on
context. For example, generation, class, race, environment, geographi-
cal location, and so on all have a bearing on how we react to terms and

labels. The use of the term 'queer' may appear liberating and empowering to an urban-based person who is secure in his/her sexuality and circle of like-minded friends and lovers, but deeply offensive and threatening to others who are isolated, live in rural communities or small towns, are still 'in the closet' or coming to terms with their sexuality. Confident lesbian, gay or bisexual activists may also find that their intellectual or political formation simply rebels against the idea that you can easily appropriate and subvert terms in this way. (The same applies to any other such label; there are still those to whom the word 'gay' or 'lesbian' appears offensive and who prefer to be known as 'homosexual'; and those who regard 'homosexual' as a clinical, pathologising, and problematic term.) Both Tatchell and Parnaby, in the passages quoted above, are in danger of overlooking the rich diversity of experiences of sexuality. One is perhaps inclined towards an urban-based 'vanguardist' approach which risks alienating the majority of non-heterosexual people (and, with rich irony, in the name of a politics of radical diversity); the other is in danger of assuming an undifferentiated experience of powerlessness in the face of structured inequality.

As we have seen, queer theory and queer politics emerged as a result of an encounter between a branch of radical lesbian and gay (especially gay male) political activism around issues such as AIDS, on the one hand, and (primarily) lesbian and gay academics working in the fields of literary and cultural studies, on the other. Tim Edwards (1998: 472 *passim*) argues that these origins help to explain a number of queer theory's weaknesses and limitations. First, he implies that the nature of queer theory – emerging within academia in the 1990s as something of a trendy field, influenced by small groups of urban-based lesbian and gay activists, and strong in its appeal to the iconoclasm of the young – predisposes it towards an exaggeration of the extent to which sexual identities as lived and experienced by most people really are fragmented and difficult to categorise. Edwards suggests that the assault on identity politics 'tends to locate queer theory in terms of a potentially utopian outcome rather than in an analysis of the present' (1998: 472).

Second, he suggests that the concentration on analysis of cultural texts is linked to a divorce from 'wider politics or grass roots activism' (1998: 473). Even queer groups such as OutRage!, Queer Nation and ACT-UP tend to be small and vanguardist in nature. The shift in emphasis within lesbian and gay studies away from fields such as history, sociology and politics towards literary and cultural analysis is an important part of the background to the emergence of queer theory and may help explain the relative lack of attention paid to political strategies.

Finally, the abstract and elitist nature of much of queer theory may help explain the impatient dismissal of identity politics and the assumption that the much-derided 'gay community' is now simply a self-imposed ghetto which is well past its sell-by date and historically redundant. Putting it slightly more polemically than Edwards, I would suggest that a new and iconoclastic branch of theory which denies the centrality of sexual identities has its obvious attractions to middle-class academics, and to mainly cosmopolitan and young 'sexual rebels'. The primary concern of the former in their daily workplace is not whether they are going to face a 'queer-bashing' by their work-mates, or a barrage of homophobic taunts, but rather whether they are going to secure tenure, promotion, or make a name for themselves by finding new topics for research and publication. The latter may well have forgotten (or, if they are very fortunate, never experienced) the trauma which still attaches to coming out as gay in this society, and, conversely, the often (quite literally) life-saving nature of assuming a positive gay identity. As Edwards puts it:

> Unless we are to presume that homosexuality is now . . . on some kind of equal footing with heterosexuality then its identity remains fundamentally necessary to the struggle for equality. Ironically, while recent decades have witnessed an ever-strengthening discourse of homosexuality, centred on opposition to older negative definitions and stereotypes, heterosexuality has for the most part remained immune or silent at a discursive level and it is difficult to see how a reverse policy of 'unspeaking' the homosexual can undermine even this discursive privilege of the heterosexual let alone make the quantum leap into its social and political importance. (Edwards 1998: 476)

As we have seen, recent feminist writings on heterosexuality have begun to question how it is lived and experienced by women and men, heterosexual and non-heterosexual. In so far as such writings address as a central concern the structured nature of gender inequality in our society, especially as experienced by heterosexual women, they offer an important antidote to some of the blind spots in queer theory – which shares with Foucault a relative neglect of any concrete analysis of patriarchy.

Sex, gender, sexuality: terminology

By now readers will be aware that many of the terms we are using – sex, gender, sexuality, identity, power, and indeed the very notion of sexual politics – are complex and contested. They are the sites of battle over their meaning (or meanings) – often politically charged battle as well as intellectual debate. Sometimes, trying to nail down exactly what a term like 'sexuality' means is like trying to hold mercury. The previous discussion of Foucault and of queer theory will have made this clear. We will now look at some common usages, beginning with the distinction between 'sex' and 'gender'.

Since Ann Oakley popularised the distinction between 'sex' and 'gender' in the early 1970s, it has become commonplace in the literature of sociology, political science and related disciplines. Oakley argued that some of the differences between 'men' and 'women' are rooted in human biology and others are rooted in culture. The former – rooted in the facts of biology – are referred to as 'sex', and the latter as 'gender'.

> 'Sex' is a word that refers to the biological differences between male and female, the visible difference in genitalia, the related difference in procreative function. 'Gender', however, is a matter of culture: it refers to the social classification into 'masculine' and 'feminine'. (Oakley 1972: 16)

In other words, sex refers to what's between your legs, and gender to what's between your ears.

Oakley's sex/gender dichotomy had a considerable influence on a generation of sociologists who were encouraged to focus on the cultural constructions of masculinity and femininity – prising open and shedding critical light on the ways in which the 'norms' of masculine and feminine behaviour are regulated, policed and reproduced in our society – and the ways in which existing power structures, relations of power, and inequalities are justified and legitimised by reference to these cultural constructions of masculinity and femininity.

The sex (biology)/gender (culture) dichotomy is still a commonly cited distinction but has recently come in for some rigorous criticism by queer theorists and other postmodernists who are unhappy with what they see as a dangerous simplification. John Hood-Williams, clearly influenced by Butler and queer theory, has disputed the notion that sex is any more natural or any less the subject of contentious discourses than is gender. Hood-Williams (1996) has acknowledged the importance of Oakley's work in developing critical thought about 'the social rather than biological determinants of a wide range of behaviours'. It had 'enabled an oppositional stance to biologisms that attempted to tie women to subordinate positions on account of a largely immutable biology' (Hood-Williams 1996: 1). However, he argues that the sex-gender distinction has out-lived its usefulness, for it rests upon three assumptions, which are often taken as 'common sense' and 'true', but which in fact are open to challenge.

The first assumption is that 'the biological realm features clear sexual dimorphism' (1996: 6). That is to say, that men are men and women are women and the two are biologically distinct and have developed differently. In fact, drawing upon the work of Thomas Laqueur (1990), Hood-Williams demonstrates that this is a fairly recent understanding of the human body, rooted in the Enlightenment, and that for thousands of years a monomorphic understanding of the human body – in which men and women were seen as variations on a single anatomical theme, with parallels and homologies everywhere in evidence – predominated.

The second assumption is that the biological and the cultural form two distinct realms. But Hood-Williams argues (and the influence of queer theory is again evident) that this is not self-evidently the case. Often our very understanding of biology, anatomy – the human body and its possibilities – is conditioned by ideological, moral and cultural values and judgements. Drawing in part on the example provided by Foucault of hermaphrodites, Hood-Williams argues that sex, as well as gender, can be ascribed to an individual on the basis of the value-judgements of those in authority as to what constitutes 'normality'. In an era in which transsexualism and sex-change operations are a reality, this point about the extent to which 'biological' 'sex' is also a social construction acquires added relevance.

The third assumption is that while sex is fixed and certain, gender behaviour is malleable and subject to change and social engineering. Hood-Williams argues that human biology is more malleable than usually assumed, and human culture perhaps less so. In other words, this assumption 'underestimates both the possibilities of medical and genetic engineering on the one hand and the *longue durée* of social relations on the other' (Hood-Williams 1997: 43).

Clearly, Hood-Williams' argument is in agreement with those queer theorists who believe that the old dichotomy between biology and sociology upon which the sex/gender distinction rests needs to be re-thought. Such a position is, in turn, vigorously challenged by feminists and others who believe that it is both fundamentally mistaken and politically dangerous. For example, Robert Willmott argues that 'the biological and the social constitute distinct, irreducible levels of reality'. He emphasises the fact that we are dealing with ontologically distinct realms, or levels, of reality which certainly interact but which require analytical separation 'in order to examine their relative efficacy' (1996: 728–9). Indeed, he argues that such a distinction – which allows us to

study the ways in which biological differences have been conceptualised at the ideological level – remains central to any project (such as
that of feminism) which aims at delineating the possibilities for socio-
cultural, political and economic change.

Willmott accuses conflationary approaches of the queer/postmoder-
nist variety, which deny that the biological and the social are distinct
levels of reality, of 'render[ing] the feminist enterprise impotent'. This
is because they remove our ability to 'explicate the complexity and
variability of patriarchy/androcentrism, that is the ways in which
women generally have been (and are) devalued and excluded to the
benefit of (most) men', and consequently 'to pinpoint what is change-
able and what is not in the context of socio-economic reality' (1996:
734).

Willmott does not dispute many of the points which Hood-Williams
makes. He concedes that our understanding of the human body does
indeed change dramatically through the ages. In recent years, the
advances made by endocrinologists, for example, have altered our
understanding of sex chromosomes. However, he argues that 'gender
ideology clearly affected the interpretations of the discovery of hormones, but this in itself does not affect the reality of hormones!
Importantly, there *is* a truth of the body, or rather bodies, human
knowledge of which is *fallibilistic*' (1996: 738). Likewise, it is obviously
true that sex differences are not absolute and that medicine, operating
to maintain 'a legal fiction of binary gender as an *absolute*' has developed surgical and hormonal interventions aimed at 'removing ambi-
guities' – sometimes with tragic consequences for the individuals
concerned. Thus Willmott's position is fully compatible with feminist
writers who argue that we need to develop a politics of the body which
recognises how our understanding of the body is itself socially constructed. But neither the fact that our understanding of the body
changes and evolves, nor the fact that there are not simply 'two
ahistorical, fixed male and female biologies', renders the sex/gender
distinction defunct. Rather, Willmott insists that '*once* embroiled in
socio-economic reality, the body/biology does not lose autonomy'.

This emphasis on the autonomy of the body – and on the importance
of avoiding the queer/Foucauldian temptation to let the body 'slip
away' – is important for two reasons. The first is that there are
important biological differences between men and women which it
would be foolish to ignore. As Willmott puts it, 'while there is biological
overlap, *men and women are ontologically distinguished by their respective
reproductive capacities* (though men and women are fundamentally not
qualitatively different kinds of people)'. It makes little sense to ignore
this. After all, a thirteen-year-old boy is not going to start menstruating

just because he is repeatedly told he is a girl. The second reason why keeping bodies in mind is so important is precisely because it is the differences in reproductive capacities which have been seized upon in patriarchal societies and given inegalitarian interpretations. Feminist scholarship has challenged the myth that biological differences provide sufficient grounds for inequality, while recognising that the reality of child-bearing has been constructed ideologically in ways which have sought to banish women from the public sphere, or place them at a distinct disadvantage within that sphere. Thus Willmott argues (*pace* Assiter) that it is not true that '*only* women are intrinsically suited to child-rearing; rather this is likely to be ideologically deemed so because of their biology and its place within the materiality of existence' (1996: 742–3).

To conclude, from this perspective the sex/gender distinction remains important. To elide sex and gender risks losing sight of the importance of material bodies, and undermining our capacity to analyse the ways in which gender ideologies reinforce male domination and reproduce inequalities through obfuscating the reality of those inequalities. The interplay between sex and gender can only be properly understood if we maintain an analytical distinction between sex and gender; for 'logically we will *never* be able to theorise about their interplay and hence nullify our capacity to pinpoint possibilities for social change' (1996: 744).

In his reply to Willmott, Hood-Williams has cited Olive Schreiner to the effect that sex differences between men and women are minor and unimportant. Men and women share 'similarities of emotion, desire and fitness' and such differences as exist between them have no determinative powers whatsoever (Hood-Williams 1997: 46–7). Certainly it is true that men and women have many more similarities than differences; and it is true also that the importance of sex differences has very frequently been exaggerated, and often with political intent. It may also be the case that Willmott is over-egging the pudding somewhat in insisting on the ontological distinction between men and women. But to accuse Willmott and those numerous feminist writers working with the sex/gender analytical distinction of, in effect, biological determinism and of reducing complex arguments about inequality to the claim that 'until men lactate our politics are at an end' (Hood-Williams 1997: 54) is as grossly unfair as it is a caricature.

This is an important debate and one which will continue for some time. By now, however, it should be clear that this study is in sympathy with those writers who argue that to treat gender as a free-floating entity, and biology as of no consequence whatsoever, in understanding how structures of inequality and patriarchal privilege are sustained and reproduced, is as untenable and politically dangerous as to argue that natural difference is a basis for gender. We need a more complex and dialectical understanding of the inter-actions, such as that hinted at by Connell, who argues that:

> The social is radically un-natural, and its structure can never be deduced from natural structures. What undergoes transformation is genuinely transformed. But this un-naturalness does not mean disconnection, a radical *separation* from nature. Practical negation involves an incorporation of what is negated into the transformed practice. A *practical relevance* is established, rather than a determination, between natural and social structures. That is to say the social process *deals with* the biological patterns given to it. (Connell 1985: 269)

The present study retains the analytical distinction between sex and gender while remaining fully aware that human anatomy and biology should never be treated as fixed and unproblematic, and that the binarisms mentioned at the start of this chapter need to be constantly interrogated.

Finally, it is not only terms such as 'sex' and 'gender' which are increasingly contested and debated nowadays. Sexuality is also a contested term. In the 1970s it was commonly used in the literature to refer to intimate erotic activity – to 'having sex' (Hawkes 1996: 8–9). On occasion, the implication was almost that if you weren't 'having sex', then you didn't 'have' a sexuality. This, of course, is nonsense. One can be celibate for long periods of time – even for life – and still be a deeply sexual being – moreover, a deeply sexual being to whom a sense of sexual identity – as gay, lesbian, heterosexual, bisexual – may well be of considerable importance.

In the 1980s and 1990s it became more common to go beyond this tendency to conflate sexuality with sex acts and to give it a broader meaning, encompassing erotic desires, practices and identities, as Stevi Jackson and Sue Scott (1996: 2) put it. Even this leaves room for debate, partly because what is erotic is certainly not fixed. As Jackson and Scott again point out, what is erotic to one person may be disgusting to another or politically unacceptable to a third; so debates rage about what are 'legitimate' subjects of a politics of sexuality and what are not.

The present study adopts Jackson and Scott's definition of sexuality which has the merit of allowing us to focus on sexual feelings and relationships, not just sex acts; and on the various ways in which we are or are not defined as sexual by ourselves and by others. This working definition of sexuality gives us room to construct a politics of sexuality which might cover a wide range of issues (including some which are beyond the range of the study, such as the desexualisation by society of the elderly, those constructed as 'disabled' and those in institutionalised care). It also has the advantage of shifting attention from a narrow focus on genital activity to a more productive focus on social relations of power. We could illustrate this point by arguing that the difference between 'gay' and 'straight' concerns not so much what people do in bed – which is actually rather similar and limited in its range. Rather, the difference lies in how people experience their lives outside the bedroom – in work, in dealings with families and communities, in their experience of society's rites of passage and in dealings with the state and with its institutions.

Part II

Sexualities, genders

Chapter 2

Modern sexualities and their meanings

Introduction

We are now ready to build on the theoretical foundations we have laid in Part I by exploring some of the ways in which forms of human sexuality have been labelled, categorised, and constructed in modern times. This will involve examining changes in some of the dominant discourses around human sexuality in our society since the nineteenth century. It will also involve looking at some of the ways in which those changes have come about, by analysing the often intensely ideological struggles which have been waged around definitions of sexuality as people, individually and collectively, have fought back against the 'truths' forced upon them by religion and science. Often such people have faced formidable odds stacked against them, and many have been crushed by the burden of stigma and isolation. Often they have displayed immense personal and political courage by simply telling different stories, bearing witness to other truths about sexuality, sometimes forming communities, and sometimes forming other identities which have challenged the identities forced upon them.

We need to keep several issues in mind before embarking on this discussion. First, we know by now that this way of investigating sexuality and social relations of power rejects any essentialism – any idea of a 'real', given, fixed and unchanging sexual truth – and seeks to understand sexualities within a changing social and political context. Moreover, this social and political context is believed to be changing, or open to the possibility of change, precisely because it is characterised by contradictions and clashing discourses. Therefore, logically, it is a linguistic and semantic simplification to talk at all about 'homosexuality', 'heterosexuality', and so on. At any given moment, and above all across time and cultures, there are many possible homosexualities or heterosexualities, and therefore in a sense there is no such thing at all as homosexuality or heterosexuality. In other words, although people in all cultures and places appear to have experienced the joys and pleasures and heartaches of being sexually attracted to, sexually active with, or falling in love with, other people, what these desires, longings, joys and agonies have meant in their own eyes and those of their societies varies enormously. These variations reflect differences in the ways in which societies, groups and individuals attach stigma or validation to various sexual acts; it also reflects the fact that human experiences of sex, love, intimacy and, crucially, power are differentiated by age, gender, race, class, wealth and social status, as well as by personality and psychology. It is for these reasons that this study will adopt the practice of speaking of homosexualities and heterosexualities.

Second, a large part of this discussion of the invention of modern sexualities will of its nature reflect the extent to which dominant discourses in our society have sought to construct particular types of person – attributing certain sexual acts, feelings and desires exclusively to each type, and drawing different conclusions about the moral worth and social positioning of each type of person so designated. However, we must bear in mind that the absolute categories invented by science, medicine, religion, law, and so on, have never been fully internalised by, or successfully implanted in, the population at large. Even in the absence of visible cultures of resistance – such as the new social movements of feminism, lesbian and gay liberation, men's groups – there are many different ways in which people happily, or often not so happily, circumvent dominant discourses or learn to live with contradictions or double standards. We will look at two examples.

(1) There is a lot of evidence that only a minority of men who have sex with other men have ever internalised or accepted as part of their self-identity either older definitions of 'the homosexual' or the more recent self-affirmative discourse of gay identity. The Kinsey report in 1948 – which gave us the arbitrary and since much-disputed figure of ten per cent of the adult population who are 'homosexual' – found that thirty-seven per cent of American men had had sex to the point of orgasm with another man at some point in their lives. In other words, Kinsey found that many men who self-identified as 'heterosexual', and often referred to their married status as affirmation of this, admitted to having had sex with other men. (Indeed, Kinsey classified human sexuality according to a sliding scale of nought to ten, with exclusively homosexual on one end and exclusively heterosexual on the other. Having decided to define as 'exclusively homosexual' those whose experiences and fantasies throughout their lifetime were exclusively of a same-sex nature, he came up with the figure of four per cent who were exclusively homosexual.) Many men may construct same-sex

sexual activity in ways which are 'non-threatening' to their heterosexual identity – as a phase they are passing through, or as something
they do when there are no women available (during military service or
in prison) – or as shared activities with their mates when watching
porno films about women. There is also the macho belief – apparently
widespread in some Mediterranean and Middle Eastern countries – that
a man who performs the penetrative role in sex with another man is
engaged in heterosexual sex, and that only the so-called passive male is
'homosexual'. It may be the case that many men who have sex with
other men are married, self-identify as heterosexual, and would never
dream of setting foot in a gay bar or club. Such men may instead seek
partners in cruising areas such as public parks or toilets, where anon-
ymity allows them to retain a heterosexual identity.

(2) It is also the case that some men and women who do identify as
'homosexual', 'gay' or 'lesbian', are out of the closet and proud about
their new-found sexual identities, may on occasion have (and enjoy)
other-sex sexual activity. The advent of queer politics in the early 1990s
has encouraged discussion of such relationships. Some people may
have redefined themselves as bisexual; others have chosen not to
embrace a new sexual identity but rather to emphasise how their
experience of sexuality points to its fluid and changing nature throughout a person's lifetime.

Ambiguity, fluidity, change, and, on occasion, contradiction may
well characterise how many of us live our lives. But this reality can be
very disturbing to those who have a vested interest in diagnosing and
prescribing how we should live. They ask, 'are these people "really"
homosexual, or "really" heterosexual?' But why do we need to ask such
questions? Why do we need to know?

Third, when investigating the construction of sexualities and sexual
identities we should remember that people may have very different
reasons and motivations for embracing or rejecting various sexual
identities. A man who has sex with other men – once in his life,
occasionally, or frequently – may reject attempts to define him as
homosexual or gay for various reasons. Perhaps he genuinely doesn't
think those are accurate descriptions of his sexuality – maybe it's the
lure of transgressive, forbidden, and until fairly recently illegal, sex
which arouses him rather than the fact that it is with men. Perhaps he
has convinced himself that he doesn't want commitment, involvement
or intimacy, liking the idea of 'functional' sex with strangers in a public
park which offers relief without commitment, and failing to see how
that makes him gay or homosexual. Perhaps he fears that to be labelled

'homosexual' or 'gay' will bring stigma, discrimination, the loss of family and friends, the loss of his job or status, public ridicule, the collapse of his social world – and so he rejects it at all cost. Perhaps he is repelled by labels and categories and refuses to see his sexual activity as anything other than private and personal.

A man or woman who rejects the label 'heterosexual' may also do so for very different reasons. Some may have taken their sexuality for granted and never really thought about it. Some may actually resent 'being forced' by the visible existence of non-heterosexuals to speak of themselves as heterosexual or 'straight'. They may feel uncomfortable with the very idea of theorising or problematising heterosexuality – forcing them to give a name to social privilege or social power which they assume is their birthright as 'normal' men or women. Some feminists argue that women's experience of love and intimacy with men is so different from men's experience of love and intimacy with women that it challenges the notion that one word or concept – heterosexuality – can define the identities of both.

Another illustration of how people have very different motivations for embracing or rejecting labels and identities – or attributing them to others – is that sometimes people understand the label or identity to mean something different from its common or technical usage. Think of the confusion over bisexuality (still confused in many people's minds with transvestism or crossing-dressing, or with transsexuality). Or think of the deliberate confusion in the tabloid press of homosexuality with paedophilia: for example, we regularly read reports about a 'homosexual abuser of boys' but never about a 'heterosexual abuser of girls'. Think also of the widespread confusion over campness – rooted in the historical attribution of effeminacy to 'the homosexual' – to the extent that a man or boy who is branded camp or effeminate is often assumed to be homosexual or gay, which of course is often not the case at all. So people may attribute labels to others who reject them, or even embrace labels and identities themselves, without understanding what they mean to others.

Finally, people may embrace one construction of sexuality, label or identity as a tactic to defend themselves against another which seems more threatening. Some of the early pioneers of sexology were themselves self-identified homosexual men (although some preferred an array of now redundant terms and labels, including 'inverts', 'Uranians' and 'the intermediate sex') who embraced the notion that homosexuality was a mental disorder or due to genetic malfunction. Today, we might accuse them of internalised self-hatred or internalised homophobia. But at the time they felt that by embracing a medical discourse on homosexuality that sought to construct it as a disorder, they could escape the more threatening legal discourse which constructed it as a crime punishable by imprisonment, or even death until 1861 in England, or a religious discourse which constructed it as sinful and evil. They felt that if they could only establish that homosexuality was a manifestation of nature, albeit imperfect nature, then they could argue that it was no more logical to imprison, persecute or brand as sinful someone for having homosexual desires than for being short-sighted.

So as we investigate the social construction of modern sexualities we have to bear all these factors in mind: the changing nature of sexualities; the fact that dominant discourses about what is homosexuality or heterosexuality have never fully reflected how people live and rationalise their sexual lives; the fact that people have very differing reasons and motivations for adopting or rejecting labels and identities and attributing them to others; and the fact that people are often genuinely confused or misinformed about the language of sexuality. Nothing is ever as straightforward in practice as it is in theory. Even when the dominant discourses on sexuality appear complex, ordinary people's lives are, wonderfully, even more complex.

Male homosexualities

The study of the construction of the male homosexual since the nineteenth century is a study of clashing discourses, political agendas and vital interests. The state and other institutions endowed with degrees of social and political power, such as the churches, the medical profession and more recently the media have sought to define the nature and fix the meanings of male homosexuality (as they have of all forms of human sexuality), and to control and regulate it. Those on the receiving end of the dominant discourses – in whom feelings of same-sex desire have awakened – have responded in many different ways. Some have sought to protect themselves from stigma, persecution, ruin, imprisonment, or worse, through forms of denial – a flight from the spectre of the 'homosexual' and all that it implies. They have sublimated or rationalised their same-sex feelings and experiences in various ways and asserted a heterosexual identity. Others asserted a positive homosexual or more recently gay identity, countering dominant discourses with the claim that homosexuality is as normal, natural and healthy as heterosexuality, and 'the homosexual' as intrinsically good a person, and useful a citizen, as 'the heterosexual'.

Of course, this is to accept the division of people into sub-types or categories labelled 'homosexuals' or 'heterosexuals' and therefore, in Foucauldian terms, partly to legitimise the dominant discourse by entering into it. As Edwards (1993: 15) puts it, 'the irony of identity politics is that in creating an opposition to state oppression, the state's power to define and regulate sexuality is inadvertently increased'. Yet as Edwards immediately adds: 'not to have an identity is to retreat into defeat, retire into obscurity, or even vanish into invisibility. Consequently, the question becomes one not of "identity or not" but of "what identity, where, why and how"?'.

Three points arise immediately. First, for those whose sexuality has been negatively constructed by the powers-that-be, as sick, perverted, insane, sinful, criminal, a danger to children and to 'normal' people, the act of claiming a positive identity through various processes of coming out may appear not only empowering, but sometimes a matter of life-and-death. It may make the difference between hanging on to sanity in the face of overwhelming social stigma, or succumbing to loneliness, guilt, self-hatred and sometimes suicide. Contemporary studies from the USA suggest that gay men and lesbians are between two and six times more likely to attempt suicide than heterosexuals (*The Guardian*, 11 August 1999). A Glasgow-based study in 1999 found that two-thirds of gay people in the city had experienced depression, seventeen per cent had attempted suicide and more than a quarter had harmed themselves (*The Sunday Herald*, 18 July 1999). Obviously, the high-risk groups include many young people who never make it past the cruel world of bullying and peer-group stigma to claim a positive sexual identity for themselves. In Britain, another study found that one-third of gay, lesbian and bisexual youngsters were bullied in secondary school, compared to ten per cent of all pupils (*The Guardian*, 11 August 1999). Suspicion of labels and categories apart, claiming a positive sexual identity which one has been denied can be a life-saving moment, literally.

Second, throughout most of the period under examination – since the late nineteenth century – legal persecution and massive social stigma meant that affirmative homosexual identities and the homosexual sub-culture tended to be forced underground and consequently became invisible to most people, including most people who experienced an awakening of same-sex desire. Without an opportunity to explore an identity other than that forced upon them by the dominant discourses, many have indeed 'vanished into invisibility'. This raises problems for the social historian. We may be looking at clashing discourses, but it has been a very uneven clash. There is little doubt as to which side has been able to shout loudest. Even today, when we do have an open lesbian and gay community of sorts and the possibility for affirmative lesbian and gay identities, these still tend to be confined to big cities and possibilities for participation tend to be undermined by mobility, income, age, and psychological disposition. It's probably a very safe bet that those who do self-identify as gay or lesbian or homosexual or bisexual – either to friends or family, or through participation in the lesbian and gay community – are only a small minority of those who are aware of same-sex feelings. So invisibility remains an important issue.

Third, by posing the question of identity politics in terms of 'what identity, where, why and how', Edwards calls on us to remember always that there can be a variety of responses to dominant discourses and a variety of ways in which people have sought to deconstruct and then reconstruct homosexuality.

The following brief summary of the various phases in the construction of modern male homosexualities draws upon the format offered by Edwards (1993: 14–30). This has the attraction of compressing and simplifying a complex body of social history, literary criticism, political analysis and history of ideas into a neat and accessible schema.

Edwards summarises the history of the construction of the modern male homosexual in five phases: damnation, criminalisation, medicalisation, regulation and reform. He hints that currently we may be in the middle of a sixth, post-AIDS, phase. He makes the critically important point that 'all of these phases or developments not only interact and connect, they, to an extent at least, coexist and are all in evidence, alive and kicking, in today's contemporary society' (1993: 16–17). The question to be asked concerns the social, political, cultural and perhaps economic reasons behind the relative rise and fall of the discourses which characterise each phase. Theodore Zeldin (1995: 121–8), whose work has a much wider historical scope, writes that 'sexual relations between men have passed through four phases, but each new phase did not put an end to its predecessor, so all four now co-exist'. Zeldin's four phases might be summarised as: homosexuality as a conservative force bolstering the social status quo (ancient times to roughly the twelfth century); damnation (twelfth to nineteenth centuries); medicalisation (nineteenth century onwards); and 'coming out of the closet' (mid to late twentieth century). The first of Zeldin's phases involves sweeping cultural and historical generalisations about the nature of the sexual relationships involved. The lack of any distinction in his schema between regulation, reform and liberation is also problematical. For these reasons, this study will tend to follow Edwards.

Damnation refers to that period in history when the Christian church was the dominant ideological influence on how Western societies made sense of sexuality. In the aftermath of the European Enlightenment and the rise of secularisation, the Church's monopoly of 'truth' gradually gave way to science, law and medicine in many industrialised countries, especially from the late nineteenth century onwards. However, religious discourses on sexuality live on with varying degrees of intensity.

In his monumental study *Christianity, Social Tolerance, and Homosexuality* (1980) John Boswell demonstrated brilliantly that the various movements to reform the Christian church in the early part of the second millennium led to an increased concern with the sexual behaviour of priests and nuns, which was extended to greater control and regulation of society at large. Before the twelfth century, the Church's teaching on homosexuality had been much less uniformly harsh than is commonly supposed. Zeldin quotes the Archbishop of Canterbury, Saint Anselm, who in 1102 demanded that the punishment for homosexuality should be moderate because 'this sin has been so public that hardly anyone has blushed for it, and many, therefore, have plunged into it without realising its gravity'. And Saint Aelred of Rievaulx praised homosexuality in monasteries as a way of discovering divine love (Zeldin 1995: 123).

The drive to control the sexual behaviour of priests and nuns led, from the twelfth century onwards, to a series of edicts against various sexual activities. As Edwards puts it, what these had in common was that they were 'prohibitions against non-procreative forms of sexuality such as sexual pleasure per se, prostitution, extramarital sex and homosexuality in the form of same-sex practices' (1993: 17). The term 'sodomy' was applied to a wide field of same-sex and other-sex practices including oral sex. The religious edict against non-procreative sexual acts meant that during the fifteenth and sixteenth centuries, the ecclesiastical authorities sanctioned the burning at the stake of women convicted of witchcraft. Feminist historical research has shown that many of these women were in effect accused of adultery, or abortion, or of being 'barren' – i.e. failing to produce children. Edwards makes the point that it was homosexual and other non-procreative sex acts which were condemned as sin, abomination, a crime against nature, worthy of eternal damnation. In other words, practices and not people as such were condemned; there were as yet no 'homosexuals'. We are dealing here with the pre-history of the modern homosexual. The idea that homosexual sex represents non-procreative sex, sex for the sake of pure pleasure, *par excellence* has therefore a long pedigree. Those for whom sexual pleasure for its own sake is a dirty or sinful thing required little imagination to attribute all manner of sickness and perversions to the modern homosexual when he entered the stage of history in the nineteenth century.

The close relationship between the ecclesiastical and temporal powers in many Western societies through the centuries has meant that, what the Church (especially the Catholic Church) condemned as sinful and evil was usually subject to a range of judicial punishments. In England, after the Reformation and before 1885, the only law against same-sex acts was that passed by Henry VIII in 1533 which prohibited 'sodomy', a loosely defined concept. In practice, there was little attempt by the state to enforce this law – it was usually reserved for political opponents. This was partly because the law required proof of 'sodomy' in the form of entry into the anus or mouth and ejaculation therein; such proof was hard to produce.

The nineteenth century saw a marked increase in criminalisation of homosexuality. In 1826, Sir Robert Peel dropped the requirement to prove ejaculation and reinstated the death penalty for 'sodomy'. The death penalty was replaced by life imprisonment with hard labour in 1861, although this was applied only in cases where 'public decency' was outraged. From 1885 onwards, the amendment to the Criminal Justice Act known as the Labouchère Amendment criminalised all sexual acts between men, whether in private or in public, as 'gross indecency', to be punished by two years hard labour. The penalty also applied to anyone helping others to commit 'gross indecency' (David 1997: 17–18). This remained the case until 1967 when very limited decriminalisation was allowed in England and Wales (this limited reform was not extended to Scotland until 1980, and Northern Ireland had to wait a further two years). This period of criminalisation constructed the modern homosexual as a criminal, a traitor to his sex and frequently to his social class and country. It thus contributed to and reinforced a discourse which held up the modern male homosexual as an example of moral weakness, lacking in manliness and patriotism and inclined towards subversion – of youth, of society, of the empire, of the army, of the nation. These prejudices are still with us; we have only to think of the eagerness with which the media pounced on the former Soviet agent Sir Anthony Blunt's homosexuality as 'proof' of his treasonable intent, or of the MacCarthyite witchhunts in the USA in the 1950s which associated homosexuality with 'communist conspiracies'. Criminalisation also forced men now branded as homosexual to live furtive lives in the shadows, often lives of deceit, or risk absolute ruin. The choice was now between the closet and the prison cell, and only a brave few risked leaving the closet. In recent years a number of works of oral history have appeared which have sought, on the basis of interviews, to record the life-stories of many twentieth-century homosexual men and women (for example, Cant 1993, Jivani 1997, Porter and Weeks 1991). A recurring theme in their stories is their sense of isolation and vulnerability. Even when anti-homosexual laws were not enforced, their presence on the statute books served to condemn the lives of many thousands of people to invisibility.

The phase in the construction of the modern male homosexual known as medicalisation occurs simultaneously with criminalisation. (The best account of this period in recent history remains that given by Weeks (1990: 11–83), upon which the following summary draws.) Karol Benkert coined the word 'homosexual' in 1869 and it was in common parlance by the 1890s. The term was soon picked up by the developing discipline of clinical psychology, which sought to explain variations in human sexuality through experimenting on patients and producing medical-psychological models. The 'homosexual' was branded by medicine as a case study in pathology. Many different theories were produced which appear distinctly contradictory and discredited from today's perspective, but still linger in our culture. One theory, popularised by the German lawyer and early advocate of homosexual law reform Karl Heinrich Ulrichs (1825–95), was that the homosexual was afflicted by a mental disorder known as inversion – the idea that he was a female mind trapped inside a male body. Conversely, a lesbian was later constructed as someone with a male mind trapped inside a woman's body. The Austrian scientist Richard von Krafft-Ebing (1840–1902) argued for decriminalisation of homosexuality on the grounds that homosexuals were mentally ill and therefore it was no more logical to criminalise homosexuality than to criminalise schizophrenia or depression. Neither Ulrichs or Krafft-Ebing had a shred of evidence for their theories. Krafft-Ebing argued that homosexuality was due to brain defects brought on by masturbation. The idea was that by excessive masturbation a male inadvertently taught himself to prefer the sex organs of his own sex rather than those of the female sex. He therefore concluded that homosexuality was a clinically defective condition which could be treated by killing the desire to masturbate.

Some of these scientists may indeed have been motivated by the desire to 'rescue' homosexuality from moral condemnation and imprisonment by introducing a discourse of medical health. For example, Ulrichs' biographer hails him as a pioneer of the modern gay movement and acclaims his (in Ulrichs' own words) 'fight for freedom from persecution and insults' (Kennedy 1988: 70). But it may be argued that these were hopelessly naïve and that, in Foucauldian terms, they contributed to new systems of control and regulation. If the homosexual was constructed as someone suffering from an illness, a brain disorder, a congenital disease, it was a short step to arguing that 'healthy' society had to be protected from contagion, and to justifying a variety of medical experiments on men against their will. After all, if such men were mentally ill, how could they possibly decide rationally that castration, electric shocks or lobotomies were not in their best interests?

Medicalisation and criminalisation often reinforced each other. This was especially the case during the last great witch hunt of homosexual men in Britain which took place between 1950 and 1955. In 1955 alone no less than 1,065 men went to prison in Britain for having consensual sex with another man and many others were fined, cautioned or put on probation. Some men sought to avoid the stigma of a prison sentence by volunteering for psychiatric and medical 'treatment', which could include chemical castration. Amongst those whose lives were destroyed in this way was the great mathematician and father of computer science Alan Turing, who reacted so badly to the effects of chemical castration that he committed suicide two years later.

The period also saw attempts by some scientists and intellectuals to challenge such discourses. John Addington Symmonds (1840–93) worked hard in the field of history and ethical philosophy to show that homosexuality had existed in all times and all places and was neither pathological nor a case of inversion. But he was terrified of being imprisoned or disgraced himself and drew back from wide dissemination of his research; after his death in 1893, his writings were destroyed by his family to 'protect' their reputation. Havelock Ellis (1859–1939) called for tolerance of homosexuality as harmless, but in his writings acquiesced in the idea of homosexuality as abnormal and was thus inhibited from confronting the dominant discourse. Edward Carpenter (1844–1929), a significant socialist intellectual and writer, went further than any perhaps in challenging the conventions of his day. Living openly with his male partner and running a semi-commune with a group of feminists, left-wing visionaries and others, he cele-brated same-sex desire (which he called 'Comrade love') as a way of breaking down barriers of class, a form of real affection, a liberation of the spirit beyond the gender roles forced on people by a capitalist society. But his work, including *The Intermediate Sex* and *Towards Democracy*, remained accessible to very few and has only recently been 'rediscovered' (Carpenter 1984). In his lifetime he was savaged by the medical profession and lived in constant fear of arrest.

The rise of industrial society, the growing power and influence of science throughout the nineteenth century, and the gradual decline of the Christian churches with the process of secularisation had all made possible an assault (in the name of science and knowledge) upon certain Biblical 'truths'. Yet for a long time scientific, legal and religious discourses on homosexuality (and other forms of human sexuality) co-existed and sometimes reinforced each other. Just as there was no absolute rupture between the phases in the construction of the modern homosexual known as damnation, criminalisation and medicalisation, so too the movement from criminalisation and medicalisation to more subtle forms of regulation was slow and partial.

Once again, the dynamic driving the change from one phase to another seems to have been that of far-reaching processes of social change, which opened up new possibilities for viewing sexual behaviour in a different light. Edwards (1993) sees the post-1945 period as one in which the state searched for new ways to regulate behaviour and reimpose order on a social structure which had been shaken to its foundations by war. David (1997) points to the importance of both the First and Second World Wars in bringing about social changes which were to facilitate the slow emergence of a homosexual sub-culture very different from the world of the late nineteenth century. Especially after 1945, there could be no turning back. Public attitudes towards women's roles had been transformed by the experience of women working in factories, on the land, driving buses, and so on. Yet a partial retreat from the pre-war modes of gender and sexual behaviour required more subtle forms of regulation. In 1957, the Wolfenden parliamentary committee report recommended a new form of regulation of homosexuality through privatisation. Homosexual acts would be legalised in private between two men over twenty-one years of age. Displays of affection between men would remain illegal in public, and sex acts between men would remain illegal in private if more than two men were involved. This implied a very limited tolerance, and certainly not social acceptance, let alone equal rights. Homosexuality would be constructed as a private perversion to which society could turn a blind eye as long as there was no challenge to the supremacy of heterosexuality as the norm. Even this limited reform took ten years to be passed into law in England and Wales, and even longer in Scotland and Northern Ireland. (Jeffery-Poulter (1991) gives a good account of the struggle for legal reform.)

Partial decriminalisation, then, involved new forms of regulation. Indeed, increased police activity against homosexual men meant a marked increase in prosecutions and imprisonments after 1967. 'Normal' society was to be reassured that tolerance had its limits. Nevertheless, the 1967 legal change did permit the emergence of a radical gay liberation movement, even if that was certainly not the intention. For the first time, men could declare openly that they were lovers – provided they were over twenty-one years old, and showed no affection in public, of course – without fear of automatic arrest; and they could campaign for further reform.

The liberalism of the 1960s, however unsatisfactory and incomplete, did help towards a further phase in the construction of the modern male homosexual – a phase in which those who had been marginalised, stigmatised and condemned to invisibility for so long could at last begin to articulate a challenge to the dominant sexual ideologies. This phase has sometimes been referred to as a period of 'reform to liberation'. The Gay Liberation Front was launched in the UK in 1970, a year after the Stonewall riots in New York, when gay men had fought back against police raids. Stonewall marked the birth of the modern gay and lesbian movement in the USA. The assertion of a new and positive or self-affirming identity involved a rejection of previous liberal notions of reform which had accepted that homosexuality was abnormal but pleaded for tolerance. Gay liberation asserted self-worth and the very label 'gay' was adopted in what Edwards calls 'a blatant assertion of positive self-evaluation over the medical, pathologised label of homosexual' (1993: 26). The essence of the new identity was the process of individual and collective re-birth known as 'coming out'. This, in its most politicised form, involved three over-lapping procedures: coming out to oneself by accepting one's homosexuality as an identity to be proud of; entering into a community by forming not just relationships but social and political alliances with others of a similar sexual orientation in safe places, and creating such safe places if they didn't exist; and coming out to the wider heterosexual society of family, friends and workplace. By openly challenging the assumption of heterosexual normality and homosexual pathology and rejecting the gender role stereotypes which often underpinned it, the new gay and lesbian identities sought to subvert existing dominant discourses on sexuality.

Of course, this is far from being the whole story. There was particularly fierce backlash, especially in the wake of the onset of AIDS in the 1980s. And just as lesbian, gay and bisexual politics have always exhibited tensions between reformist and more utopian impulses, so too, lesbian, gay and bisexual identities have been constantly interrogated by questions pertaining to gender, race, and degrees of affluence. We will return to these issues later. For now, it should be emphasised that the construction and deconstruction (subversion?) of male homosexualities is still very much an on-going process.

Lesbianisms

While medicine, science and the criminal law were the significant forces in constructing and bringing to public attention the phenomenon of the male homosexual, it was in late nineteenth- and early twentieth-century literature that public images of lesbian women were first presented. Several women writers, in particular Radclyffe Hall (1880–1943) whose novel *The Well of Loneliness* was famously banned under the Obscene Publications Act in 1928, have been identified as important figures in this development. It has been argued by Weeks (1990: 87–111) that whereas male homosexuality was constructed against the grain of mainstream male sexual identity – the association with effeminacy, weakness, and disease, and the suggestion of a failed man, a pseudo-woman – lesbianism before the present century (and before it was named as such) merged more easily into the general pattern of female interactions. It was silent because un- thinkable, because an autonomous female sexuality was unthinkable. Under such circumstances, representations of strong and intense ro- mantic friendships between women could escape the stigma of sexual perversion.

The emergence of lesbianism in the twentieth century, in the sense of its increased visibility, was in large part due to the growing realisation that women in general had sexual needs and desires which were not simply 'kissed into life' by men. So we can argue that the different historical origins of lesbian identity perhaps highlight a number of related elements which have traditionally shaped images of and atti- tudes towards lesbians. Among these are the social roles assigned to women; prevailing definitions of female sexuality; and the ways in which lesbians have defined their own identities.

The social roles of women have traditionally been determined pri- marily in relation to assumptions about their family responsibilities. Female identity can be seen to have been largely defined both by, and in terms of, men and the procreative function. For example, the fact that lesbianism was largely ignored by nineteenth- and early twentieth- century medicine and science can arguably be seen as a reflection of the male dominance of these fields, and of the dominance of masculinist assumptions – sometimes shared by the handful of women scientists who were published in the mainstream – about women's primary or even sole role as wives and mothers. If lesbianism was considered at all, early scientific studies tended to present it in terms explicable to men: (1) as a characteristic of prostitution, of fallen women, that is to say immoral or evil women, 'whores', who had fallen from the state of feminine grace; or (2) as pseudo-maleness. The dominance of these ideas has continued right into this century. During the Nazi holocaust, whereas homosexual men were a separate stratum within the concen- tration camps and were forced to wear the pink triangle on their camp uniforms, the Nazis officially classified lesbians as prostitutes forcing them to wear the black triangle insignia which the Nazis applied to prostitutes, vagrants and 'common criminals' and often to work as prostitutes servicing German soldiers. (This is why the black triangle badge, not the pink, is regarded by many contemporary lesbian activists as the authentic badge of lesbian defiance and self-visibility.)

Other popular 'explanations' for lesbianism which emerged in the first half of the twentieth century also clearly reflected the dominance of the idea that an autonomous female sexuality was inconceivable and that lesbianism could be understood only in male-centred terms. Lesbianism was presented variously as the outcome of rape or abuse by a male father figure, as residing in an hysterical fear of pregnancy, or as the preserve of 'unattractive' women who really wanted men's attention. All these myths are still with us. Another, which has rather fallen from favour, was that illegitimate female children were more likely to turn out lesbian because of the lack of a 'normal' mother-figure role model and a consequent inability to develop fully into their 'natural' roles as wives and mothers.

What might nowadays be regarded as lesbian relationships between middle- and upper-class women, but at the time were regarded as 'romantic friendships', were common in the nineteenth century and carried no stigma. Not only were they desexualised, but they were presented as fully compatible with heterosexual marriage – that is, as non-threatening to a female identity which was defined by, and in relation to, men. This construction still echoes today, even in an era in which same-sex relationships between women have been sexualised within popular culture and medico-moral discourses applied to them. Same-sex activity between women is frequently presented in pornography aimed at a male heterosexual audience in ways which present 'lesbianism' not as an expression of female sexual autonomy but as a titillating foreplay to men's possession of and enjoyment of women's bodies.

Despite the gradual adoption of the term 'lesbian' from the 1890s onwards, lesbianism remained a largely invisible social phenomenon until the 1960s. A specific lesbian sexual identity emerged later than the gay male sexual identity; subcultural development was also slower, reflecting more limited possibilities for bars, clubs and a commercial scene. Women tended to have considerably less financial autonomy and spending power than men, so access to commercial and shared spaces was restricted. This invisibility was, and still is, reflected in the criminal law. In general, lesbians have not been subject to the criminal law on the same scale as gay men. An attempt in 1921 to extend the criminal law to lesbians failed and, to date, there are no common law or statutory offenses specifically directed at lesbians, although lesbian acts have been prosecuted in Scotland as a form of 'shameless indecency'.

The theme of lesbian invisibility can also be detected within social constructions of sexual activity. It has been shown that in most

Western cultures, sexual activity has traditionally been defined princi-
pally in terms of its procreative function. As such, vaginal intercourse
has been widely portrayed as the 'normal', 'natural' and 'most satisfying' form of sexual activity. The assumption that sex necessarily
involves vaginal intercourse was enshrined in the legal definition
of rape in the UK until 1994 when the Criminal Justice Act was
amended to include for the first time a definition of anal rape. Such
a view can be seen to have affected not only how other forms of sexual
activity are evaluated as sexually satisfying or arousing, but also
whether they are regarded as sexual acts at all. Diane Richardson
(1996: 278) has suggested that lesbians are often depicted as participat-
ing in foreplay rather than 'real sex'. Another common portrayal of
lesbian sex is as a mimicry of heterosexual intercourse involving the use
of penile substitutes. Such myths may be seen to reflect traditional
male-centred assumptions about female sexuality which emphasise
vaginal orgasm.

In common with male homosexual identity, lesbian identity has
traditionally been defined by dominant discourses in terms of deviant
sexual preference/activity. Such an interpretation can be detected
within the widely held view that lesbianism is incompatible with
motherhood. The implication of this seems to be that lesbian mothers
pose some sort of sexual threat to children – although not perhaps as
great a threat as homosexual or gay fathers are often constructed as
posing. As an assumption, this can be linked to the challenge which the
reality, the existence, of lesbian motherhood presents to dominant
ideologies of gender and family, which arguably reflect patriarchal and
heterosexist ideas. These have portrayed motherhood as a state to
which all 'normal' women aspire. Indeed, motherhood generally invites automatic assumptions of heterosexuality. Such values have been
reinforced in UK legislation such as the Local Government Act 1988
which prohibits the 'promotion of homosexuality as a pretended
family relationship'. Whatever the difficulties experienced in translat-
ing this piece of legislation into practice, there is no doubt that it was
intended to prevent schools, libraries and other bodies financed by
local authorities from stocking books and other materials which portrayed gay men and lesbians in family situations – in stable relationships, and especially bringing up children.

Indeed, so powerful is the discourse which equates women with
motherhood and motherhood with heterosexuality, that Monique
Wittig (1992) has argued that to be lesbian is to repudiate the very
category of woman, through repudiating the inequality inherent in
patriarchy and heterosexuality.

Over recent decades, lesbians have struggled to extend definitions of their own identities beyond the boundaries of the sexual. During the 1970s, lesbianism was desexualised by many lesbian feminists who asserted that lesbian identities should be seen primarily in terms of a political strategy involving the rejection of male-dominated hetero-sexist oppression and not in terms of what certain people did in bed or who they did it with.

The emergence of a specifically lesbian political activism from the early 1970s onwards has to be set against the background of a triple marginalisation and oppression which many lesbian activists experi-enced during the 1960s and early 1970s First, the broader gay liberation movement was overwhelmingly dominated by white middle-class gay men both in Britain and the USA, and within it many women felt marginalised by sexism. Second, and crucially, marginalisation oc-curred within the broader feminist movement. Emily Hamer (1996: 191–211) recounts how many heterosexual feminists in the 1960s and early 1970s were reluctant to take up issues of concern to lesbians for fear of discrediting feminism as a whole by making it a laughing stock in the eyes of male-dominated society. In Betty Friedan's infamous phrase, lesbians were branded the 'lavender menace'. Third, these feelings of marginalisation within both the gay and feminist move-ments were, for many, compounded by a media discourse which sought to define what it meant to be lesbian. As Hamer puts it:

> The media seized upon 'loony' lesbian stories as a way to attack not only all lesbians but all feminists. The stigmatization of lesbian feminists as fat, ugly women in dungarees was used to attack lesbians and feminists regardless of what they actually thought about lesbian-feminism. This meant that lesbianism quite generally came to be seen as a politicized identity, and many lesbians who had not seen their lesbianism as political had to accept that other people now did. (Hamer 1996: 201)

The emergence of a politicised lesbian identity and the passionate debates which accompanied it further underline the enormous diver-sity of human experiences of sexuality, and of identity politics. For not all those who agree that lesbianism is a political identity agree on what that identity is, and not all women who identify as lesbian agree that it is a political identity. At the heart of recent debates has been the issue of whether lesbianism – given its specific historical trajectory, rooted in the subordination of all women and the denial of female sexual autonomy by patriarchy – should be seen as a distinct sexual identity for some women; or as a potential political identity for all women, regardless of whether or not they have sex with other women.

Adrienne Rich, whose 1980 article 'Compulsory Heterosexuality and Lesbian Existence' (reproduced in Jackson and Scott 1996) stimulated a vigorous debate, is probably the most outspoken and best-known proponent of the position that lesbianism is a potential political position for all women. Rich argues that we must draw a distinction between what she called lesbian existence and a lesbian continuum. Lesbian existence refers to the historical presence in our society of women who self-identify as lesbians. Their sense of identity may not be rooted in sexual practices but rather in a sense of self of women who are emotionally and politically bonded primarily to other women independent of men. By a lesbian continuum she means that there exists 'a range – through each woman's life and throughout history – of woman-identified experience, not simply the fact that a woman has had or consciously desired genital sexual experience with another woman' (Rich 1996: 135). Such a continuum includes many more forms of primary intensity between and among women – the sharing of an inner life, bonding against male tyranny, giving and receiving practical and political support, and resistance to attempts to regulate female sexuality and women's roles in society and within the family. A lesbian continuum may embrace all women who can move in and out of it, regardless of whether they identify themselves as lesbian or not. It forms a culture of sisterhood, solidarity and resistance to male power embedded in patriarchy.

Rich saw compulsory heterosexuality as the key mechanism of control of all women, ensuring, by defining other sexualities out of existence, the perpetuation of male domination. Lesbianism – both through the existence of self-identified lesbian women and through the various bonds which potentially exist between all women located somewhere on the lesbian continuum – becomes the focal point of political resistance to patriarchy. It is thus seen as not primarily – or even at all – about genital sexual acts, but about the realisation of the male-free potential of all women.

Against this position other lesbians and feminists have raised a number of objections. As Weeks (1987: 45) points out, three criticisms have been fundamental. First, the notion that lesbianism is a potential political identity for all women – a sort of political vanguard of the women's movement – has been criticised as based on a romantic presentation of women's bonds. It seems to suppose the pre-existence of a powerful female solidarity of sisterhood which is always there but constantly suppressed or driven underground by patriarchy. Similar criticism has been levelled at Marx's notion of class consciousness: that it supposes the existence of a consciousness which actually has to be created; that it underestimates the complex nature of how power discourses affect people's subjectivities; and that it underestimates real contradictions within the oppressed group – in Marxism's case, the working-class, in radical lesbian feminism's case, women. Take, for example, contradictions between white women and black women or working-class women and bourgeois women. If a black, working-class, 'heterosexual', married woman decides she has more in common with her black, working-class husband than she has with her white, middle-class, lesbian employer – is she suffering from false consciousness induced by patriarchy? This would seem to be Rich's position. Other lesbians and feminists have argued that such a conclusion would not only be elitist but would risk distorting the complexities of the construction of women and thus obscuring the sort of politics needed to bring about real change.

Second, Rich and the radical lesbian feminist school have been criticised by a feminist writer such as Cora Kaplan as trapped in naturalistic essentialism. Kaplan (quoted in Weeks 1987: 46) writes of Rich that for her, 'female heterosexuality is socially constructed and female homosexuality is natural . . . Political lesbianism becomes more than a strategic position for feminism, it is a return to nature'. This, she argues, brings about a narrowing in political focus: women are seen as always oppressed by compulsory heterosexuality, always socially controlled by men, who stand outside history. The danger is that women can be constructed as perpetual victims and sufferers. The ways in which women through their struggles have changed the forms of heterosexuality and challenged masculinity by engaging with it can be overlooked.

A third criticism which some lesbian feminists have directed at Rich is that she ignores the specifics of lesbian sexuality, and thereby contributes to a desexualisation of lesbianism. Such writers take the view, according to Weeks, that 'the elevation of female sexuality in general into a semi-mystical bonding, where bodily contact and genital pleasure are secondary or even non-existent, denies the possibilities of female eroticism, including the real potentiality of lesbianism' (1987: 46).

It might be added here that a fourth criticism has been levelled at Rich's school of radical lesbian feminism by lesbian feminists such as Beatrix Campbell (1987:19–39). Campbell argues that a retreat into naturalism and separatism risks seeing men and not male-dominated institutions as the enemy; that a focus on heterosexual sexual practices or acts rather than on the forms of sexual relations as the target leads logically to the conclusion that every heterosexual act serves the function of punishing and controlling women; and that this can lead to heterosexual or bisexual women being stigmatised as collaborators with the enemy. Ironically, this seems to lead to an implosion of the very solidarity and sisterhood, the possibilities of which Rich set out to map.

Diane Richardson (1996) has written of the resexualisation of lesbian identities over the past decade under the shadow of AIDS and discussion of safer sex. Others (for example, Schneider 1992) have noted the political divergences which have opened up between lesbian feminists who have worked with gay men in joint campaigns around issues such as AIDS and campaigns for law reform, and radical lesbian feminists who have tended to criticise such work as serving a male agenda, and have chosen instead to emphasise separatism. It is possible that the construction of modern lesbianism as a desexualised, political identity for all women may inadvertently offer succour to a conservative and misogynistic discourse. Anna Marie Smith has analysed how, in the UK, such a discourse has sought to set 'harmless, sex-free lesbians' against 'perverted, sex-mad gay men'. For example, she quotes Lord Halsbury, speaking in the House of Lords in 1986, who declared: 'Lesbians are not a problem. They do not molest little girls. They do not engage in disgusting and unnatural acts like buggery. They are not wildly promiscuous and do not spread venereal disease' (Smith 1994: 208). Smith argues that official discourses around AIDS in both the UK and USA have over-sexualised gay men – who are defined entirely in terms of sexual promiscuity – and desexualised lesbians. This, she argues, reinforces a traditional discourse which views women as passive, demure, moderate and non-assertive. She implies that there is a need to resexualise lesbianism in the sense of reclaiming a right to and reasserting the existence of woman-to-woman sexual acts.

These debates about what lesbianism is, what its potentialities are, and what it means to women in general, illustrate the great complexity of the human experience of sexuality and of identity politics. The social construction of lesbian identities also 'testifies to the historical denial of a particular form of female desire – and the struggle necessary to affirm it' (Weeks 1987: 47).

Heterosexualities

What is heterosexuality? What does it mean and how has it been constructed? Is it changing? Many people find these difficult questions to pose. Kitzinger and Wilkinson (1993) report a reluctance on the part of many feminists to acknowledge a heterosexual identity. The women they are describing never in their writings or public pronouncements gave any indication of a non-heterosexual existence, often lived in a steady relationship with a man, but resented being labelled as 'hetero-sexual' in many cases because they felt this to be an inadequate description of either their politics as feminists or their experience of life as women.

Many male writers on masculinity speak of masculinity, rather than heterosexuality, as their sexual identity. They write of 'male sexuality', 'masculine sexuality', the 'sexuality of men', effectively conflating their gender and sexual identities. Yet it is often the case that they are universalising from their own experience as men whose sexual desires, feelings, needs and fears are directed towards women. Their hetero-sexuality remains unnamed, and subsumed within their masculinity. By equating masculinity with their sexuality, they ignore gay and bisexual men who are often confined to the limbo of non-men.

The question of heterosexuality is not just a question of sexual attraction, or relationships, between men and women. Modern hetero-sexuality is every bit as much a social construction as modern homo-sexuality or lesbianism, and can only be understood in terms of meanings, discourses, power relations, power within relationships, and the institutionalisation of norms which produces privileges as well as disadvantages for groups according to how they are labelled.

Indeed, even a superficial, 'common-sense' definition of heterosexu-ality which rests upon the notion of sexual attraction between men and women will not suffice. Not all men who are sexually and emotionally attracted to women, and vice versa, are, or see themselves as, hetero-sexual. And how do we deal with the phenomenon of the rapist, abuser, sadist – typically but not exclusively male – who derives sexual pleasure from abuse of power? Is he sexually and emotionally attracted to women? Or is he motivated by hatred and fear of women, and sexually excited by power? At a deeper and more disturbing level, is other-sex or opposite-sex attraction at the heart of heterosexuality, or is it a mixture of attraction and repulsion, desire and fear, 'need for' and 'alienation from'? Some writers, of a liberal or even conservative shade, see the misogynist (for example) as an anomaly, an exception. Others, includ-ing radical feminist theorists, and many liberal psychologists or psy-cho-analysts such as Heather Formaini (1990), see misogyny as inherent in heterosexual masculinity, in the dominant forms it takes in our society. They see it as reflecting deep-rooted power differentials between men and women stretching far back into history or even pre-history, which condition relationships between men and women. Others, still, see misogyny as an inherent aspect – active or dormant – of the dominant forms of masculinity, whether heterosexual, gay or bisexual.

Similar debates surround the subject of sado-masochism. The eroticisation of power has its corollary in the eroticisation of powerlessness and while this applies both to men and women it has especial political and moral resonance for feminists. Heterosexual men in general have been notoriously reluctant to air the issue of male masochism – although all the evidence from numerous surveys of sex workers to a casual perusal of sex-line adverts in the tabloid press suggests that masochistic desire amongst British heterosexual men is widespread. And anti-sexist heterosexual male theorists sympathetic to feminism have been embarrassed about problematising and politicising their fantasies of sexual domination of women. Some feminist writers have argued that eroticisation of male domination and female submission, sanctioned and reproduced by the dominant culture, is central to the institution of heterosexuality and can even affect the nature of homo-sexual relationships. Sheila Jeffreys argues this point in a passage which is worth quoting at length:

> The 'difference' between the sexes which is supposed to give the excitement to heterosexual sex, is, I would argue, not natural but political, a difference of power. Heterosexual desire is formed out of, and requires for its excitement and continuance, the subjection of women. But it is not limited to opposite-sex couplings. Lesbians and gay men can experience heterosexual desire too, through the repro-duction of gender through butch/femme role-playing, other stylised forms of gender power difference such as sado-masochism or through eroticising race, class or age differences. The opposite of heterosexual desire is homosexual desire: desire based upon sameness instead of difference of power, desire which is about mutuality and which is more suited to the egalitarian future that feminists which to create. Heterosexual women and men can experience homosexual desire, but the structural power differences that regulate the relations be-tween women and men can make this particularly difficult to achieve. (Jeffreys 1996: 76–7)

Here, Jeffreys clearly reformulates the notions of homosexual and heterosexual desire in terms of equality (or its absence), arguing that we are all enmeshed in the institutions of heterosexuality, which reflect profound social and political inequalities between men and women in patriarchal societies. In other words, when we study the social con-struction of heterosexuality we come face to face with a powerful ideology of heterosexuality which continually gets in the way of a democratisation of male-female relations and reproduces inegalitarian-ism through the eroticisation of powerlessness. However, Stevi Jackson has a point when she writes, 'to argue that the power hierarchy of gender is structural does not mean that it is exercised uniformly and evenly at the level of interpersonal sexual relations, nor that our practice and experience is wholly determined by patriarchal structures and ideologies. There is some room for manoeuvre within these constraints. To deny this is to deny heterosexual women any agency . . . It certainly cannot be assumed that if women like heterosexual sex we must all be wallowing in a masochistic eroticization of our subordination – the consistent message of the radical lesbian position' (Jackson 1996: 29).

Feminists, as the contributions in Kitzinger and Wilkinson (1993) make clear, and those male theorists who have addressed power imbalances in heterosexual relationships in their writings on masculinity, (amongst whom are Cohen (1990), Hearn and Ford (1991), and Seidler (1991), are also divided over the strategies needed to free male-female relationships from the sexism and heterosexism which informs institutionalised heterosexuality. Some radical lesbian feminists, such as Monique Wittig (1992), see heterosexuality itself as inherently inegalitarian and a withdrawal from heterosexuality in favour of a chosen lesbian identity as the only way to subvert gender inequality. This option is rejected as either unrealistic or undesirable by feminists such as Stevi Jackson (1996, 1996a) and Marie-Jo Dhavernas (1996) and, not surprisingly, by virtually all (mainly heterosexual) male theorists working in this area. Most feminists and heterosexual male theorists have instead focused the discussion on ways in which to combat gender inequalities and democratise other-sex relationships. In so doing, they are drawing a conceptual distinction between on the one hand, other-sex desire, other-sex sexual acts and relationships, and on the other, heterosexuality as an institution – as a site of certain forms of privilege and inequality and specific forms of regulation. To critically deconstruct heterosexuality as an institution is not to invalidate other-sex relationships, any more than to critically deconstruct discourses on homosexuality is to invalidate same-sex relationships.

When we investigated the construction of male homosexuality in modern times, we considered not why some people are sexually and emotionally attracted to others of their sex, but the various meanings society attributed to their feelings, relationships and lives through its ideological discourses, institutions and sites of power. We also looked at how this impacted on the lives, social standing and health of the people constructed as 'homosexual'. A parallel assumption can be made for heterosexuality: that what requires investigation is not the existence of male-female attraction, desire and relationships but what 'heterosexuality' has come to mean in our society.

There are three important issues. First, as Kitzinger and Wilkinson

(1993) point out, heterosexuality is frequently not experienced as a political identity but rather as something which is simply taken for granted. As two of the contributors to their book put it, 'who would want to mobilize around being straight?!' (Gill and Walker 1993: 71). The answer is probably that while very few feminists or anti-sexist 'straight' men have mobilised politically around being straight, some on the religious or moral right wing have sought to do so as part of the backlash against perceived advances by gay men and lesbians. This may increase the reluctance of feminists and 'progressive' straight men to claim a heterosexual identity and to ask themselves what it means to be straight nowadays. There is perhaps an embarrassment that it might be seen as either unnecessary or as part of the backlash. In other words, there is no simple symmetry between heterosexual identities and gay, lesbian or homosexual identities and we cannot trace the evolution of the former in quite the same way as we did the latter.

Heterosexuality is so inscribed in the norms of society that it is frequently invisible. Changes are certainly taking place – fuelled by economic and cultural change – which cause heterosexuality as lived and experienced by most people to shift over time. But whether it is debates over men sharing housework and child-rearing, the 'crisis' of marriage and behind that the broader crisis of male-female relationships in adjusting to social change, or the increased sympathy for (or at least tolerance of) lesbian and gay demands for equal legal rights, all these developments in heterosexuality are usually approached and conceptualised in piecemeal form and rarely provoke any debate about the changing nature of heterosexuality itself.

A related issue is that we all, in a real sense, live in heterosexuality whether we are heterosexual or not. Society is heterosexual, its laws, institutions, and values are imbued with the assumption of heterosexuality. We almost all grow up in families where heterosexuality is assumed. We are educated in schools where it is universalised; work in environments where it is taken for granted; are affected by marriage laws, tax laws, inheritance laws, residency laws, and laws governing how we behave in public, which afford privilege to heterosexuality as the only recognised form of being. Most people take this so much for granted that the very use of the word 'privilege' may cause surprise. Yet that which is granted to one group of persons and denied to others can indeed be described as privilege. We inhale heterosexuality with the air we breathe. This is really what is meant by institutionalised heterosexuality or heterosexuality as a site of power.

So it becomes impossible to imagine a heterosexual sub-culture or a heterosexual community in the same conceptual framework as a gay sub-culture or lesbian community. There may of course be sub-cultures within heterosexuality but that is rather different. This has important implications for sexual identities and sexual politics. Those who are constructed as 'homosexual' or 'lesbian' or who come to recognise themselves as non-heterosexual may be forced reconstruct their lives and identities against the norm – in opposition to the dominant discourses. Those who recognise themselves reflected in society's mirror, even if only partially, may find it easier to go with the flow. Even if they are deeply unhappy with aspects of their lives and relationships, they may not make a link between this state and the dominant forms which heterosexuality takes at present. In other words, whereas women who are profoundly dissatisfied with the position of women in society and their own personal experiences of relationships with men may 'come out' as feminists, and some straight men who are unhappy with sexism or heterosexism may try to rethink their masculinity, it is much less usual for heterosexuals to 'come out' as 'straight' in the sense of rethinking, reworking and reclaiming their heterosexuality. This may be either because it seems unnecessary to them to challenge heterosexual privilege, especially if it is not perceived as privilege, or because straight identities alternative to the dominant discourses on heterosexuality do not seem a serious possibility.

A third important issue is that heterosexuality has been constructed around the notion of fundamental gender differences. Men and women, we are told, don't speak the same language; don't communicate in relationships because they are so fundamentally different; we 'can't live with them – can't live without them'. That this idea finds powerful resonance in popular culture is shown by the phenomenal publishing success of John Gray's *Men are from Mars, Women are from Venus* series of paperbacks. And yet it is this apparently unbridgeable gulf, this battle of the sexes, which is constantly eroticised in our culture. 'New men', we are told, are simply not sexy to women; liberated women or feminists kill the male libido. An enormous amount of cultural energy has gone into maintaining and reproducing the eroticisation of gender difference rather than opening up the possibilities of changing it. This underlines the close connection between gender and sexual identities and means that, if we wish to study the social construction of heterosexualities, we are required to study the social construction of gender – which we move on to in the next chapter. The tyranny of the gender dichotomy may also explain why many writers (especially writers on masculinity) tend to write of 'male sexuality' and 'female sexuality' when they are really describing male and female heterosexualities. Heterosexuality remains unspoken and non-heterosexual masculinities and femininities are condemned to invisibility.

The construction of heterosexuality around fundamental gender difference also raises the problem of whether there is really any such thing as a shared heterosexual identity. Do men and women, apart from being attracted to each other, experience heterosexuality very differently? If that is the case, then what is it exactly that is hegemonic? Is it a particular construction of male heterosexuality, the values and assumptions of which are embedded in our culture, our institutions and the state through patriarchy – and from which not only non-heterosexuals feel alienated, but also many heterosexual women and perhaps men as well?

A heterosexual politics which points the way to better and more satisfying other-sex relationships as well as addressing questions of gender inequality and sexual inequality in society surely needs to start with male and female heterosexuals exploring the possibility of working together to change heterosexuality in ways which make it more satisfying to both. They also need to tackle the phenomena of homophobia and heterosexism which function to 'police' gender hierarchies and punish transgressors. This is widely recognised by writers such as Lynne Segal (1994) and David Cohen (1990). Yet in theory, as in people's lives, mutual suspicion and contradictions abound. Many women have experienced the reluctance of the heterosexual men in their lives to make the sort of far-reaching changes to their gendered individual and group behaviour which would involve giving up a certain amount of male privilege as well as doing hard work emotionally. Many heterosexual men react with suspicion against feminism, seeing it as excluding them, or complain that if they do try to change their sexist behaviour, they are laughed at.

Two approaches to studying the construction of heterosexuality might be called the 'external' and 'internal' narratives. The former takes as its starting point that modern heterosexuality has been largely constructed as the opposite of homosexuality. This is not to deny that when the term 'heterosexuality' was first popularised – by the American psychiatrist James Kiernan in 1892– it referred to a sexual perversion 'in which individuals of opposite sexes engaged in non-procreative sex for pleasure alone' (Nye 1999: 196). However, as Chauncey points out, at the end of the nineteenth and the beginning of the twentieth centuries heterosexuality was simultaneously defined as normality and deployed to police masculine intimacies: ' "Normal" men only became "heterosexual" men in the late nineteenth century, when they began to make their "normalcy" contingent on their renunciation of such intimacies with men. They became heterosexuals, that is, only when they defined themselves and organized their affective and physical relations to exclude any sentiments or behaviour that might be marked as homosexual' (Chauncey 1999: 199).

If negative characteristics and attributes are projected on to the homosexual, then the positive attributes of humanity are constructed as intrinsic to heterosexuality. Heterosexuality is natural, healthy, mentally fit, strong, morally upright, infused with the values of family, hard work and patriotism and socially necessary. It expresses, through the medically, legally and morally sanctioned forms of procreative sex (and nowadays for the most part non-procreative sex also, at least within marriage) the purest form of human sexuality. It is the norm against which human behaviour is measured. In this construction, what is not 'good' is either projected on to sexual minorities, or seen as a deviation from or betrayal of heterosexuality itself. Thus, through deploying the language of 'perversions' to construct some acts (e.g. child sex abuse) as intrinsic to homosexuality but as involving a deviation from 'normal' masculine or feminine behaviour which are taken to be synonymous with heterosexuality, heterosexuality itself is never allowed to be questioned. A *cordon sanitaire* is drawn around it.

The advantage of the external approach to the study of heterosexuality is that it puts dominant discourses under the spotlight. It draws attention to ways in which criminalised or stigmatised forms of sexual behaviour, from rape and abuse to consensual sado-masochism, are projected on to others or hidden by being 'deheterosexualised' in order to protect the integrity of the dominant discourse. It highlights how heterosexuality is closely linked to discourses of 'correct' gender roles – 'real' men and 'real' women. The potential danger of this approach is that, in isolation from other approaches, it can make heterosexuality seem monolithic; it runs the risk of ignoring the plurality of hetero-sexualities as lived by people.

The 'internal' narrative looks at ways in which gender role differentiation and gendered forms of power – as well as racial and class forms of power – affect relations between men and women, and inter-male and inter-female relations. It focuses on the ways in which clashes and struggles amongst different heterosexualities can contribute to producing change. The emphasis here is on how patriarchal forms of power differentiate people's experience of heterosexuality. For example, heterosexual feminists have argued that women's relationship to issues of heterosexual privilege is very different from (and more complex than) men's. Likewise, race and class background condition people's relation to patriarchal power or the patriarchal state and their relationships with each other. The advantage of this approach is that it highlights a plurality of identities and experiences, exploding the myth of a monolithic or homogenous heterosexuality, and challenging us to look at the different experiences of men and women. The potential danger is that it could lead us to dissolve the category of heterosexuality altogether, thereby perpetrating the invisibility of heterosexual privilege and of discrimination against non-heterosexuals.

Both these approaches to the study of the construction of heterosexuality focus on key sites of cultural, political and social power – key institutions – which are theorised as central to the reproduction of heterosexual power and, many feminists would say, of the patriarchal power that lies behind heterosexuality at present. These include: patterns of marriage, family organisation and parenting; economic work and the division of labour; the segmentation of society into public and private spheres; the gendering of love and emotions – with emotionalism ascribed to women and gay men and suppression or control of emotionalism to 'real' or heterosexual men; and political, ideological and moral sites of struggle over what is 'normal' and socially desirable. It is only through a concrete, empirical, case study of each of these sites of power, informed by theory, that we can approach an understanding of what heterosexuality is in our type of society, how it impacts on people's lives, and what else it might become.

Bisexualities

It is only very recently that self-identified bisexuals have begun to claim and assert a separate sexual and political identity for themselves, and that books which consider seriously the construction of bisexuality have entered the academic curriculum. Bisexuality has been almost totally ignored both by social scientists and by medical, legal and religious formulators of dominant discourses on sexuality. Even today, it is striking how many textbooks by feminists and by lesbian and gay scholars, as well as by anti-feminist and anti-gay writers, ignore the issue of bisexuality. Bisexuals have found themselves trapped in the heterosexual/homosexual dichotomy, and have continued to experience hostility, rejection, or even a refusal to believe that they really exist, from within both heterosexual society and the lesbian and gay communities.

Freud wrote of 'the innately bisexual constitution of all human beings' and believed that there was an original bisexuality of which both homosexuality and heterosexuality are derivatives; and moreover, that there remains a bisexual potential in all human beings (Garber 1995: 25–6). However, subsequent generations of Freudians tended to abandon this formulation and concentrate on the construction of heterosexuality as the natural, normal state from which homosexuality was a perversion, ignoring bisexuality altogether. We cannot trace the historical evolution of the construction of bisexuality or of bisexual identities in the same way that we considered homosexuality or lesbianism, or survey attempts to theorise bisexuality as we did with heterosexuality. Bisexuality remains under-researched and under-theorised.

What we can do is to look at some of the myths and stereotypes surrounding bisexuality in our culture and consider what they tell us about the construction of bisexuality, and about how bisexuality may threaten sexual identities and certainties rooted in the gay/straight, homo-/hetero- dichotomy. We can also look at recent attempts by bisexual activists to explore what a bisexual politics might involve.

Amanda Udis-Kessler (1996: 45–57), in a useful and stimulating essay upon which the following account is largely based, provides a check-list of stereotypes of bisexuality which are commonplace in our culture. She then interrogates these stereotypes in a critical way. She lists ten main stereotypes:

- bisexuals are confused, undecided or going through a phase. Ultimately they will settle down as either homosexual or hetero-sexual;
- people who say they are bisexual are really heterosexual but are experimenting, playing at being cool, or fooling around;
- people who say they are bisexual are really gay or lesbian but still have one foot in the closet;
- bisexuals are promiscuous and cannot be trusted in a relationship. They are attracted to everybody;
- bisexual men pick up HIV while having promiscuous unsafe sex with men and spread it to their 'innocent' wives and girlfriends. They are thus the mechanism by which AIDS enters the hetero-sexual population;
- bisexuals are shallow, narcissistic and lacking in morality;
- bisexuals are traitors to the cause of lesbian and gay liberation. They pass as straight in order to enjoy heterosexual privilege and dilute the cause of lesbian and gay liberation;
- bisexuals will always leave their lesbian or gay lovers when tempted by the lure of 'normality' and heterosexual privilege;
- bisexuals are desperately unhappy and are always searching for true peace of mind;
- bisexuals have the best of both worlds. They have twice as many available potential partners, and are more in tune with the full range of their sexuality than either homosexuals or heterosexuals.

There is no doubt that many bisexuals will recognise most if not all of the above myths and stereotypes. They form part of a popular discourse about bisexuality that reflects the anxieties of a society which is both fascinated and frightened by the subject. What is interesting is the way in which most of these myths reflect the profound unease which many people feel about the very existence of bisexuality. It is seen as threatening the homosexual/heterosexual and male/female dichotomies, or binarisms, which underpin our gender and sexual identities to such a large extent. In the case of the first three stereotypes, there is a refusal even to acknowledge the existence of bisexuality. It is simply wished out of existence. You can either be homosexual or heterosexual but anything else is just a phase, just playacting, not real. As Udis-Kessler argues, this reflects an ideology of essentialism which dismisses the idea that sexuality may be fluid, not fixed, and that its forms can change over a person's lifetime. This ideology assumes that there is a 'true' sexuality which we are working our way towards and that bisexuality is not really 'true' or 'serious' because it is a transition towards that other state. But there are two interesting points she makes in reply to that.

First, can it not be that homosexuality or heterosexuality might be a transition for some people towards bisexuality? There are plenty of life-stories to be told of, say, women for whom lesbianism and its associated political identity was a transition on the road from heterosexuality to bisexuality; or men for whom heterosexuality was a transition on the road from homosexuality to bisexuality.

The second point is more fundamental: who is to say when a transition begins and when it ends? Who is to say 'you have finally arrived. This is your "true" essential sexuality. You have finally discovered it. Previous experiences are not really valid because they were just experiments'?

As Udis-Kessler points out, transitions are not a rehearsal for life. Life is a series of transitions: points of arrival become new points of departure, and vice versa. So why should we assume that the way we experienced our sexuality ten or twenty years ago is necessarily less 'true' or important than the way we experience it now, or that the way we experience it now will necessarily be the same in ten or twenty years time? Obviously this applies not only to bisexuality, but it is an argument which those – including some lesbian and gay activists – who accuse bisexuality of being a sort of 'false consciousness' seldom get to grips with.

Clearly, then, issues of visibility, acceptance and, above all, authenticity are important for bisexuals. Jo Eadie (1993: 140) has claimed that lesbians and gay men, anxious to create safe spaces where they are not subject to homophobic rejection or oppression, may (consciously or unconsciously) seek to exclude bisexuals on three main grounds. First, that bisexuals can easily slip into 'heterosexual privilege' and behave in heterosexist ways – for example, some lesbian activists have expressed great reluctance to share organisations with bisexual men who might treat them as sex objects. Second, that bisexuals might 'dilute' the common experiences of the oppressed group in question; although the same argument can certainly be used to oppose the idea that lesbians and gay men share common ground or common agendas. Third, that the admission of bisexuals into lesbian and gay social spaces and organisations causes fears and anxieties associated with the fact that bisexuals stand in a very different relationship to societal relations of power.

Such concerns obviously reflect the marginalisation of lesbians and gay men in our culture and the feeling that they must stick together and fight to define and defend their own territory. Unfortunately, as soon as this happens, as with every oppressed or stigmatised group, it can lead to others being oppressed or stigmatised in turn. With something as intimate and hard fought-for as the right to sexual self-definition, this is a special temptation. For many lesbians and gay men who have had to fight, and continue fighting, for the right to exist as self-defined lesbians and gay men, anything which seems to threaten that identity by sowing the seeds of ambiguity can end up being resented. But it is logically difficult to see how some people can assert their own claim of right to self-definition and chosen identity whilst denying others the same right. Moreover, the comfort and security of the ghetto can of course result in its inhabitants becoming, in Foucauldian terms, embroiled in new forms of regulation and self-policing. In particular, the fear that bisexuality threatens the hetero-/homosexual dichotomy upon which modern gay or lesbian identities – as much as heterosexual identities – depend may reflect an element of insecurity and internalised homophobia which many lesbians and gay men continue to struggle with. Behind the suspicion of 'getting involved' politically, socially, or, indeed, romantically with bisexuals may well be the unarticulated fear that bisexuality somehow threatens to invalidate modern lesbian and gay identities.

Such tensions have prompted different responses on the part of bisexual activists. Some activists have sought to deconstruct sexual identities altogether through an embrace of queer theory. Jill Humphrey (1999), for example, clearly sees 'queerdom' as, at the very least, offering an escape path for bisexuals, transgendered people and, ultimately, all of us from the tyranny of the hetero-/homosexual dichotomy. Other activists have sought to advance the construction of positive bisexual identities through mapping the possibilities for a bisexual politics. This project is not without its difficulties. Sharon Rose speaks of the frustration of bisexual activists who come up against the fact that, for many people, the primary need which bisexual organisations meet is their need for mutual support and affirmation. They then move on to other political causes, perhaps influenced by the fact that the laws and social conventions governing their sexual and public lives are framed in terms of the hetero-/homosexual dichotomy, and there are few legal, social, political and economic institutions or structures which address bisexuality directly. Consequently there are few targets for a specific bisexual politics to focus on. She writes of the 'unwillingness [within the bisexual community] to impose a collective [political] dogma' (Rose 1996: 215–6). It is certainly true that in most Western countries a bisexual politics is either non-existent or in the very early stages of formation. It is, nevertheless, interesting to reflect on what such a politics might involve. Most bisexual activists seem agreed that at least three issues would be fundamental to the construction of politicised bisexual identities.

The first concerns the question of raising visibility and consciousness. Given the relative lack of discourses around bisexuality, and the corresponding lack of images of bisexuality in popular culture, the lack of bisexual social spaces, and the fact that many bisexuals in relationships feel under intense pressure to suppress or keep silent about one part of their sexuality, raising consciousness and visibility can be seen as an intensely political act.

The second issue involves challenging processes of exclusion within other 'progressive' movements. We have already commented on negative attitudes towards bisexuality within parts of both the feminist and the lesbian and gay movements/communities. This is again linked to the issue of invisibility. A bisexual within the lesbian and gay community, for example, will usually find that she or he is assumed to be lesbian or gay. Alternatively, we usually make assumptions about a person's sexuality based on the sex of the person they are having a relationship with; the possibility that they may be bisexual often eludes us.

Finally, as we have seen, a third issue involves challenging 'monosexual' essentialism and thus raising questions about the fundamental nature of sexuality. The term 'monosexual' has been coined by some bisexual activists to describe those whose erotic desires are targeted on one sex only. There is no doubt that some activists see the existence (or perhaps 'rediscovery') of bisexuality as posing a challenge to 'monosexuality' and raising the possibility that we all have the potential for a more multi-faceted sexuality than our culture tends to admit. In such a construction, a bisexual politics emerges, not as a struggle to advance the interests and rights of a minority, but as a possible pathway out of 'monosexuality' for all.

Conclusion

Throughout this chapter, a number of themes have recurred. First, that sexual identities and categories are fluid, not fixed. Second, that struggles to challenge and subvert the dominant constructions of various forms of human sexuality – those constructions and meanings which have been articulated by powerful social, political and cultural institutions – have often been intensely political. Third, that these struggles, whether on the part of those who were branded 'perverts' or 'abnormal' or on the part of well-intentioned individuals within the power structures, have tended to bear fruit when they have coincided with wider processes of social and technological change which have allowed gendered and sexualised relations within society to be called into question. Fourth, that new forms of regulation, policing and control – new 'normalising' mechanisms – have often emerged even as the old seemed (partially) to retreat.

The medical profession, for example, may have retreated from some of the sexualised obsessions of the late nineteenth and early twentieth centuries, including the fear of adolescent masturbation which saw doctors manufacture and sell a range of anti-masturbation devices to Victorian middle-class parents, or the denial of female sexuality altogether. But new forms of medical power have emerged. A range of 'illnesses' and 'disorders' – from (mainly) female depression, to (mainly) female eating disorders, to (male and female?) mid-life crises, to (male only?) impotence – is highly gendered and sexualised. For example, the act of constructing depression as a mainly female problem which can be treated with anti-depressants involves the medical profession in a series of complex, gendered power relations. And it is likely that even greater profits are to be made from the sale of drugs such as Viagra to sexually anxious Western men at the start of the twenty-first century, than were made from the sale of 'erection harnesses' and other anti-masturbation devices to sexually anxious Victorian parents at the end of the nineteenth.

As definitions of sexual health and constructions of what human sexualities mean change, it is important to strive to consider these debates against a background of wider power relations. It is important also to pay attention to how changing discourses on sexuality can involve shifts in the balance of power amongst different social institutions, groups and professions. For example, we have seen how a shift in the balance of power took place in the nineteenth century in industrialised countries from the church to the medical and scientific community (with considerable overlap). Leonore Tiefer (1993) has written that another great shift has characterised the closing decades of the twentieth century: from the medical and scientific community to the mass media. Again, there is considerable overlap. Just as the medical profession in the late nineteenth century often consciously avoided a direct challenge to religion and even reinforced discourses of sin and damnation, so today's mass media may in some respects reinforce the status and prestige of doctors – so many newspapers, magazines, and television talk shows feel that they must have an 'in-house' doctor or scientist to offer 'expert advice'. Such a shift in the power to define social normality – from religious and scientific elites to the mass media – might be seen as democratic but it is not necessarily so. As Tiefer puts it, 'the combination of scientific (read: biological) "news" and health-expert advice in the nonfiction media reinforces the impression that sex is very important without providing the kind of information ordinary readers or viewers can actually use. People end up with the directive to consult a professional expert – not the most empowering message' (1993: 26). Again, we are cautioned to be ever alert for new forms of regulation and control.

Finally, we have seen that the construction of sexual normality and sexual perversion has been intimately connected into the regulation and policing of gender behaviour. The delineation of masculinity and femininity – and the fixing and maintenance of the boundaries be-tween them – is the basis upon which constructions of heterosexuality as normal and righteous, and of non-heterosexuality (and even non-reproductive forms of heterosexuality) as abnormal and perverted, rest. It is therefore to the construction of gender identities and gender behaviour that we now turn.

Chapter 3

Gender ideologies and gender regulation

The politics of sexuality is inextricably interconnected with the politics of gender. Both were at one time subsumed under the umbrella of 'sexual politics', a term used to encompass both feminist and gay politics, to denote opposition to both male domination and heterosexual hegemony. (Jackson 1996b: 1)

Introduction

As the above quotation from Stevi Jackson makes clear, gender and sexuality are interconnected concepts. We have seen from our study of heterosexuality and homosexuality that male heterosexuality has tended to be defined in terms of masculinity and male homosexuality in terms of 'the feminine'; there is thus a close interconnection between the denigration of male homosexuals in most Western cultures and the devaluing of what are regarded as the traits of femininity. There is an intimate relationship between homophobia and misogyny. So one could argue that the privileging of heterosexuality in our type of society is really about male power over women (McIntosh 1993: 40). Writers such as Jackson and Mary McIntosh have argued that a 'decoupling' of gender politics and the politics of sexuality can lead to a form of gender blindness on the part of many gay writers in particular and thus to a loss of political radicalism. McIntosh, for example, argues that 'for gay male theorists, gender has lurked in the wings, and when it has appeared it has usually been in the guise of "manliness" or "effeminacy" – a component of the individual's psychic profile – rather than in the more elaborated form of family patterns and power relations' (1993: 40). A similar criticism has been levelled at queer theorists, both male and female. By making the homosexual/heterosexual (rather than male/female) dichotomy central to their analyses and, in a sense, 'down-grading' the issue of gender to questions of performativity, queer theorists are in danger of underestimating the force and material power of ideologies of masculinity and femininity, and the extent to which our experiences of sexualities are gendered. McIntosh argues that 'queer theory should not forget that the heterosexuality in terms of which we are defined as other is a highly gendered one, so that our otherness and the forms and meanings of our dissidence are also gendered' (1993: 47). For Weeks (1998: 148), McIntosh's comments conceal a more pointed criticism of queer theorists, namely that they 'are in danger of displacing all other social contradictions [than the homosexual/heterosexual] from serious consideration, and of forgetting in the process Foucault's injunctions about the dispersed nature of power'.

This chapter seeks to emphasise the importance of the study of gendered experiences and gender ideologies for a radical sexual politics. It begins by briefly discussing the complexity of gender identities and then moves on to discuss some aspects of gender ideologies, raising some points also about the methodological problems involved in theoretical writings on masculinity and femininity. After a discussion of some examples of how our experience of social and personal life is highly gendered, the chapter concludes by examining how the hierarchy of sexualities functions to police gender boundaries.

Intersecting identities: cultural constructions of gender

As Nancy Bonvillain (1995: 1–11) argues, cultural constructions of gender 'make use of sexual differences between males and females, but they are not constrained in a predetermined manner by these sexual differences. If they were, roles performed and values attached to women's and men's behavior would be identical in all societies. This clearly is not the case'. Indeed, ever since the pioneering anthropological work of Margaret Mead in the 1930s (Mead 1935), the enormous variations in male and female social roles across time and amongst cultures have been extensively studied. It is commonplace within sociology to argue that ideologies of gender – which teach us the appropriate behaviour expected and rewarded by others, mould our personalities to conform to society's norms, and repress or punish nonconformist behaviour – are transmitted to children from birth. What is important here is the fact that gender ideologies are not in any sense monolithic, but highly differentiated. That is to say, ideologies of gender behaviour intersect with ideologies rooted in other material hierarchies which structure our lives, such as race, class and nationality. Moreover, hidden ideological messages about gender are often 'symbolized in religious beliefs and practices', and language itself functions as an important medium for the transmission of gender ideologies (Bonvillain 1995: 1).

For years, feminist scholars and activists have grappled with the differentiated nature of gender identities. We have already seen that some writers argue that the categories of 'men' and 'women' are meaningless: that, for example, poverty-stricken women workers in the so-called Third World have little or nothing in common with a rich, white, female executive of the multi-national corporation involved in exploiting them. Yet male social privilege and female exploitation are so prevalent in the contemporary world that most feminist writers would argue that, though patriarchy may be highly differentiated and gender identities may intersect with other important identities, patriarchal power is real and political struggles against forms of exploitation and marginalisation rooted in women's common experiences remain valid.

Before examining some of the efforts made to theorise masculinities and femininities it is important to remind ourselves of how gender ideologies and identities may intersect, shape, and be shaped by, other important ideologies and identities. Much work, for example, has been undertaken on the subject of race. It has been shown that ideologies of racism are often highly gendered and sexualised. The prevalence of pornography which eroticises the legacy of slavery – with black men portrayed as savage, well-hung, and animal-like, and black women portrayed as powerless, promiscuous sluts readily available for the pleasure of white men – is an obvious example. hooks (1996) has argued that American culture is permeated with images of black people and of interracial relations rooted in the legacy of slavery. She underlines the problem confronting feminists who treat 'women' as an undifferentiated category by angrily accusing white feminists of partially ignoring the rape and abuse of black women. The stereotype of black men as lazy and feckless and black women as producing endless children outside marriage is another example of how racist and sexist myths overlap and reinforce each other.

The sexualisation of Asians in white European and North American pornography as passive and demure is a further example of racialised and sexualised power. Indeed, the projection of sexual passivity on to racial, national or ethnic groups which have been conquered or exploited is a recurring theme. Examples might include the eroticisation of the 'Jewess' in European literature and of Indian women and boys at the height of British imperialism. In times of war – in our own times from the Vietnam war to the terrible conflicts in Bosnia and Kosovo – the use of rape and sexual torture to reinforce notions of racial superiority or national conquest is well documented.

Mac an Ghaill (1996) provides an interesting illustration of how ideologies and myths of nationality, ethnicity, class, gender and sexuality can intersect. Studying Irish gay men living in England, he provides evidence of how many of these men feel 'feminised' and powerless, on grounds of both their nationality and their sexuality. This powerlessness is most keenly felt by the working-class men in Mac an Ghaill's sample who experience a triple-marginalisation. This occurs: within the (otherwise) protective confines of the Irish working-class immigrant community, on the grounds of their homosexuality; within the lesbian and gay scene, on the grounds of their class and nationality; and within English society as a whole. The middle-class men in his sample were better able to 'assimilate' (and, one might suspect, enjoy the advantages of the prevailing forms of patriarchy).

Victoria Goddard's study of women in Naples highlights the ways in which control and regulation of women's sexuality through the deployment of gendered concepts of 'honour', 'shame' and 'pollution' function to delineate the boundaries and reinforce the identity of the (male-dominated) group (Goddard 1987). A parallel can be drawn with many societies in which rigid notions of what constitutes membership of the ethnic group or caste, and what are the acceptable laws governing inheritance, are reproduced at the ideological level through a series of taboos on (mainly) women's sexual activity. Such taboos are often rooted in religion. Nancy Bonvillain (1995: 211) argues that 'through religion, social constructs are rendered timeless and unalterable . . . a social order said to have sacred origins cannot be resisted or questioned without shaking the foundations of religious belief'. Thus, in Hinduism, for example, social constructions of male and female roles are 'rendered timeless' through dual representations of the goddess: benevolent goddesses are portrayed as faithful wives, dangerous and vengeful goddesses are unmarried. The message here is that when women are independent and control their own sexual behaviour they are dangerous to society. The cult of the Virgin Mary within Christianity, and the systems of taboos on female sexuality within Islam and Judaism, convey similar messages.

Class also intersects with gender and sexuality, and is, in turn, both gendered and sexualised. The eroticisation of power differentials is intimately connected with questions of economic inequality. From the Contagious Diseases Acts of the late nineteenth century, which sought to regulate the sexuality of working-class women (identified as sources of moral pollution) at the same time that these women (and working-class youths) were targeted and preyed upon sexually by Victorian 'gentlemen', there has been a long history of eroticisation in popular culture of 'rough trade' and, conversely, of the power of rich men. Class, gender and sexuality interact in other ways: ideologies of masculinity and femininity are very often fragmented along class lines, and notions of what constitutes, for example, 'lady-like' behaviour or behaviour characteristic of 'real men' often reflect intense social class conditioning.

This brief overview of how identities and ideologies intersect raises again one of the fundamental issues in debates between socialist and feminist theorists on the one hand, and post-modernists on the other: whether we can speak in terms of some forms of oppression and exploitation which are fundamental (class?, gender?), and others which are derivative. Even if we accept that types of inequality and oppression rooted in capitalism and patriarchy are fundamental and near-universal, it is important to resist any temptation to treat masculinity and femininity as being in any way monolithic. Rather, our understanding of the ways in which ideologies of masculinity and femininity govern our experiences can only be enriched by focusing on the ways in which oppressions and identities can overlap, sometimes reinforcing and sometimes contradicting each other, sometimes hindering attempts at political mobilisation and sometimes helping to cement political alliances.

Ideologies of masculinity and femininity: the critiques of 'men's studies' and feminism

It is now several decades since Simone de Beauvoir famously argued that one is not born a woman but becomes one through culture, and that the social and cultural processes involved in moulding women in Western societies construct woman as the opposite of man (de Beauvoir 1953). That is to say, femininity is constructed as that which is not masculine. However, the masculine often remains invisible, implicit, universalised. In many European languages, we speak of 'mankind', 'man', 'men' when we mean the human race in general; and in both the natural and social sciences male scientists have very frequently universalised on the basis of male experience. Since de Beauvoir wrote, a great deal of work within the social sciences has sought to shed light on the masculinity/femininity dichotomy and to render both visible. If women are constructed as non-men, then men are equally constructed as non-women; the dynamics of this duality need to be explored if the gendered aspects of political, economic and social power are to be grasped.

Even today, masculinity remains more invisible than femininity. For example, there is still a tendency, albeit diminishing, to confine the study of gender to the study of women, and to conflate gender studies and women's studies. This is perhaps understandable in the sense that much theoretical work proceeds from a feminist perspective and feminist praxis is primarily about the advancement and liberation of women. Yet it runs the risk of assuming that men do not have a gender – that somehow only women are gendered beings. This, of course, is nonsense. It is difficult to see how we could ever hope to reach a state of gender equality unless masculinity comes under the microscope as much as femininity.

Recently, a growing literature on masculinity has emerged, often under the rubric of 'men's studies', and often influenced by feminist theoretical writings. According to Judith Squires, 'there is still reluctance within much feminist theory to engage fully with the literature on masculinity. Yet its insights and developments are essential and profoundly helpful to a full understanding of gender theory'. Moreover, 'given the extensive theorization of masculinities now in existence, the notion that gender might be synonymous with women, while masculinity remains untheorized, has now been overturned' (Squires 2000: 75). Much of this growing literature on men and masculinities has been concerned with the existence of a supposed 'crisis of masculinity' in contemporary Western societies, and much of it has been reactive to elements of this crisis. These are said to include: fundamental changes in employment patterns and in the nature of work, which have challenged masculine identities and self-confidence; changes in the nature of families and patterns of child-rearing; and the impact of both feminism and gay visibility upon hegemonic heterosexual masculinities. We will consider this literature on masculinity first, before moving on to examine whether masculinity can be said to be 'in crisis' at present.

The fact that masculinity is everywhere, but until recently has not been seen everywhere – not rendered visible and problematic – means that the study of masculinity is much more complicated than it might appear. It is not surprising that social scientists have different opinions on defining and theorising masculinity. Robert Connell (1995: 68–71) has distinguished four main strategies for approaching the study of masculinity according to their logic of explanation, although they are often combined in practice. These are respectively essentialist, positivist, normative and semiotic.

Essentialist definitions of masculinity usually pick a feature that defines the core of the masculine and try to hang an account of men's lives on that. This feature might be risk-taking, aggression, rationality, responsibility, (or, conversely, irresponsibility), competitiveness, the 'nature' of man as 'hunter and provider', sexual promiscuity, or the 'sacred' vocation of men as leaders (often justified by reference to patriarchal religions). The weakness in essentialist approaches, as Connell points out, is that the choice of the 'essence' is quite arbitrary and often contradictory.

Positivist social science defines masculinity in terms of what men actually are, which can be rendered clear by empirical research. As Connell makes clear, this approach is not without its difficulties. There is no description without a standpoint: one has to have some basis upon which one determines which facts are selected as either significant or not, or about the relative importance and degrees of emphasis given to various acts, practices, characteristics and so on. Apparently neutral descriptions about what men do and what men are themselves are underpinned by assumptions about gender. Moreover, critics of positivism argue that it is more useful to use the terms 'masculine' and 'feminine' to point beyond categorical sex differences to ways in which men and women differ among themselves in terms of gender behaviour. In other words, we should investigate 'masculinities' and not assume a single masculinity.

Normative definitions recognise these differences and offer a standard or norm: masculinity is what men ought to be, as defined by our culture. This notion allows that different men approach the standard to different degrees, and that cultural variation exists. But normative approaches also entail paradoxes. Connell highlights the fact that such a norm may actually reflect a masculinist ideology, used to police people by using their internalised insecurities and perceived inadequacies to control their behaviour. Are we to say, sociologically, that the majority of men are 'unmasculine', if they fall short of this norm?

Semiotic approaches define masculinity through a system of symbolic difference in which masculine and feminine roles and identities are contrasted. In effect, masculinity is defined as not-femininity. This approach to masculinity (and gender in general) has most obviously appealed to queer theorists and has proven effective in cultural analysis. For example, books by writers such as Mark Simpson (1994, 1996) have highlighted the extent to which men act out, or perform, certain scripts of masculinity. A rich school of cultural analysis inspired by semiotic approaches has identified a catalogue of signs, gestures, forms of body language and speech, and cultural inscriptions which define 'what makes a man a man' in our culture. However, Connell suggests that, useful though these approaches are, they are limited in scope. They do not directly address issues of personality, internalisation of roles, or the insights of psychoanalysis. To grapple with the full range of issues about masculinity Connell suggests that we need ways of talking about various kinds of relationships. He suggests that, 'rather than attempting to define masculinity as an object (a natural character type, a behavioral average, a norm) we need to focus on the processes and relationships through which men and women conduct gendered lives' (Connell 1995: 71).

We need an approach to both masculinity and femininity which is dynamic. To stick with masculinity, we could focus on ways in which men and women take sets of expected attitudes and react to them: accepting, rejecting, changing, feeling forced to conform to certain behaviours, reacting against the norm in other ways. However, a psychoanalytical perspective which ignores the role of material forces in shaping the range of real choices available to us is unlikely to get us very far. So we are striving here towards a blend of perspectives which would recognise that the study of gender ideologies must take account of both (a) the force of psychoanalytical theories which point to ways in which people divide themselves up into many different selves with reference to different situations and relationships – for example, a man acting differently in his roles as husband, father, colleague, employee, friend, and so on, but also, for example, as a gay man in a heterosexual environment compared to a gay man in a gay environment; and (b) the power of material forces such as class, race, employment, degrees of freedom and autonomy in shaping the range of choices available.

Such an approach would start with the view that masculinity is a flexible concept, though not infinitely flexible: material forces and dominant discourses do limit the range of possibilities in any given situation. Consequently, it is better to adopt a flexible way of investigating it and to view masculinity as a range of ways in which men respond to what they perceive as social expectations of masculinity, the practices through which their masculinity is established and the effects of these practices on those around them and on the men themselves. This approach undermines the illusion that masculinity is uniform, monolithic and innate. Instead, we are confronted with a variety of masculine forms. Different masculinities exist in terms of men's differential location in different relations. Brod and Kaufman (1994: 107) write of 'distinctions between gay, nonhierarchic heterosexual, and hierarchic heterosexual; between white and black; between nonfathers and fathers; unpaid careers, paid careers and noncareers; and nonviolent, violent and military masculinities'. This approach arguably represented a big step forward in sociology. But, again, it is important to note the point made by Connell (1995: 76) that we must beware of another simplification which is that of thinking that there is a single black masculinity, or a single working-class masculinity. Instead, masculinities are perhaps more accurately understood in terms of complex associations of more than one social division (class, race, and so on).

Thus we can recognise black, middle-class masculinities, or white, gay masculinities, amongst others. (Brod and Kaufman 1994: 111).

Linked to this is the distinction between hegemonic and non-hegemonic masculinities. Hearn and Morgan point out that:

> ... the concept of 'hegemonic masculinities' ... point[s] to the dominance within society of certain forms and practices of masculinity which are historically conditioned and open to change and challenge. Thus today such a model might be white, heterosexist, middle-class, Anglophone, and so on. This implies that men too, within a society that may be characterised as 'patriarchal', may experience subordinations, stigmatizations or marginalizations as a consequence of their sexuality, ethnic identity, class position, religion, or marital status. (Hearn and Morgan 1990: 11)

The 'men's studies' literature has not only produced different approaches to defining masculinity, and opposing views on the relationships between social structures and individual actors, it has also produced different political perspectives on gender identities and ideologies. Kenneth Clatterbaugh (1990) mentions six main contemporary perspectives: conservative, profeminist, men's rights, spiritual, socialist, and group-specific. There are clear parallels between many of these political perspectives on masculinity and similar perspectives on femininity.

The conservative perspective is clearly rooted in essentialism – the belief that traditional ideologies of masculinity and femininity are manifestations of male and female nature, and therefore it is 'natural' for men to be politically and socially dominant. Clatterbaugh (1990: 9) points out that moral conservatives see married heterosexual, law-abiding, patriotic masculinity as a social and moral code created by society in order to over ride and control men's antisocial tendencies: 'it is the civilised role which men play when they are fathers, protectors and providers'. Femininity is the corresponding social and moral code society has evolved to contain, domesticate and tame men's natural aggressiveness. 'According to *biological* conservatives, virtually all social behaviour is a manifestation of men's natural tendencies as selected through an evolutionary process.' Moral conservatives vehemently oppose feminist demands for gender equality as interfering with the 'natural order of things' and undermining social cohesion by provoking family breakdown and depriving male children of adequate male role-models. They attribute the so-called crisis of masculinity to unreasonable and unnatural feminist agendas.

Profeminist male theorists 'argue that masculinity is created through male privilege and its corresponding oppression of women, although they allow that traditional masculinity is also harmful to men' (Clatterbaugh 1990: 10). Radical profeminists tend to echo radical feminism 'in holding that masculinity is created and maintained by misogyny and violence against women, and that patriarchy is the social and political order in which masculine privilege is reproduced'. They refuse to accept patriarchal masculine behaviour, working against male violence and hierarchical patterns of political organisation. Liberal profeminists, not surprisingly, echo liberal feminism in maintaining, as Clatterbaugh puts it, 'that masculinity is a set of restrictions that are imposed on both men and women but which are not insuperable and can be reformed'. In their writings they tend to concentrate on the need for individual men to combat sexism by changing the nature of their personal and professional relationships with women.

The men's rights perspective tends to depict men, rather than women, as the main 'victims' of recent gendered economic and social changes in Western societies. Some are consciously part of the anti-feminist backlash, concerned with ways in which feminism has allegedly disempowered men. In this, they overlap considerably with the conservative school. Some areas of concern raised have included the alleged oppression of men in divorce cases, access of divorced, unmarried or separated fathers to their biological children, the operations of the Child Support Agency in the UK, the alleged neglect or denial of men's support for women, and the ways in which changes in male employment patterns lead to men being discarded as disposable objects. The last concern can easily turn into resentment against women's presence as competitors in the labour market and a determination to defend male privilege in the workplace. The men's rights perspective tends to argue that men are the primary victims of a sexism generated by feminism.

The spiritual perspective 'is founded on the conviction that masculinity derives from deep unconscious patterns' which 'are best revealed through a tradition of stories, myths and rituals' (Clatterbaugh 1990: 11). Much more popular in the USA than in the UK, this form of mysticism basically argues that men need to reach down deep into their psyches and 'reconnect' with an authentic masculinity from which they have been separated by social organisation since the industrial revolution. This has its manifestations in the search for a 'golden age' of lost masculinity – associated with proponents such as Robert Bly (1990) who has pioneered the movement of so-called 'wild men'. This movement has organised weekend retreats in the forests where men dance naked around the camp fire and 'rediscover' the primitive 'hunter' in themselves. Obviously this reflects a form of essentialism, reinforced by mysticism and retrospection, which has more in common with a conservative position than a belief in progress.

The socialist perspective treats masculinity as a material reality, grounded in class structures and in economic inequality. It sees gender ideologies and roles as constructed around the pursuit of power and profit, not human growth. It sees contemporary forms of masculinity and femininity as reflecting alienation from part of our human potential – an alienation rooted in class society. Forms of masculinity and femininity can be understood only through the social context which is said to be capitalism. The socialist perspective on masculinity concurs that male alienation – from self, from other men, and from women – can be fully transcended only when the economic base of society has been fundamentally altered away from the pursuit of profit, alienation of human labour, and competitive individualism – all of which are said to be reflected in the dominant construction of masculinity. A similar approach to the study of femininity has been developed by socialist feminists.

The group-specific perspective developed as a critique of standardised discussions of masculinity which presumed a universal and monolithic masculinity (often based on a white, heterosexual and middle-class perspective). It emphasises new explanations and different evaluations of masculinity and points to alternative agendas for change. For example, perspectives developed by gay male writers and by black writers might be said to fall into this category.

These perspectives are not mutually exclusive and some can be combined easily with others.

In approaching the subject of masculinity, and indeed femininity, it is important to bear in mind the methodological limitations of various writings as well as the possible insights on offer. One way of highlighting some of these limitations is to think lateraly and to regroup our theorists, not according to the perspective they claim to offer but according to their personal point of departure. Thus, recent writings on masculinity and men fall into three broad areas: writings by heterosexual men; writings by gay or bisexual men; and writings by women – overwhelmingly feminists, although belonging to different schools of feminism.

Jeff Hearn (1987: 38) has written that 'a central difficulty in the study of men and masculinity, specially the study of men and masculinity by men, is to do with inequalities of power'. In other words, men continue to occupy more positions of power in our society than do women, and to derive a whole range of privileges from being men – including economic and political privileges. This is perhaps especially true of men who produce the works of theory, including academics and writers. They are usually middle-class men with fairly secure incomes, and in so far as these privileges are related to gender, they may well be blind to them. The same reality applies to sexuality: a male hetero-sexual writer may overlook or take for granted what appears to a gay man or a woman as privilege. Hearn argues, that claims of self-knowl-edge must always be suspect and always closely examined for evidence that they may have overlooked inequalities of power. Thus, some feminists have criticised some writings on the crisis of masculinity by male academics as self-indulgent and self-pitying – or even self-serving – material which down-plays masculine privilege.

Even when 'straight' male theorists take gender inequalities fully into account in their study of masculinity, they often stand accused of ignoring other mechanisms of oppression. Many of these studies are generalised from a white, middle-class, heterosexual masculinity against which other men's experiences are measured. As Edwards (1993: 1) argues, 'men's study of masculinity added some insights into masculinity and male experience though frequently excluded full consideration of sexual orientation and heterosexuality as a compo-nent of masculine identity'. Some straight male writers on masculinity have recently begun responding to these criticisms while others remain reluctant to problematise the relationship between masculinity and heterosexuality. For example, there is still a marked dearth of material by heterosexual male theorists on the centrality of homophobia within ideologies of masculinity.

Gay male scholarship also has its blind-spots. Both feminist and gay male writings on sexuality and gender have celebrated personal ex-perience as a counter to what they see as the pseudo-scientific and rationalist pretensions of much male heterosexual work on the subject. Such writing avoids talking of 'the personal' explicitly, whilst actually assuming that male heterosexual experiences hold true for everyone. Yet in celebrating personal experience and making it part of one's theoretical point of departure, one needs constantly to be reminded of the need for critical self-reflection. For example, there is no easy or straightforward relationship between gay sexuality and masculinity; gay men experience masculinity in as great a variety of ways as heterosexual men, are connected to masculine privilege in complex ways, and relate to women in all sorts of ways. Universalising from personal experience is always a great temptation and a methodological trap.

Moreover, the stress on sexual difference which is strong in gay male social theory has been chiefly concerned with documenting sexuality's importance. This stress on male sexuality may well leave out gender aspects. For example, feminists such as Stevi Jackson (1996) can with justice bemoan the fact that much gay writing contains hidden sexism; it ignores inequality between men and women. Gay writing on gender and sexuality is concerned with the advocacy of equality and liberation; but this equality is frequently seen as equality with heterosexual men, not with women. As Jackson puts it, when gay male theorists advocate equal human rights, male heterosexuality is often taken as the standard on which human rights are founded, and hence the issue of rights is posed in terms of equality between men.

Feminism has obviously exercised a formative influence upon the emergence of 'men's studies'. That said, we have already noted Judith Squires' claim (Squires 2000: 75) that some feminists have been reluctant to engage with the new men's studies. Some feminists have been suspicious of male writers tackling issues of gender at all because of the perceived tendency for such men to refuse to acknowledge their social power as men, and how they use that power in their daily lives and relationships, including within the academic profession and in the classroom. It has sometimes been argued that men's studies is simply an attempt by 'the boys' to hi-jack for themselves the scarce resources available to women working in the field of gender studies; or that the social sciences in general are 'men's studies', forming as they do part of the so-called male-stream. No doubt there are genuine issues of power and exclusion here which need to be addressed. But the danger of such a dismissive attitude towards critical studies of masculinity by male writers is that it reinforces the stereotypical view that gender research is really something which is best left to women because it doesn't really concern men. In other words, an essentialist view of masculinity (and femininity) may lurk beneath the surface of such prejudices.

Hammersley (1995) identifies the emphasis on the validity of personal experience as against the conventional (and, it is claimed, masculinist) emphasis on scientific method as a common methodological concern of feminism. This sometimes results in an insistence that only women can do feminist research and that only women researchers can truly understand women and their situation. This raises the question of whether women writers can study men as well. Do women have access to truths about the social worlds of both men and women which are not available to men because of masculine privilege? It's not impossible to argue this but it sounds implausible.

Finally, the feminist emphasis on personal experience ought to warn against any tendency to regard all men – gay, straight, black, white, rich, poor – as standing in roughly the same relationship to patriarchy. Yet some radical feminist writers continue to write as if the masculine experience of patriarchal society is monolithic. This criticism could be directed at those radical feminist critics of pornography who simply conflate gay and straight pornography, implying that gay pornography is as misogynistic as straight male pornography (see, for example, Dworkin 1981, and Jeffreys 1996). The argument here is that gay pornography glorifies inequalities of power between men and women because the so-called passive male in pornographic depictions is really a 'substitute female'. This is a highly debatable argument which ignores issues of context, meaning and personal experience. It could just as readily be argued that gay male pornography which depicts one man in a so-called passive sexual role and another in a so-called active sexual role, far from being degrading to women, is highly subversive of traditional masculinist assumptions. The ambiguity of such an image, after all, is derived in part from the fact that the 'consumer' may identify with either man so depicted.

Although these brief comments have drawn attention to some of the methodological issues which some feminist writings on masculinity have raised, it must be said clearly that some of the most stimulating and influential work on masculine ideologies and identities has been undertaken by feminist theorists. Two outstanding examples are Lynne Segal's path-breaking study, *Slow Motion: Changing Masculinities, Changing Men* (1990) and Susan Faludi's more recent *Stiffed: the Betrayal of the Modern Man* (1999). Segal's book alerted us to the persistence of gender inequalities and to the formidable obstacles in the path of any profound undermining of masculine power. Inequality, she argued, is 'nourished by the grim authority of images of masculinity, the inviting cosiness of images of femininity'. On the other hand, she did identify a range of subversive masculinities – of gay men, black men, non-sexist heterosexual men, men who were being changed by 'greater involvement in childcare and domestic work and by being required to pay attention to the demands and interests of women' (Segal 1990: 308–9). Her cautiously optimistic conclusion was that fundamental economic structural changes meant that 'the absurdity of the traditional gendered divide between public and private is daily more apparent' (1990: 319), and that, although many men might well mount a tooth-and-nail defence of masculine privilege, a more equitable outcome to the much-vaunted 'crisis of masculinity' was certainly possible.

Writing nearly a decade later, Faludi paints a bleak picture of a generation of American men in profound crisis. Her interviewees are mostly angry, disillusioned men haunted by economic and marital instability, by the cultural undermining of their masculine values and solidarities, and by their inability to adapt emotionally to social and personal change – an emotional damage which many attribute to a generation of post-war fathers who were silent and remote, absent or violently abusive. Faludi's conclusion is that contemporary men have

'experienced so many of the same injuries as women, the same humi-
liations' (1999: 603) and yet seem incapable of finding a progressive
solution to this crisis of masculinity (that is, one which challenges
patriarchal ideology rather than reinforcing it). This, she argues, is not
because men as a group are determined to hang on to the reins of
power, which she believes have slipped through the hands of most men
already, but because they lack a strategy, a sense of direction, and a clear
target for their anger. In the end, it is feminism's battle against the
tyranny of gender which offers men a 'glimmer of an opening' –
'because as men struggle to free themselves from their crisis, their task
is not, in the end, to figure out how to be masculine – rather, their
masculinity lies in figuring out how to be human' (1999: 607).

The message, then, from feminist writers such as Segal and Faludi is
clear: the crisis of masculinity reflects the inadequacy of traditional
gender ideologies and the damage inflicted on both men and women
by the tyranny of gender dichotomies. The only real solution is a
struggle by both men and women to overcome gender and to become
fully human.

Feminist writings on gender ideologies have been emphatically
concerned with issues of inequality of power. Hammersley (1995)
identifies four main themes in feminist research methodology. We
have already discussed two of these – a central concern with gender
asymmetry, with the fact that human social relations of all kinds are
heavily structured by differences in the social position of women and
men and by differences in power; and the emphasis on the validity of
personal experience. A third feminist methodological concern has been
that the relationship between researchers and researched should be a
reciprocal one, that 'hierarchical' distinctions between researchers and
researched should be broken down so that they are on the same level.
Finally, there is the idea that the goal of feminist research should be the
emancipation of women, and in that sense research should be subordinated to the political aim of the women's movement which, as
Hammersley puts it, 'is not just the study but the overcoming of
women's oppression and exploitation' (1995: 47).

These admirable methodological concerns do leave feminist writings
on gender open to other potential traps or weaknesses. Obviously,
many feminists are aware of these and indeed have pointed out the
pitfalls.

First, the effect of concentrating on gender inequalities may be to
strip away other relevant aspects of the phenomenon studied, and its
context. For example, inequalities between women related to class;
inequalities between men; the relationships between power and sexuality, race, and so on. As Hammersley says, 'while we need to subject

social research to assessment for male bias, feminist bias is also a danger' (1995: 51).

Second, the emphasis on subjective experience carries the danger that feminists may encourage treatment of some of the woman researcher's or indeed the woman interviewee's own experience and assumptions as beyond question, possessing an absolute and innate validity – when in fact they require scrutiny and constant interrogation. Otherwise, it is very tempting to treat what one wishes to believe as proven by experience. This is the sort of criticism which has been levelled, by men, but by some feminists also, at a writer such as Andrea Dworkin. Dworkin has been accused by critics of a sort of 'experiential absolutism': the notion that if you disagree with her, you are by definition wrong, because her views are rooted in her experience as a woman and the experiences of other women she has worked with, and these experiences carry their own validation and are beyond criticism.

A third potential problem which has been identified is that it is often not possible to implement non-hierarchical relationships in research because this is at odds with the nature of the surrounding society. The idea of non-hierarchical relationships in research, whilst undoubtedly very attractive to many, runs the risk of masking power differences between professionals doing the research and those they are studying or researching. Take the example of a feminist academic, researching low-paid women factory workers in the clothing industry, who wishes to interview such women and explore their experiences. She may well go and live amongst them for a few weeks or a few months, and even share their work and their pay – before returning to her university to write up her research. Even though she may make every effort in good faith to break down hierarchy, she may well remain – by virtue of education, social status, economic security – outside the world of the women she is studying. A failure to recognise this, and to reflect self-critically on its full implications may serve only to reproduce essentialist myths of the 'all women are really the same' variety.

Finally, the concern to link feminist research into gender issues with women's struggle for emancipation opens up other methodological problems. First, academic feminism is open to the charge that academic marxism used to face when it was influential: that it may be led by political bias and knowingly or unknowingly distort results to produce politically attractive conclusions. Of course, it is also true that many of those who level such charges are guilty of hypocrisy as they mask their own biases behind a veneer of objectivity. Second, there is a problem with dividing the world into oppressors (men) and oppressed (women) which has been recognised by those feminists who have engaged with

Foucault. It may be true, they argue, but it is not the whole truth. If you dispense with the idea that there is a single source of oppression, then different people will be classed as both oppressors and oppressed from different points of view and not only men will emerge as oppressors in every situation. This issue has been highlighted by black feminists who have challenged the neglect of racism by white feminists.

Bearing these debates and issues in mind, we are now in a position to examine some of the myths and beliefs which feminist writers have identified as central to female identities as constructed by ideologies of femininity in the contemporary Western world. The exploration of this theme has been a hallmark of second-wave feminism.

Probably one of the best known texts of (liberal) feminism which addressed the nature and power of ideologies of femininity was Betty Friedan's *The Feminine Mystique*, published in 1963. In this highly influential as well as much-criticised book, Friedan argued that the setbacks and disappointments which American – and by extension, Western – women suffered after the Second World War, when men returning from the war expected women to vacate the jobs and roles they had taken on during the war years and return to the home, were underpinned and sustained by a coherent ideology of femininity. This ideology is what she called the 'feminine mystique'. Friedan argued that the feminine mystique blinded women to their real interests and potential. Women are socialised into believing that the fulfilment of their femininity represents the highest value they can aspire to, and this femininity acts as a powerful ideological myth which sustains social and economic inequality between men and women.

Friedan believed that the ideology of femininity addressed women as, by nature, mysterious, intuitive and life-giving beings who, by virtue of their vocation of motherhood, are quintessentially different from men. Obviously, the ideology of femininity has a particular appeal to women and endows them with a certain status and sense of purpose. But even as it puts women on a pedestal it simultaneously tells them that the root of their problems has been their envy of men and that they should instead accept their feminine vocation. This involves an acceptance of sexual passivity, male domination, and motherhood as the ultimate aspiration of every woman. Thus, the ideology of the feminine mystique provides a rationale for social policies and labour market practices which aim at keeping women in the home and justifying patriarchal power. It also produces massive alienation on the part of many women who find themselves trapped in a suburban nightmare of domesticity, the only escape from which is, for many, reliance on anti-depressants (over-prescribed by a male-dominated medical profession) or alcohol.

Friedan's brand of liberal feminism has been criticised by other more radical feminists and by socialist feminists. They have highlighted a number of problems, in particular her advocacy of women's ability to transcend this situation through individual effort. Judith Evans, for example, writes that 'Friedan's remedy is not conceived of as changing the system, in a revolutionary way. For she wishes – and here it could be pointed out that the analysis is liberal in its assumptions about action and responsibility – women to take their (individual) fate into their own hands by seeking education and careers . . .' (Evans 1996: 34). Other criticisms are that Friedan ignores differences amongst groups of women and plays to the agenda of white middle-class women; that she is far too optimistic of the possibility of transcending the division of domestic labour (a criticism also made of her 1981, book *The Second Stage*) which remains, even at the beginning of the twenty-first century, sheer drudgery for many women; that she is dismissive of the concerns of radical feminists about sexual politics; and that she argues for equality between women and men on the basis of a fundamental sameness. As regards this last, Evans points out that many feminists see Friedan's argument as potentially dangerous – leading possibly to the acceptance of new myths of homogeneity and intolerance of diversity. If we argue for equal rights on the grounds that we are all the same, then we have to ask who it is that defines this sameness. Having said that, Evans acknowledges that by the 1980s Friedan had shifted her stance considerably on the question of sameness versus difference. Indeed Friedan, during the 1980s, appeared to back away from the analysis inherent in her earlier work, calling upon feminists to 'affirm the differences between men and women' (quoted in Faludi 1992: 355), and distancing herself from women's struggles over abortion rights and the politics of rape and sexual violence to such an extent that Susan Faludi could see her as almost part of the intellectual backlash against feminism carried out in the name of 'post-feminism'.

Nevertheless, Friedan's *The Feminine Mystique* was one of the first works to focus attention on the idea of gendered ideologies and she supported her research by a rigorous look at some of the factors which helped to disseminate the ideology of femininity including, for example, how women's magazines changed their content and editors as men returned from the war; how women were encouraged to stay at home through an increased emphasis on ideologies of mothering, supported by changes in the practices of psychoanalysis, psychology, education and social work; and, of course, the huge influence of advertising in propagating consumerist illusions and myths of beauty. These ideas have been influential, and new generations of feminist writers – not all of them liberals – have sought to build upon these insights and analyse aspects of the ideology of femininity as it exists today.

For example, there has been a vigorous debate within feminism about ideologies of mothering and their role in the construction of women and of ideas of gender difference. In the early days of the women's liberation movement, the emphasis was often on 'challenging the myth that motherhood was woman's inevitable destiny' (Rowbotham 1993: 205) and on asserting that for women happiness did not necessarily come only through motherhood – a myth which risked closing down a whole range of possibilities for women. Later, feminist activists would divide between those who argued that 'motherhood was a source of power for women that men seek to control' and that women ought to reaffirm motherly values of nurture; and those who argued that this was a self-defeating political concept which led to an idealisation of motherhood and left women trapped in a form of biological determinism (Rowbotham 1993: 206).

Brannen and Moss (1993: 207–11) have argued that one of the main aspects of the dominant ideology of motherhood in post-war years was the idea that when children are small, ' "normal" motherhood is a full-time activity precluding employment, and that the mother has the major responsibility for all aspects of the child's development'. They argue that this ideological tenet has inhibited women from gaining full-time employment and has left many women who do work either full- or part-time feeling guilty and anxious. It has meant that there has often been 'a grudging acceptance of maternal employment, but not positive approval'; and has been used by conservative politicians to reinforce notions of the traditional family, denying that the state should do anything to help working mothers through child care policies. This links with another aspect of the ideology of motherhood, what Woollet and Phoenix (1993: 216) call 'mother-blaming' – the idea that social problems related to juvenile delinquency can be blamed on poor mothering (as opposed to poor parenting). Indeed, Aminatta Forna has argued that 'a great deal has been said and written about motherhood. The only purpose of the bulk of what has already been published is to tell women how to do the job better' (Forna 1999: 2).

Forna makes a formidable case for the prevalence of the myth of motherhood and the damage it inflicts upon women in contemporary society. Taking issue with the post-feminist view that the entrance of significant numbers of women into the workforce in recent decades means that women have achieved equality with men, she argues that women are still left, overwhelmingly, with the burden of housework and child-rearing (1999: 225). 'Motherhood', she writes,

is the largest single remaining obstacle to women achieving equality in contemporary, post-modern society. The problem is not children, having children, or the love and care of children, but the framing of Motherhood and the endurance of the myths which surround it . . . Today's 'problem with no name' is the myth about Motherhood. The myth denies that the problems of hundreds of thousands of women are real or valid and instead insists that they are natural and inevitable. (Forna 1999: 260)

These problems include the severe curtailment of personal freedoms and life choices, financial dependency, limited access to resources, which undermines women's ability to compete on equal terms with men, and increased vulnerability to manipulation and control by the medical profession and the courts. Forna sounds a distinctly pessimistic note, arguing that 'the Motherhood myth is growing more powerful and is enjoying a popular resurgence, propelled by the insistence on linking ideas about Motherhood to every social ailment from crime statistics to personal happiness' (1999: 261). Nor does the increased emphasis within popular culture upon fathering necessarily change things for the better, as the evidence overwhelmingly suggests that fathers are not taking anything like an equal share of caring and childrearing. The emphasis on fathers' rights can just as easily reinforce gender inequalities rooted in the patriarchal family as challenge them.

Although post-feminists such as Naomi Wolf stand accused by Forna (1999: 11) of underestimating or neglecting the importance of myths of motherhood in reproducing profound gender inequalities, Wolf has highlighted another persistent aspect of feminine ideology which calls for some examination. In *The Beauty Myth* (1991), Wolf argues that part of the backlash against women's advancement in the social and economic spheres has been the articulation of highly constraining myths of beauty. These myths tell women that conformity to certain standards of beauty is now a 'legitimate and necessary qualification for a woman's rise in power' (Wolf. 1991: 28) and that any woman who is not beautiful, as so defined, has only herself to blame. In other words, that 'beauty' can be earned by hard work and enterprise. This last myth, of course, has facilitated the exponential growth of highly lucrative cosmetics, fashion, and dieting industries. Thus, huge profits are made from the manipulation and control (and, sometimes, starvation and destruction) of women's bodies.

Wolf also analyses how myths of beauty have become part of what are known as 'genuine occupational qualifications' for many jobs in the UK and the US –she calls this the 'professional beauty qualification' or PBQ. Wolf gives numerous examples of cases where the courts have upheld the rights of employers to sack, demote or punish women who are deemed too old, unattractive, or insufficiently 'feminine' – cases which have no male parallel. These are examples of how women's access to the labour market has depended on their acceptance of a hyper-sexualisation of their personae in a way which does not apply to men. It is a reinforcement of gender hierarchies, as in women being told that they are too old; that they are expendable over the age of thirty-five. Wolf argues that the PBQ filters down throughout society to many occupations, especially those in the service sector in which women predominate – waitresses, bartenders, catering staff, public relations and customer care jobs. In this way, the ideology of femininity, backed up by the harsh reality of economic discrimination, helps to police millions of women.

Gender divisions and paid work: the 'public' sphere

Men and women in industrial societies have had different cultural and historical experiences of work, due to the material basis of the gendered division of labour. Women, when in paid employment, have tended to be engaged in necessary and productive economic and social tasks such as childcare, food production, clothing, health care and teaching; men have tended to be engaged in industrial manufacturing, economic accumulation, creation of wealth, administration, war, and exercise of state power (Cockburn 1991). Recent decades have seen momentous changes in the structure and nature of the labour market in post-industrial countries. The decline of many traditional masculine occu-pations – in particular, jobs-for-life in the heavy industry and manu-facturing sectors – and the entrance of many women to the labour market are developments which have been heralded by some com-mentators as either contributing to the so-called crisis of masculinity, or alternatively as proof that one of feminism's key demands – eco-nomic equality – has largely been met. In reality, the picture is much more complex. We have seen that material practices, justified by reference to ideologies of gender, continue to constrain women's economic advances. Moreover, the concentration of women workers in part-time, low-paid and often seasonal jobs means that, even in the wealthy countries of the West, women continue to earn significantly less than men. The problem goes deeper. European Union findings published in June 1999 (and based on figures for 1995) show that the UK continues to have one of the worst gender gaps in pay in the EU, with women workers paid just 73.7 per cent of what men earn for the same jobs (*The Guardian*, 9 June 1999). Significant differences remain, also, in participation rates in paid employment. For instance, UK figures show that just over three quarters of women aged between the ages of twenty-five and forty-four were either in employment or seeking work in 1997 (up from only half in 1971), compared with 91 per cent of men (*Social Trends 29*, 1999). These findings support Walby's contention that three main issues need to be addressed when looking at the gendered division of work: women generally earn less than men, do different types of job, and have lower rates of labour force participation (Walby 1986).

It has also been noted by feminist scholars that whenever women enter the ranks of a particular occupation in large numbers, the overall earnings of both men and women within that occupation tend to decline, as the status and prestige associated with the occupation are reduced. An example is the clerical profession. In the late nineteenth century, most secretaries and clerks were men; by the end of the twentieth century, most were women. Indeed, 1998 figures show that 28 per cent of all women workers in the UK are employed in the clerical/secretarial sector, compared to 8 per cent of men workers (*Social Trends 29*, 1999). Pringle (1992) has shown that not only has the status and earning power of this sector decreased as it has been 'feminised', but the relationship between (female) secretary and (male) boss has come to mirror women's subordination to men in non-work relationships. The secretary comes to perform a range of 'tasks' – from coffee-making, to 'looking good', to managing the boss's social, familial and leisure schedules, to covering up for his marital infidelities – which have nothing to do with her professional expertise and everything to do with her subordinate position within the ideological matrix of masculinity and femininity.

Much of women's (usually unpaid) work has taken place in the so-called private sphere, much of men's in the so-called public sphere. Feminist analyses have aimed to demonstrate that 'the analytical separation of the public and the private – of home, work and politics – leads to an incomplete understanding of the structural inequalities in contemporary societies' (McDowell and Pringle 1992: 121). Seidler describes how this split between public work and private work affects men and women in different ways:

> It has served to reinforce the subordination of women economically and socially by assigning them to the area apparently outside of 'production' of domestic labour, reproduction and the socialization of children. Even in the last 50 years or so when women have become integrated into the workforce this inequality has been largely maintained; there has been a kind of job segregation by sex which seeks to extend the exploitation of women as the 'caring' servicers of labour in the home into the service sectors of employment, and into areas of

industry requiring particular dexterity and patience. This transition is then presented as 'natural'.

For men, this split has had an ambiguous effect. In broad terms, it has given us, right across class lines, an economic superiority to women, and an ideology to justify it. But it has also fostered an emotional alienation from life outside work, from the home. (Seidler 1991: 127–8)

Patriarchal power structures reflect male occupation of public sphere – politics, administration, societal organisation. Patriarchy also involves, and is reproduced by, highly gendered masculine and feminine behaviour. As Cockburn argues, 'due to its systemic nature, patriarchy is not something in which membership is optional', and

men may strive to change their personal lives so as to be more equal with women with whom they are close. But being male they continue to be seen by others as members of the patriarchy, and they are bound to share, even if unwilling, in the benefits it affords men. (Cockburn 1991: 8)

She goes on to argue that men have an interest, even if they don't always recognise it, in organising together to work alongside women in changing those hierarchical relations of dominance in the public sphere – the world of work – which impose a masculinist discipline and exact a heavy emotional price from men. As well as exacting a heavy emotional price, patriarchal modes of production confer many privileges and advantages on men, including greater economic power, status, prestige and more time for leisure.

Since the 1970s, feminist scholars have developed a body of sociological theory which studies the extent to which organisations construct sexuality, and are in turn constructed by it. This work has examined sexual dynamics in the workplace and it has sometimes been argued that suppression or control of sexuality is often a central element in organisations. Witz, Halford and Savage (1996), for example, have studied a number of professions and found that managers have often promoted mixed-sex working environments as a way of cutting down on the time spent on banter amongst workers and raising productivity. Indeed, managerial control often encourages 'an acceptable level of heterosexualisation of office culture' (Witz, Halford and Savage 1996: 183) as a means of promoting gendered competition and reinforcing hierarchy. What is deemed to be 'unacceptable' – and to cross the line into sexual harassment – varies between occupations and work environments, often to the detriment of women workers. Thus, the researchers found that nurses were usually expected to accept a considerable degree of verbal and even physical harassment from (male) senior consultants; on the other hand, the banking profession has traditionally sought to control sexual liaisons between staff to a great extent – not out of concern for the harassment of junior female staff but rather in the belief that overt sexualisation of the working environment might threaten the bureaucratic efficiency and work culture of the banking organisation.

Adkins and Lury (1996) have shown that women workers are often overtly sexualised. This can take several forms. Women working in the service sector (waitresses, bartenders, and so on) may be required to dress in sexually alluring or provocative ways which simply do not apply to men. The skills of caring, nurturing, and dealing with emotionally fraught situations, which are deemed by gender ideology to be hallmarks of femininity, may be exploited in certain stereotypical (and usually underpaid) 'female' occupations – nursing, childminding, counselling and customer services being obvious examples. In these ways, the labour market is overtly gendered and ideologies of femininity and masculinity are deployed to maximise profits.

Bureaucratic organisations with a strong masculinist ethos may demonstrate desexualisation, in the sense that emotional concerns and problems are either ignored or handed over for 'solutions' to professional counsellors. Indeed, in many occupations which impose heavy emotional demands upon men – the police, the ambulance service or people dealing with horrific accidents – an occupational culture is often produced which is intensely sexist and superficially cold-hearted as a means of dealing with emotional involvement and preserving masculine constructs intact. Again, professional ideologies – of ethics, confidentiality, impartiality, and objectivity – may reproduce themselves as ungendered and desexualised.

Naomi Goldenberg (quoted in Formaini 1990: 125) has argued that male work culture tends to revolve around work with machines and the administration of things, where people are defined almost as machines. That is to say, when dealing with the administration of people – whether as students, employees, patients, citizens or subjects – men tend to invoke the ideology of rationalism and professionalism to disentangle themselves emotionally and to depersonalise the situation. This may well be a useful and perhaps necessary way of deflecting personal responsibility for decisions. But the ideology of rationalism can also obscure a great deal of stress and unhappiness (and harassment of other workers), and can mean that women enter the workforce alongside men at a distinct cultural disadvantage. It could be argued, *pace* Goldenberg, that this means that male decision-making often takes place in a vacuum. Although distancing through rationalism appears necessary in modern societies, given the social structures into which we are inserted, it may also lead to a form of leadership, including political leadership, which detaches itself from those needs and problems of life which cannot be quantified and solved by administrative means.

Formaini (1990: 125–33) suggests that work provides men with a number of important psychological benefits. First, it protects them against unwanted emotional involvement. The workplace bestows its own camaraderie and closeness, yet the ideology of work embodies certain clearly recognised boundaries. One's workmates know and respect certain 'no-go' areas where unrequested familiarity will be regarded as intrusion. Second, work bestows a sense of identity. Formaini agues that women are encouraged to define themselves more in terms of their relationships and attachments to others; men are encouraged to define themselves in terms of what they do. Work bestows a powerful sense of value and identity, of worth and self-definition. This situation is changing. Changes in the economic structure have led to a relative marginalisation of hard physical manual labour – once seen as embodying one type of manly ideal – whilst the onset of mass unemployment has left many men unable to live up to the 'dominant expectation which shaped our childhood and adolescent image of the future . . . that of getting a job, earning a living, making a career' (Seidler 1991: 126). There is a clear class differential. Middle-class men employed in creative professions – those often expressing greatest satisfaction with what they do – are also more likely to see work as a means to self-knowledge and fulfilment. However, there is no clear correlation between work satisfaction and the amount of time devoted to work in a man's life, Men in jobs which they regard as boring, alienating and repetitive often devote much more time and energy to their work – and derive a sense of identity from it – than economic necessity alone dictates. This is despite the fact that much evidence exists that overwork results in ill health, stress, burn-out, poor relationships, and feelings of deprivation as a result of not spending as much time as workers would like with partners, children, friends, and so on.

It has sometimes been argued that working-class ethics may be healthier in psychological terms – allowing workers to keep their distance from their employers. However, the decline of traditional working-class traditions of solidarity, rooted in the experiences of mass production, and the move into a so-called post-Fordist era where workers are more atomised and diversified, together with attempts to foster so-called Japanese-style work practices emphasising devotion to the corporation, may impose additional psychological and emotional burdens on people.

Many middle-class men devote themselves to their occupation, company, or organisation with a dedication which cannot be explained in terms of rational benefits over costs. Such an ethos places women attempting to enter the professions on an equal footing with men at a distinct disadvantage, given the burden of child-bearing, child-rearing and housework which women still overwhelmingly carry.

The gender-differentiated effects of patterns of paid work upon men and women can be illustrated by a brief look at the impact of unemployment and retirement. It has often been noted that many men find it very difficult to cope with retirement. Surveys have highlighted the male fear of retirement revealing that many men want to work beyond retirement age and fear loss of meaning and direction in their lives. Retirement in heterosexual couples often involves a major change in the balance of power: it is then that women come into their own. Men tend to live shorter lives after retirement than women. Unemployment also seems to impose huge psychological burdens on men. Formaini (1990: 125–33) claims that it can result in the virtual disintegration of the personality in some men, and that studies show the vulnerability of middle-aged men especially to unemployment: they are more likely to suffer mental illness and breakdown. Other research, cited by Formaini, claims to show that heterosexual men sometimes use immersion in the world of work as an escape from their female partners, and that such men often feel threatened by the work achievements and earning power of their partners and even their children.

It is clear that the relationship between ideologies of masculinity and femininity and the gendered division of work is changing. Changes are being brought about by a combination of changes in the nature of production and women's challenge to men's domination of the public sphere – through demands for equal pay, equal job opportunities, a shared burden of unpaid domestic labour, and changes in the ethos of the workplace. Of course, change is never painless or straightforward. As we have seen even in this brief survey, the material forces resisting change are formidable. Such steps towards overcoming the gendered division of work as have occurred seem to leave intact the hierarchical and competitive nature of work in the public sphere, where people's lives are subordinated to the demands of profit and production. Even where a certain 'feminisation' of management style – more people-centred or people-friendly – is recognised as beneficial not just to women or men but to the organisation itself, Cockburn has documented the ways in which organisations draw a new line in the gendered context of work. On the basis of her study of four types of organisation

– civil service, high street retail, local authority and trade union – she concludes that:

> women may join in the exercise of power; they may even change the style of management; but they are unlikely to be permitted to change the nature of the organisation. Having more women in management, even women 'doing things in womanly ways' . . . does not guarantee a feminist revision of the goals and structure of the organisation, nor of its operations in the labour market. Without such a revision women will step into power in an organisation which, convivial though it may be for managers, continues to exploit women as workers and consumers in the same way as before. It will be mainly white women among the men at the top, exploiting women, many of whom will be black, at the base. (Cockburn 1991: 73)

Cockburn cites some depressing evidence of male resistance in organisations to the advancement of women in the workplace, including male reluctance to press for, and take advantage of, gains such as paternity leave and job-sharing which would allow men to play a fuller role in domestic labour and child-rearing. Her research suggests that while men welcomed a few days off in the event of a new baby, very few would seriously consider a career break or a prolonged period of paternity leave to raise children. She concludes that a profound gender division of labour will take more than a few years of equal opportunities to break down.

To conclude, it can be argued that, although many men still cling to the privileges and psychological advantages which the patriarchal division of work seems to bestow on them – or, as Faludi argues, simply do not know how to respond to structural changes seemingly beyond their control – there is now considerable evidence that both men and women pay a high price for the tyranny of gender ideologies in the labour market. This price is paid in terms of economic and financial independence, emotional well-being, health, and possibilities for both family life and personal development.

Gender divisions and emotion work: the 'private' sphere

Feminist scholarship's deconstruction of the analytical separation between the public and private spheres has opened up for scrutiny and analysis another area in which gendered ideologies have clearly constrained and conditioned human behaviour and relationships – the area of 'emotion work'. The phrase covers a range of emotionally and physically demanding activities, from the exhausting work of child-rearing to the daily tasks of listening, counselling, mediating and peace-making which are central to the preservation of peace and unity within families, to similar tasks which are central to the maintenance of all human relationships. Clearly, this work and the emotional skills which accompany it are of central importance to human beings. Yet feminist scholarship has uncovered considerable evidence that emotion work is unevenly shared between men and women, and that the types – or perhaps levels – of emotional skills which men and women exhibit are different. Naturally, this involves something of a generalisation; in-deed, it could be argued that the presence of so many exceptions to the general rule is proof of the ideological (as opposed to 'natural') basis of this aspect of masculinity and femininity.

Jean Duncombe and Dennis Marsden (1993) imply that struggles over emotion work and reciprocity in intimacy may well form a new frontier in the battle for gender equality. Their argument is that men, in general, seem less skilled than women at identifying and expressing their emotions and less likely to perceive and therefore be influenced by the emotions of others. They identify significant gender differences in the willingness or ability to disclose emotionally and to work at sustaining intimacy and trust in relationships. Duncombe and Marsden argue that women's (socially constructed and sanctioned) skills in emotion work impose additional burdens within families and can be commercially exploited – as we saw earlier in this chapter – in the service sector or caring professions. They raise the question as to whether ideologies of masculinity and femininity have in fact devel-oped broadly separate emotional cultures for men and women.

Stevi Jackson, in her deconstruction of myths of romantic love, has pointed to one of the ways in which these broadly separate emotional cultures may come about. Jackson (1993: 212) quotes Rosaldo to the effect that 'feelings are not substances to be discovered in our blood, but social practices organised by stories that we both enact and tell'. She examines how we make sense of our feelings and relationships through learning what love is supposed to mean and acting out a script which we adopt as our own. Jackson's central argument is that love is a gendered learning experience – boys and girls learn different scripts. Men are not encouraged to develop competence in locating themselves within discourses of emotions – it is through the idiom of sexual bravado and conquest, not the language of romance, that masculinity is asserted. Encouraged to locate the central core of their identities in the 'external' world, men often learn to express feelings of love or friendship through 'doing things' and in shared activities rather than intimate disclosure. Women, by contrast, are socialised into defining themselves in terms of relationships and, through the pervasive idiom of romantic fiction, are encouraged to embrace not only disclosure but the notion of self-sacrifice in the name of 'love'. Jackson also points out that material power differences between men and women, for example, 'the emotional and physical labour they perform for men within households and families' (1993: 217), underpin these romantic fictions. This point is reinforced by research carried out by O'Connor (1991), who highlights not only how financial and material constraints hinder many women's ability to maintain intimate friendships outside marriage, but also how women's desire to save their marriage and avoid the jealousy of their husband may lead them to sacrifice such close friendships. Wendy Langford (1999) has argued that the feminine themes of sacrifice and redemption (through romantic love) often lead to women becoming trapped in an alienating dynamic of male domination and female submission.

There has been a great deal of recent research on how a male fear of intimacy can damage and stultify men's capacity for meaningful relationships, whether these are friendships which involve sex or not. Sociological and psychological research suggests that many men have a real problem with emotional disclosure. This seems to operate on a number of levels. First, men may associate emotions with weakness and vulnerability. Seidler (1991: 69) argues that this is central to contemporary masculinity in our society and forms part of a deep cultural inheritance. Men are socialised from an early age to eschew weakness and to deny or sublimate feelings which seem to threaten their sense of control over themselves. The implication is that self-knowledge, which would seem to be the prerequisite for being at peace with oneself and being capable of loving others, can come into conflict with the masculine ideal.

Second, the fear of disclosure in relationships seems to operate to police relations between men, which often reflect the masculine ethos of containment, aggression, competition, and fear of 'feminisation' through being exposed as vulnerable and dependent in the eyes of another man, even a close friend. Not surprisingly, several of the contributions in Nardi (1992) argue that male friendships are often perceived by men as less satisfying than their friendships with women.

This, however, leads on to a third aspect of the male fear of intimacy – a tendency for men to expect others, especially women, to do the emotional work needed to sustain a relationship; and a corresponding inability or unwillingness to offer the same level of emotional support in return. Seidler (1992) argues that in the absence of a person in their lives prepared to fill the 'feminine role' of emotional carer, many men learn to live without friendship or intimacy even while desiring it. In other words, the fear of change can outweigh the fear of loneliness. With the advent of feminism and of fundamental social and economic change, more and more women are unwilling to accept such a raw deal in terms of emotional support, and are demanding greater reciprocity in relationships. This often touches a raw nerve in men, bringing an aggressive and dismissive response.

As many of the contributions in Nardi (1992) make clear, the ideology of masculinity stigmatises intimacy between men, and seeks to lock intimacy between men and women within the confines of heterosexual coupledom in which given gender roles tend to ascribe primary responsibility for sustaining the friendship, relationship or marriage to the woman. This ideology is never unchallenged, of course, but it is dominant still. For example, Karen Hansen (1992), writing of men's friendships with women in New England before the American civil war, notes how difficult it was for a man and a woman to have an exclusive, reciprocal, intimate but non-romantic (platonic) friendship unless they were blood relatives. Her point is that such friendships existed, but were not socially sanctioned. Indeed, they were so difficult to sustain that men often developed intense (non-sexual) friendships with their biological sisters, as her research purports to show. It still seems to be the case that a close, intimate, equal friendship between a man and a woman which is not going to end up in sexual coupledom is made difficult, not only by an individual man's stunted capacity for intimacy but also by social pressure – the expectation that such friendships are sexually suspicious, and even perhaps carry a certain social stigma.

As regards men's friendships with each other, it is arguable that for all men the positioning of men in the social structure has encouraged the formation of sociable relationships but restricted the potential for self-revelation within them. Typically, male friendships, especially those which revolve around work or sports, have in fact taken the form of 'mateship', or 'buddyship', which, Formaini (1990) argues, acts as a poor substitute for friendship. Such relationships involve the imposition of a code of behaviour which demands a macho image and a denial of the feminine, and the imposition of external appearances over inner truth. In such relationships, men often tend to find that their conversation with each other revolves around subjects rooted in an external world where masculinity is constructed as being in control: politics, sport, business. Men are usually unable to discuss sexuality with other men, according to Formaini's research.

Of course, this involves a huge generalisation. It ignores, for example, the question of sexual orientation. Research has found significant differences between gay-identified and heterosexual men – although much more research remains to be done on this topic before we can draw any firm conclusions. Nardi (1992a) suggests that a majority of gay-identified men do discuss sexuality, emotions and the intimate details of their lives with other close gay male friends. More than seventy per cent of Nardi's sample reported having discussed everything or almost everything about their own sex lives with their best friend, and more than fifty per cent discussed everything or almost everything with close friends. However, Nardi's sample is of mainly youngish gay men within the metropolitan area of Los Angeles and how representative this is of non-heterosexual men in general is open to question. Intriguingly, Nardi's research also tells us much about both the limitations and possibilities of masculinity in general: the gay men in his sample often see sex as a path to intimacy – as men in general so often do; but as members of a marginalised community they have developed a greater sense of mutual caring and emotional sharing, which all men are capable of.

Feminist (and feminist-inspired) scholarship claims that the uneven division of emotion work between adult men and women, with all the concomitant problems and unhappiness which that can cause in human relationships, is precisely linked to the relative absence of men from the world of child-rearing – the so-called 'private' sphere – an absence underpinned by economic inequalities and realities. The inculcation in children of ideologies of gender begins at a very early age. Formaini (1990) argues that we observe the inferior status of women from early childhood – how women are treated by men inside the home and outside in the world – and that this inferiority is underpinned by the separation of men from the world of child-rearing and emotional responsibility, out into the world of work, business, success and freedom. Boys learn that even though they love their mother, they love someone who is defined as inferior. For boys, this sets up a process by which a split in the male personality hardens into a form of misogyny which contains a measure of self-hate. Masculinity teaches men to hate the part of themselves as men which loves something they are told is inferior.

The entrance of the boy into the external world – school – involves a further process of socialisation through peer groups and rites of passage which works upon this constructed split in the male personality. A young boy has to learn not only to separate from his mother, but to suppress his love for her, and his ability to show emotions: he is not allowed to cry after a certain age, or to show weakness. The demands of masculinity impose a sense of loss and deprivation at this point in development.

This affects men's later ability to enter into mature, loving relationships, or to assume full responsibility for their emotional commitments. The argument is not that men do not feel very deeply, nor that they are not capable of tremendous feelings of love; but that those feelings come to overwhelm and terrify. The split in the male personality manifests itself both as a powerful capacity for love and a powerful resistance to love. The resultant neurosis lies behind the tendency to 'botch' relationships by running away precisely when the relationship is becoming important. Masculine ideology manifests itself in the internalised sense that men have to protect themselves from too close an attachment. Once again, we have an illustration of the heavy price ideologies of masculinity and femininity demand; and of Forna's point, that enduring myths of motherhood, as opposed to social and political emphasis upon good parenting, underscore women's social disadvantage and are a formidable obstacle to overcoming gender inequality.

The policing of gender boundaries

Having examined some of the more salient aspects of ideologies of masculinity and femininity, and how they impact on people's lives, we will look at how gender ideologies are enforced and gender identities policed. This is a complex matter. An important question which calls for examination is the intimate connection between traditional ideologies of gender and the maintenance and reproduction of the norms of heterosexuality.

Recent research by sociologists into the attitudes of young people in the UK has highlighted this connection. Holland et al.(1996), for example, worked with young women and men in Manchester and London between 1988 and 1992 and found that double standards about gender behaviour and sexual reputations were still very much alive. Young men who were sexually active with different partners were widely regarded as 'studs' and emerged with enhanced reputations in the eyes of their peers, whereas young women who acted in a similar fashion were stigmatised as 'slags'. The researchers concluded that 'masculine young men have power in ways in which feminine young women do not' (1996: 241) and that the fear of stigma and loss of reputation mean that young women police their own behaviour through the psychological mechanism the researchers refer to as 'the male in the head'. The young men, by contrast, maintain their social prestige and power through exaggerated maleness:

Since heterosexual masculinity is socially constructed in opposition to femininity and homosexuality, men cannot simply step out of social maleness. To be a man is to be not-women, not-gay, not absorbed back into a mother/son relationship. A man who rejects heterosexual conquest, who makes himself a willing wimp, may call himself a new man, but in terms of the double standard he is a loser. (Holland et al., 1996: 251)

Moreover, such a man often risks injury through bullying, beatings, or so-called 'queer-bashing'. The authors conclude that 'male resistance to masculinity [is] physically dangerous'.

Debbie Epstein's work with lesbian and gay teenagers also reveals high levels of homophobic harassment and bullying within schools. Epstein's research shows that harassment of lesbian and gay teenagers and of those perceived to be gay is related to sexist harassment of women. It is also relatively widespread within schools culture, and can be seen as part of the process by which young people are forced to 'learn the script' of heterosexuality and conform to that script, or pay a heavy price. Indeed, the policing of gender boundaries is so invidious that Epstein shows that 'for men, both the avoidance of stigmatisation and the production of acceptable masculinities seem to depend, at least in part, on harassing women and other men' (Epstein 1996: 217). Thus, many gay teenagers tried to avoid persecution themselves by directing homophobic insults at other young people.

Further research by Anoop Nayak and Mary Jane Kehily (1996, 1997) into why teenage school boy culture can be so intensely homophobic found that, by acting out rituals of homophobic abuse, young men create a masculine self-identity for themselves and convince them-selves that they are entering into a world of adult masculinity. Homo-phobia not only polices behaviour which threatens the boundaries of gender or introduces ambiguity; it bestows on the homophobe a sense of security and manliness. Homophobic language and behaviour can therefore be seen as part of a performance of 'hyper-masculinity' which 'is enacted to expel fears, desires and the vulnerability of ambivalence' (Nayak and Kehily 1996: 225). The consequences of this 'performance' for those who are stigmatised as 'poofs' or 'bum bandits' and treated as traitors to their gender can be loneliness, depression, and disintegration of self-respect.

Other writers have discussed the extent to which homophobia functions to ensure the strict demarcation of male and female gender roles in adult life. Segal (1990) argues that homophobia is central to the construction of adult masculinity – the fear of being branded a 'poof' or 'faggot' acts to police men's intimate behaviour and socially expressed attitudes. Building on Foucault, she suggests that homophobia works to police and constrict men's friendships in the context of an era of mass bureaucracy and mass production in which close friendship between men is seen as dysfunctional or threatening. For example, it is possible to identify specific forms of homophobia which operate in this way – such as the homophobia which is part of the military code and which lays down strict limits to intimacy between men in the name of toughness, denigration of the feminine, and 'proper functioning' of the military machine. In this ideological code, the stereotyped 'weak', 'feminine' man – so often the victim of relentless bullying and abuse within the armed forces – becomes a metaphor for the reduction of military strength. Or one can point to the homophobia associated with forms of imperialism, which attributes 'effeminacy' to those deemed racially inferior and extols the virtues of sexual abstinence and emotional coldness as characteristics of the superior, imperial, 'race'. Again, this type of homophobia may be associated with the metaphor of 'the enemy within' – alleged traitors to the nation (masculinity). Thus, we have witnessed homosexuality projected on to political enemies by many states and powers in this century. The anti-communist witch-hunts of McCarthyism in the USA in the 1950s went hand-in-hand with anti-homosexual witch-hunts; the USSR and like-minded Stalinist regimes attacked homosexuality as a sign of (pro-Western) 'bourgeois decadence'; and, in the UK, at the height of the Cold War panics over the Philby, Burgess and Maclean spy scandals, homosexuality was held almost as evidence of treasonable intent. Segal also believes that homophobia's other forms include that of an agent to reinforce the economic function of the family and the gendered division of labour. Until recently, men who did not work or who stayed at home while their female partners went out to work were open to the charge of being effeminate. Homophobia can also police family life – a man who walks out on his wife and children, or who fails to assert patriarchal authority within the family unit, might feel himself suspected of weakness.

Clearly, one of the most persistent myths central to homophobia is that homosexuality is both weak and effeminate and simultaneously threatening to heterosexual men. At first sight, this might seem contradictory. If homosexuals are so weak and 'unmanly', why does homophobia seem consistently to generate panic attacks about the havoc which homosexuality has the potential to unleash upon 'real' men? Segal sheds light upon this by pointing out that all men have a need to be 'passive', to be held and to be loved, but these needs and feelings clash with the dominant construction of masculinity – with masculine ideology. This produces feelings of shame and guilt about the fact that men are often vulnerable, afraid, and in need of protection. One whole part of men's humanity is thus perceived as 'the enemy within one's self', to be contained, repressed and struggled with lest it reveal just how fragile a construct masculinity really is. In this way, homophobia can be understood as not merely intimately connected with misogyny, but a way in which many men project on to the existential Other – the 'homosexual', or 'effeminate' man – their hatred and fear of, and embarrassment over, what they perceive as the feminine part of their own nature.

Dollimore (1991) agrees, and points out that the association of masculinity with opposition to homosexuality combines within itself two classic dichotomies – that of masculine/feminine and that of homosexual/heterosexual. In this way, homophobia polices the boundaries of gender and constricts and constrains all of us. The unmasking and decentering of homophobic myths and stereotypes thus becomes a matter of primary importance, not only to gay men, lesbians and bisexuals, but to everyone who feels alienated from traditional ideologies of gender and who aspires to liberation from sexism and patriarchy.

Part III

Sexual politics

Chapter 4

Contemporary debates and challenges

Introduction: a sexual revolution?

We live in an era of unprecedented social, economic and cultural upheaval and change. Employment patterns, family patterns, and long-cherished beliefs, certainties and identities rooted in class, religion or nationality are all either in crisis or changing rapidly, often beyond many people's control or comprehension. A sense of who we are, where we belong or fit in, and what is our community can become critical. And in such an era of rapid change, many of our anxieties – as we watch the world we grew up in change beyond recognition – can become focused on issues of gender and sexuality. That is why Jeffrey Weeks and others have argued that the politics of sexuality becomes a sort of barometer for measuring wider personal and social anxieties over cultural change. Weeks (1995: 4–5) argues that 'anxiety about the sexual has, like mysterious creatures scuttling under the floorboards, implicitly shaped many of our public debates for a long time', but that what is new about the contemporary era is that 'worries about changing sexual behaviour and gender and sexual identities have become the explicit focus for debates about the current shape and desirable future of society'.

This chapter explores what it means to be involved in sexual politics, and whether it can really be said that we have lived through a period of 'sexual revolution' since the 1960s. It seeks to illustrate some of the concerns which motivate, and some of the challenges which face, those involved in sexual politics by focusing on a number of debates under way between feminists and postfeminists, within lesbian, gay, bisexual and queer politics, and within so-called men's politics.

To become involved in sexual politics usually means recognising not only that gender and sexual identities and behaviour are political issues in the sense that they are the object of state control and regulation and of battles between social forces and ideologies, but also that the struggle to gain control over one's body and its capacities and pleasures, the struggle for self-definition and self-determination for choice is seen as central to the constitution of the human subject. In that sense, coming to terms with both your gendered identity and your sexuality, in the sense of assuming responsibility for both, and asserting the right to name, change and redefine your gendered role in society and your sexuality, is integral to the reformulation of your view of the world. This search for self-knowledge and for a reinvention of your sense of identity – bearing in mind Foucault's reservations about the regulatory function of new discourses – often involves a real change in who you are, how you perceive yourself and your place in society, and how you relate to others and to the state. It involves a real change in how you respond to the discourses on gender and sexuality (or, if you prefer, ideologies) being expounded daily through television, radio, the popular press, schools and colleges, church pulpits and religious tracts, courts, police and penal service, political elites, and of course the family and immediate kinship or neighbourhood community. It can involve an empowerment. And it is that sense of empowerment which can politicise and radicalise and pose a real subversive challenge to the forces which regulate and govern our gendered and sexualised identities.

Most writings on sexual politics agree that a key defining process here is that which has become known as 'coming out'. The phrase 'coming out' has now entered popular parlance to cover a wide range of situations, common to which is an individual's attempts to assert a positive identity based on self-acceptance, pride and visibility in the face of powerful messages which seek to obliterate that individual through shame and invisibility. It is best thought of not as a one-off event or moment but as a lifelong process. Once you take the first uneasy steps out of whatever closet your life experience and social formation may have put you in, there is really no turning back. You have embarked upon a challenge which will confront you for the rest of your life, assuming – as we have to assume – that we don't experience in our lifetime a sexual democracy in which sexual and gender discrimination, oppression, and even differentiation belong to history.

The phrase 'coming out' was until recently almost exclusively associated with the process of claiming, integrating within oneself and asserting a chosen identity as lesbian, gay or bisexual. Its meanings and application have now broadened. Potentially, everyone faces the challenge of grappling with the constitution of their sexuality, with disempowerment and with gendered or sexualised oppression (perhaps women more than men – but men too, perhaps gay more than straight – but straight too, perhaps black more than white – but white too, and so on . . .). And everyone has to take a decision whether to 'come out' in that sense or not. For example, women 'come out' as women when they confront issues of gendered oppression – the rape, violence, abuse, contempt, discrimination, manipulation, denial of their subjectivity and their experience, which they have suffered. Heterosexual men 'come out' when they confront issues of sexism and homophobia, face up to issues of male privilege and their responsibility in the context of relationships, and defy what they feel are the dominant expectations of the way they should behave as men, even at the risk of derision or laughter. In this sense, the experience of coming out – confronting the challenge of personal, social, and political change, and fighting against powerful ideologies which deny one's full humanity and seek to cloak one in invisibility – constitutes a common experience of all those engaged in radical or progressive sexual politics. An exception, of course, would be those – such as conservative and patriarchal men's groups – who have a vested interest in ideologies of exclusion and in presenting male privilege as natural and pre-ordained.

When the empowerment conferred by 'coming out' is experienced as a political commitment and a new sense of belonging or community, we can speak of a politics of sexual identity. Obviously, the community of women with its sense of sisterhood, and the lesbian and gay communities, spring to mind. It is important to emphasise right away that identities both change and overlap. A politics of sexual identity is by definition a politics of constant change, self-questioning and self-doubt (as well as self-affirmation), although like every form of radical politics it has its share of dogmatists, fundamentalists and those who risk getting trapped in a ghetto of the mind and the heart.

We are all the bearers of multiple identities. Moreover, identities do not appear out of thin air but are the product of social forces. Forms of oppression and discrimination, power and control do not all revolve around gender or sexuality (there are such things as racial, class and sectarian discrimination and oppression, after all). For these reasons few would argue that their sexual identity is their only important identity or that they can, either in theory or practice, base solely on sexual identity a political project which seeks radically to transform the society we live in.

It can be argued that various 'cultures of resistance' have grown up in response to systematic attempts by the state, church and medical profession to name, define and construct identities – categories of people – on the basis of ascribed gender and sexual behaviour. The concept of 'cultures of resistance' is rather a broad and nebulous one, spanning the worlds of fashion, music, politics, art, theory, alternative patterns of collective living, consciousness-raising groups, counselling and self-help groups, or simply safe spaces where people can enjoy themselves (such as pubs and clubs) or have sex (such as the legendary swinging parties and suburban orgies which are part of the mythology of the 1960s). There is no agreement as to whether all sexual sub-cultures are synonymous with cultures of resistance; or whether all cultures of resistance are political. When people meet, for example, to celebrate transgressive sexual pleasure as an end in itself, are they all, by virtue of resisting the dominant construction of gender and sexuality, necessarily engaged in political defiance? Is defiance of the law, or of conventional morality, in itself a political act, a positive affirmation of the personal as political? Or do certain sexual sub-cultures – for example, the heavily commercialised side of the gay scene or the whole SM scene (both straight and gay) – simply reinforce aspects of an oppressive status quo through trumpeting consumerism, fetishisation of beauty and youth, or eroticising power and violence? And that is not even to mention the sub-culture of paedophilia which the great ma-jority of writers on sexual politics would see as oppressive, abusive and beyond any claim on the sympathies or support of those involved in sexual politics or the politics of sexuality.

This seems to touch upon a bone of contention which runs through virtually all contemporary sexual movements and sub-cultures – and will also allow us to 'locate' debates between feminists and postfemi-nists. Linda Grant (1993) characterises this as a battle between millen-arianism and what she calls libertinage. Grant's choice of terms is perhaps unfortunate, given the association of millenarianism in pop-ular consciousness with apocalyptic religious fanaticism and of liber-tinage with immorality. But, as we saw in Chapter 1, Grant uses these terms to distinguish between what we might call sexual optimism and sexual pessimism. For her, millenarianism posits the possibility of a future in which relations between men and women have become more egalitarian, more fulfilling, more democratic, less alienating or abusive: a sexual democracy. Time and time again, in the idealism of the feminist and lesbian and gay movements of the 1960s and 1970s, one comes across the hope, the belief, that it is within human potential to construct such a society – to transcend fear, prejudice, violence, aggression, hatred. We have here a vision of a genderless society – to match the Marxist utopia of a classless society – in which a common humanity will replace the categories of male and female, homosexual and heterosexual. There have been severe disagreements about how progress towards the desired utopia can be secured – whether it is through legal and political reforms, education of public opinion, economic change, rejection of and withdrawal from existing patterns of social regulation into alternative social structures (such as commu-nes), or revolution. These disagreements run through the debates between differing schools of feminist thought and politics – radical feminists, socialist feminists, liberal feminists, and so on. But the belief in the future is central.

Libertinage, by contrast, involves a movement away from the pursuit of fundamental social change towards sexual hedonism and individualism. Authenticity is to be sought through the pursuit of pleasure. As Grant puts it, the libertine approaches the pursuit of pleasure as an amoral enterprise, rejecting the clear sense of morality and of moral community inherent in sexual optimism as self-deluding puritanical nonsense.

Grant suggests that this conservative, consumerist, hedonistic message is suited to the postmodern, 'end-of-ideology', and essentially right-wing times in which we live. It is an era in which capitalist consumerism claims to offer a solution to all our worries (provided we have the money to pay for the appropriate 'lifestyle'), and in which socialists, feminists and others who hanker after profound social and political transformation can be presented as outdated, unfashionable, or puritanical. This message may also be suited to a period in history in which a certain disillusionment with the so-called sexual revolution of the 1960s is evident. It can be seen as having cheated women of sexual self-determination, or as having failed to deliver its promised liberation from sexual oppression. Certainly it is important to bear in mind the wider political context – the apparent collapse of socialism and the 'triumph' of capitalist consumerism, the growing power of transnational corporations which seem to undermine traditional political strategies for social change, the growth of consumer rights and Internet campaigns as substitutes for mass political activism – when examining the challenges which postfeminism, queer politics and other manifestations of postmodernism pose for so-called millenarian sexual politics.

Debates between feminists and postfeminists

The 1980s was a tough decade for millenarian politics in general in Britain and North America. The 1990s – which began by being heralded as the 'caring 90s' – has been an even tougher decade in much of Europe, as hopes of peace, progress and greater humanity are battered senseless by the resurrection of nationalist, ethnic and religious hatreds, those prejudices and age-old conflicts which many had hoped were buried for ever. At times it seems that nothing can be taken for granted and that all the so-called humanist achievements since the Enlightenment are under attack. How secure or well-grounded were those achievements anyway?

In Britain and America, the 1980s was a decade of backlash (Faludi, 1992) against millenarian sexual politics. Many in the women's movement have been astonished to discover that 'gains' which they had thought were permanent – such as the legalisation of abortion, divorce, or the right of women to enter the labour market – have been under attack in some countries. Equal pay legislation has been undermined by the economic crisis which has seen a major growth of low-paid, part-time and largely female jobs in all industrialised countries. The right of women to choose to have a child outside marriage or bring up children on their own has been attacked by those who blame single-parent families for social malaise and crime – and who shamelessly call for single mothers to be locked away in religious institutions, or encouraged to give up their children for adoption. In the UK, Section 28 of the Local Government Act of 1988 (Section 2a of the Scotland Act) was the first legislative move in over twenty years explicitly aimed against the claims of lesbians and gay men to be treated on an equal basis with heterosexuals. In many states of the USA, the Christian Right has succeeded in having passed into law by popular referendum legislation which removes legal protection from gay men and lesbians in housing and employment, and permits discrimination. The Child Support Agency (CSA) in the UK has issued rulings effectively making many single mothers financially dependent on the fathers of their children, thus threatening their independence and privacy and possibly even safety, as well as laying a financially heavy burden on many men.

Of course, this is only part of the story. There have also been renewed movements in favour of lesbian and gay rights which have achieved some successes, and a new wave of activism against the CSA, although some of this has taken an ambiguous attitude towards single mothers. However, this new wave of activism in sexual politics has to some extent been characterised by an embarrassment over feminism. Several writers have observed that many women who hold attitudes and views which are clearly influenced by feminism are nevertheless unwilling to describe themselves as 'feminists', seeing the term as too strident or restrictive. Is there a link between this and the visible depoliticisation of large numbers of young gay men and lesbians who take for granted freedoms which are really very recent indeed – the freedom to go to a gay pub or disco, form a college society, meet with others their own age and form relationships reasonably openly? Is it that millenarian idealism is taking a battering in both cases, with pragmatism and caution on the one hand, and consumerism on the other, making large numbers of people unwilling to accept an ideological approach to sexual or gender politics which they suspect feminism or gay activism involves?

Against this sustained assault on feminism we have to set the rise to fashionability and media favour of postfeminism. Postfeminism rejects feminism as a cult of 'victimhood'. The best-known spokesperson for this position is Camille Paglia who has famously written: 'sexual freedom, sexual liberation – a modern delusion. We are hierarchical animals. Sweep away one hierarchy and another will take its place' (quoted in Grant 1993: 20). This seems to suggest that as things are so they shall remain. Indeed, one of the big issues at stake in debates between feminists and postfeminists concerns whether or not sexual politics has to be a politics of profound social transformation.

The meaning of postfeminism is confusing to many. On the one hand it can present itself as enjoying an evolutionary relationship with feminism – as encapsulating a 'maturing' of the feminist project. On the other hand, it can be seen as seeking to undermine, discredit and dance on the grave of second wave feminism – as forming part of a strident anti-feminist backlash. Brooks (1997: 8) argues that postfeminism has its roots in the breakdown of the consensus surrounding second wave feminism due to pressures from three directions. These are the critiques mounted by black feminists and others of the 'racist and ethnocentric assumptions of a largely white, middle-class feminism'; the problematising of sexual difference and sexual identity; and the intersection of feminism with postmodernism. Such a position can lead one to see postfeminism as a necessary corrective to some of the 'homogenising' and 'totalitarian' assumptions of feminism, and as a natural 'sister' of queer politics and Foucauldian analysis. Coppock, Haydon and Richter (1995: 3–14), however, argue that postfeminism appeared 'out of nowhere' in the late 1980s and early 1990s and was soon trumpeted by the mass media – which created its own postfeminist celebrities, most notably Camille Paglia – in celebration of the claim that women had now achieved equality with men and no longer had need of the feminist project. Indeed, as they point out, postfeminism lacks any analysis of the gendered, structural inequalities which are part of contemporary liberal capitalist societies. Instead, it seems to take at face value the argument that liberal initiatives such as equal pay legislation and equal opportunities policies have of themselves solved the problem of gender inequality. 'Qualifications, access, promotion and job security are assumed to have been accepted and established principles of equality, prevailing in all organisations and their management structures' (Coppock, Haydon and Richter 1995: 4). The argument is that 'superwomen' nowadays can have it all – high-flying careers, children, success in the worlds of both the family and business. Indeed, it is even argued that the pendulum has swung too far in women's favour, with men unfairly blamed and victimised by feminists (a position articulated by Paglia).

The consequence of the absence of any analysis of the structural inequalities inherent in capitalist and patriarchal society is that post-feminism, certainly as expounded by Paglia, denies that there is any real conflict of interests between men and women, gay and straight. We have reached the end of sexual history. (There are echoes here of Francis Fukuyama's thesis [1992] about the triumph of Western liberal capitalism). Women can take power if they want to, and if they do not – or experience disappointment and disillusionment – then they have only themselves to blame and should perhaps reconsider whether they have tried to have too much in life. A barrage of media discourses has told young women that we live in the era of 'Girl Power' (which, according to the Spice Girls, included Mrs Thatcher) and that anything is possible for them. Of course, when these young women come up against the 'glass ceiling' which still exists in so many walks of life, pop psychology is at hand to reinforce the message that feminism 'has gone too far' and rendered women unhappy.

Postfeminism also suggests that women can overcome sexual ex-ploitation almost by an act of will – by celebrating sexual pleasure, not 'whining' on about how wicked the penis is. The penis, in fact, is wonderful! Rape, abuse and battering of women by men is either wished out of existence, or downgraded as a matter which feminists have wickedly exaggerated, or blamed on women themselves (as we will see shortly). Male sexual aggression is celebrated as biological fact. According to Paglia, all great culture, art and civilisation has been created by men and is the product of masculine energy and genius: 'if civilisation had been left in female hands, we would still be living in grass huts' (quoted in Coppock, Haydon and Richter 1995: 6). Paglia's celebration of this crude version of sociobiology leads her to proclaim that 'male lust . . . is the energising factor in culture. Men are the reality principle. They created the world we live in and the luxuries we enjoy. When women cut themselves off from men, they sink backward into psychological and spiritual stagnancy' (Paglia 1993: 24).

This reactionary nonsense is occasionally presented by some of its exponents as 'power feminism' battling against its predecessor, 'victim feminism'. This allows feminists and socialists to be constructed as born 'victims', forever whining, complaining and trying to change that which cannot be changed: biology, destiny or sex as power. The central message to women seems to be: forget utopianism, accept your hor-mones, free yourself by competing with men on men's terms. There is no need to engage in millenarian dreaming about dismantling hier-archies because women can now climb to the top of hierarchies. There is no need to 'castrate' men – which Paglia accuses feminists of wanting to do – because women can 'have balls' too. In short, women can fuck as well as men. It is interesting that, at a time when many gay men under the shadow of AIDS have turned away from penetrative sex, some postfeminists have begun to celebrate sexual penetration. 'It's not that I don't like a penis inside me', jokes the postfeminist lesbian comedian Lea de Laria, 'it's just that I don't like a man on the end of it'. The message is that women can empower themselves by emulating the boys.

Rape, Camille Paglia writes, is a risk women must learn to live with. Women must accept that humane or egalitarian eroticism will never be possible because male sex is by its nature violent, dark, aggressive and powerful. Women must learn to live with it, and stop trying to change it or pretend they are superior. In one of her most contentious – or to many people, downright offensive – passages, Paglia writes:

> Rape is one of the risk factors in getting involved with men. It's a risk factor. It's like driving a car . . . go for it, take the risk, take the challenge – if you get raped, if you get beat up in a dark alley in a street, it's okay. That is part of the risk of freedom. That's part of what we demanded as women. Go with it. Pick yourself up, dust yourself down, and go on. We cannot regulate male sexuality. The uncontrollable aspect of male sexuality is part of what makes sex interesting. And yes, it can lead to rape in some situations. What feminists are asking for is for men to be castrated. (Paglia 1993: 63)

Feminists have been accused by another postfeminist, Katie Roiphe, of more or less inventing the myth of date rape in order to encourage women to wallow in victimhood. Roiphe (1994) appears to argue that unless women define themselves as victims, victimisation has not occurred. This is surely tantamount to blaming the victim for being assaulted. If rape within intimate heterosexual relationships is just a risk which women must accept, then date rape is almost defined out of existence. The British feminists Kelly, Burton and Regan (1996) have argued that this effectively returns women to the position of more than twenty years ago when rape was by definition 'stranger rape' because rape within marriage, by male relatives or within close relationships was scarcely recognised.

In the late 1990s, a number of British feminists argued forcefully against some of the postfeminist ideas arriving in the UK from the USA and receiving much attention in the media. They argued that rejecting the possibility of radical change, of any transformative project, coupled with a celebration of male sexual aggression as creativity, and of biology as destiny, amounts to rejecting the possibilities of sexual politics and surrendering to patriarchy, to the dominant construction of male subjectivity.

Lynne Segal, for example, has described Paglia as 'basically a very conservative 1950s Freudian who refuses to engage with any of the developments of the last 30 years' (quoted in *The Guardian*, 19 September 1998). Segal has pointed out that in Britain at the end of the twentieth century, 80 per cent of women still earn less than their male partners – and that the central concerns of feminism such as fairness and equality of opportunity, far from have being achieved, are still as elusive for many women as ever. Indeed, she argues that 'deepening global inequalities, assaults on welfare, renewed paternalistic and "workforce" rhetoric, have successfully undermined precisely those goals for which the women's movement once fought so vigorously' (writing in *The Guardian*, 17 August 1998). Segal's *Why Feminism?*, published in late 1999, analyses with considerable rigour the many social, economic and political obstacles to genuine gender equality which still exist and which postfeminism ignores. Segal unapologetically affirms the continuing need for feminism in an era in which the contradictions between markets and morality are more glaring than ever, and reasserts feminism's vision of a better future.

Many feminists would argue that the widespread media attention given to Paglia's work is a telling commentary on how far the struggle to change the nature of gendered power relations has yet to go, and also on the ability of the media to latch on to and popularise a message that is constructed as hip, iconoclastic, and full of good sound bites. A lot depends on where you stand in relation to the two key propositions which underpin postfeminism: that feminism has achieved most if not all of its objectives as regards gender equality; and that there are no longer any fundamental social contradictions or power inequalities between men and women, or gay and straight – just as there are said to be no longer any fundamental contradictions rooted in class, for example. If you accept those propositions, then the doctrine of personal empowerment and celebration of sex, detached from any social project, perhaps makes sense. But if you reject them, it falls down.

In a somewhat different vein, the young British feminist Natasha Walter has recently published two books which seek to take on board some of Paglia's claims about so-called 'victim feminism' without agreeing with her central rejection of most of the main tenets of feminist thought. Walter does regard Paglia as a feminist. In *The New Feminism*, published in 1998, Walter portrays a deeply divided Britain in which gendered poverty and inequality between men and women is still very much a reality:

We lack equality and everything that comes with that. We lack the commitments to parental leave and flexible working that would make men and women equal players in the workforce. We lack support for women facing grinding poverty, for women bringing up their children alone in miserable conditions. We lack training and education for women in dead-end jobs. We lack legal support and refuge housing for women fleeing violence. We lack women's voices in the highest courts and debating chambers of the country. (Walter 1998: 9)

Walter's prescription, however, is for a 'new feminism' which concentrates on a reformist agenda of social and economic amelioration – and which almost reads like a New Labour manifesto. This new feminism retreats from many of the concerns of radical sexual politics, decoupling the personal from the political, emphasising its acceptance of family and heterosexuality, and 'embracing power'. At a superficial level this is of course entirely reasonable. All feminists want women to be empowered, and family life can be wonderfully enriching and self-affirming. Moreover, the optimism of Walter's analysis is infectious. She paints a picture of a generation which 'has learnt that you can have it all, but you can't have it all at the same time' (1998: 231) and which is ready to create a better balance between work and home, liberating both men and women to enjoy the pleasures of both. Her five-point plan for this new feminism involves: revolutionisation of the world of work; creation of a national network of childcare; 'encouraging' young men to take on their fair share of domestic work; supporting women who are trapped in poverty; and supporting women who face sexual and domestic violence (1998: 222–3). The problem is that Walter lacks any theory of patriarchy or of male privilege. She does not really analyse the strength of misogyny and the nature of the forces arrayed against her optimistic vision of future gender relations. She assumes that the new feminism will be embraced by young men as well as young women and that a benevolent, non-patriarchal state can be persuaded (presumably through a New Labour government) to implement its key demands. Her approach is pragmatic, almost non-ideological, and her feminism one which includes men as well as women and welcomes Conservatives as well as socialists – in her own words, a 'solid, unimpeachable bourgeois revolution' (*Independent on Sunday*, 18 January 1998). She seems to embrace aspects of traditional femininity in an attempt to make her own brand of new feminism attractive to young British women who are aware of the barriers women still face but are uninterested in appearing too radical. Germaine Greer has criticised this version of British pragmatism as 'unenlightened complacency' designed to reassure the 'faint-hearted' (quoted in *The Guardian*, 26 February 1998).

Perhaps stung by this charge, Walter's introduction to her second book – an edited and disparate collection of often exciting and passionate essays – emphasises that 'all the writers here rage against inequality. None is complacent. And that lack of complacency, that desire to build a better society in which men and women are more equal, is something that is found all around us now' (Walter 1999: 4). Is it really? Well, perhaps in the circles Walter moves in. But there are millions of working-class (and other) women, trapped in poverty, powerlessness and abusive relationships, who do not see the desire for gender equality 'all around them'. Ironically, Walter, far from disproving Greer's charge of complacency, gives it credence. That said, many of the voices expressed in this book bear witness to the healthy state of British feminism – its passion, conviction and strength. But they also bear witness – not least in those contributions which flatly reject Walter's own decoupling of the personal from the political – to British feminism's uncertainty about its future strategy and future priorities.

Walter's decoupling of the personal from the political reflects her fear that feminism is perceived by many men and women as too eager to impose so-called political correctness in the sphere of sexual relations, and too repressive of sexual desire. However unfair this might be it does highlight a challenge which postfeminism and Walter's new feminism pose to those involved in progressive sexual politics. This challenge is to define the agenda of sexual politics so that the pursuit of social change is not at the expense of the individual's right to express and enjoy her or his sexuality, and the expression of that sexuality is not at the expense of others' right to self-determination. In rejecting the individualism of consumer capitalism, there is always a danger that feminists (and gay activists opposed to so-called queer politics) will lapse into puritanism and denial of sexuality. Many feminists and gay activists are suspicious of a consumerist culture in which political involvement and struggles for social justice sometimes seem to have been replaced by talk of 'lifestyles' and emphasis on spending power. It is as if 'the personal is political' has become replaced by 'the personal is pleasurable', or 'shopping is political' (or perhaps just 'shopping is pleasurable'?) as a slogan for our times. Is it the case, such activists may ask, that we are veering off into hedonism, or selfishness? Are people more inclined to mobilise in defence of their right to have sexual pleasure – including freedom to consume pornography or have an orgy – than to oppose injustice or change society? Is the politics of sexual identity now reduced, in the writings of Paglia, the popular culture of Madonna, or the commercial gay scene, to a series of images we consume? While these are valid and necessary questions, and while sexual politics demands a much more rigorous analysis of the corrosive and dehumanising ideology of consumerism than is often on offer, it will not help the cause of progressive sexual politics for feminists to ignore the sort of worries expressed by Walter or to lapse back into a censorious mode. (We shall return to this aspect of debates between feminists when we discuss the question of pornography in the next chapter.)

A major contribution to the revitalisation of British feminism was the publication in 1999 of Germaine Greer's *The Whole Woman*. Greer is essentially a socialist feminist, both visionary and razor-sharp in her critique of contemporary reality (even if her polemics are arguably sometimes misplaced), who has little time for the compromises involved in new feminism or New Labour. In *The Whole Woman* she dissects the postfeminist illusions of gender equality by pointing to the many ways in which women still face exploitation and exclusion in the fields of health, sex, work, education and politics, amongst others. A central theme of the book is that young women in today's society face even greater pressures than did their mothers' generation to starve, mutilate, and punish their bodies in order to conform to stereotypes of femininity; in that sense, ideologies of gendered oppression, far from having waned, have gathered strength. A central thesis of the book is that the way to combat this oppressive reality is to recognise that women have been sold a liberal version of gender equality which has, in fact, forced them to compete on masculinity's terms in a never-ending struggle which they can never win, and that the alternative is a politics, not of equality understood as 'sameness' but of liberation. Such a politics of liberation may well involve women 'separating' from men's company and rediscovering the necessity and liberating power of sisterhood. Greer writes that:

The personal is still political. The millennial feminist has to be aware that oppression exerts itself in and through her most intimate relationships, beginning with the most intimate, her relationship with her body. More and more of her waking hours are to be spent in disciplining the recalcitrant body, fending off the diseases that it is heir to and making up for its inadequacies in shape, size, weight, colouring, hair distribution, muscle tone and orgastic efficiency, and its incorrigible propensity for ageing. More of her life is wasted cleaning things that are already clean, trying to feed people who aren't hungry, and labouring to, in, from and for chain-stores. (Greer 1999: 329–30)

Not surprisingly perhaps, much media hype distorted and trivialised this argument – portraying Greer as an authoritarian who sought to 'dictate' to women whether they should wear make-up, and constructing an entirely spurious confrontation between 'new feminists' and 'old feminists' (Greer). But what Greer is actually offering here is a cogent critique of the dehumanising effects of rampant consumerism, and her book ends with a ringing affirmation of second wave feminism's continuing relevance to hundreds of millions of exploited women in the developing countries especially. Even so, Greer's book contains some glaring contradictions. For a start, she emphasises the biological, cultural and psychological differences between men and women in language which would appeal to any sociobiologist and argues that the failure to recognise these differences lies behind many women's unhappiness. Yet she does not fully explain how, if biological sex really is destiny in this way, the world can be fundamentally changed. Moreover, given that patriarchy persists and men still hold most positions of economic and political power, it is not clear how change can be brought about through separatism. Unless, of course, patriarchy is destined to collapse as a result of its internal contradictions (in the manner of classic Marxist analyses of capitalism).

A very different perspective indeed informs Ros Coward's *Sacred Cows: Is Feminism Relevant to the New Millennium?*. Coward argues that feminism has become the victim of its own success and has been too ready to ignore the ways in which society has changed in response to its demands and to presuppose that men are more powerful than they actually are (Coward 1999: 211–12). Coward's argument is subtly different from that of the postfeminists. She does not argue that feminism has 'gone too far', or that women are now the 'powerful' and men the 'victims'. Rather she contends that this view too is 'stuck in an old model of sexual power, where one sex consistently has power across the board'. She also mounts a fierce attack on the reactionary politics of the UK Men's Movement (see below). The problem with Coward's emphasis on masculine confusion and feminist ideological blindness, however, is that one could just as easily muster the available social and economic evidence to argue that feminism has not gone far enough and that there is still not enough masculine confusion at the top of business, politics and so on.

Oona King has contributed to these debates about the future direction of feminist politics by arguing that,

the new feminism must broker a compromise between 'difference' feminism and 'equality' feminism. The modern woman sees truth in both. Equality feminism champions a woman's right – and ability –

to compete on the same terms as men in a man's world. Difference feminism argues that the man's world is innately incapable of offering women real equality of opportunity. Instead of women changing to suit the rules, difference feminism believes the rules should change to suit women. The fact is that these rule changes would also suit any enlightened man. (King 1999: 59)

King acknowledges that, despite the advances of equality feminism, 'rights on paper for the majority of women mean nothing in practice', and she affirms that the personal remains political whilst arguing that this must not be interpreted as a 'reductionist argument about whether feminists wear lipstick' (1999: 59–60).

This brief review of some of the current most salient debates between feminists and postfeminists has identified a number of common and recurrent themes: the extent to which second wave feminism has achieved most of its goals; whether feminism has gone too far or not far enough in its battle to change gendered power relations; whether feminism as an ideology is still relevant in the so-called postmodern world; whether society is still patriarchal; whether profound social contradictions still characterise our type of society; and whether feminist strategies for change should emphasise sexual difference or sexual sameness. The intensity of these debates and the prominence they have received in some sections of the press is a measure of both the impact feminism has had since the 1960s and the backlash it has endured since the 1980s.

Some debates within lesbian, gay, bisexual and queer politics

As we saw in Chapter 2, partial decriminalisation of male homosexuality in England and Wales in 1967, however incomplete and hedged in by moral and police campaigns against homosexual sex, made it easier for a homosexual politics to emerge and begin to challenge the invisibility which had cloaked so much of homosexual life. The immediate aftermath of legal reform saw the launch of the Gay Liberation Front (in 1970) and a brief but intense period of gay and lesbian radical activism. However, this was not sustained for long. The 1970s saw splits between gay male and lesbian activists, and a marginalisation of political activism as many gay men eschewed politics for personal pleasure, celebrating their new-found 'freedom' by seeking sexual and social comforts on the emerging gay commercial scene. Small groups of political activists grew even smaller, and much of the remaining political energy was directed into founding gay and lesbian telephone helplines, counselling services, consciousness-raising groups and so on.

The 1980s was to prove a decade of both catastrophe and renewed hope. The catastrophe, of course, came in the form of the impact of AIDS which claimed thousands of gay lives in the developed countries of the western world, and cast a dark shadow over the celebration of sexual pleasure and greater social visibility. It was brutally manipulated by forces on the homophobic moralising right and by sections of the mass media which whipped up an unprecedented campaign of insults, prejudice, hatred and calls for state repression of gay men in particular. Renewed hope came when a sense of helplessness, pain and despair in the face of this onslaught gave way, within the gay and lesbian communities, to immense anger, and anger in turn gave way to a burst of political energy which saw a huge political mobilisation at the end of the 1980s. What the homophobic right had hoped would prove a God-sent opportunity to force homosexuality underground more firmly than ever actually proved a turning-point in lesbian and gay determination to smash heterosexist discrimination and neglect of lesbian and gay lives.

The two key events in the UK were first, the woeful neglect of gay and bisexual men who were infected with HIV, especially those who went on to develop AIDS, during the Thatcher governments of the 1980s. Homophobic prejudices within government meant that no action was taken to formulate a government policy on AIDS until at least 1986. And secondly, the introduction by the Conservatives of the notorious Section 28 of the Local Government Act of 1988. Section 28 prohibited local authorities from 'promoting the acceptability of homosexuality as a pretended family relationship'. This was a direct attack on the rights of gay men and lesbians to have their relationships recognised as valid and emotionally caring, and on the ability of schools to deal with same-sex relationships in a non-condemnatory fashion. (Both these developments will be analysed in more detail in Chapter 6.) Schneider (1992) has argued that the involvement of many lesbians in AIDS work – caring for gay male friends who were dying or ill or bereaved and campaigning around funding and education and human rights issues – helped to heal the divisions between gay men and lesbians which had opened up in the 1970s. Certainly, the campaign against Section 28 saw the involvement of large numbers of lesbians and gay men working together. If issues such as the age of consent might be seen by some lesbian activists as 'male' issues, this was assuredly not true of Section 28 which, with its construction of same-sex relationships as sick and anti-family, directly attacked many lesbian mothers living with their children. The end of the 1980s in the UK saw huge demonstrations involving tens of thousands against Section 28, and the beginning of 'direct action' shock tactics by lesbian activists – who, for example, abseiled into the House of Lords to register their protest and seized a BBC newsroom during a live broadcast.

In 1989 a new lesbian and gay rights group, Stonewall, was created in the UK. Reformist rather than radical, Stonewall was founded by several leading actors and 'celebrities' (including the actor, Ian McKellen) and was to concentrate on quiet campaigning behind the scenes for legal reforms in the direction of sexual equality, including lobbying politicians and other powerful figures. Stonewall's successes and limitations were to highlight both the achievements of so-called 'assimilationist' strategies and the risks of failing to challenge 'invisibility' head-on and becoming prisoners of a parliamentary agenda over which, ultimately, lesbian and gay campaigners had only limited influence.

Stonewall set itself the goal of establishing a respected and effective parliamentary lobby group, backed up by networks of letter-writers and fund-raisers. Increasingly, it would rely on celebrity donations and fund-raising events by pop stars, television and other personalities. It also produced a series of well-researched and informative surveys including bullying in schools and workplaces, rates of suicide and attempted suicide amongst lesbian and gay young people, discrimination in employment and housing, which provided sympathetic politicians and commentators with ammunition they needed in challenging homophobic prejudice. Similar work was undertaken in Scotland by Outright Scotland and later by the (Scottish) Equality Network, which would increasingly work alongside Stonewall. Undoubtedly such work was important and helped to change attitudes; but covert influence is notoriously difficult to measure. Stonewell provoked unease and anger amongst some lesbian and gay activists because it seemed to be singularly failing to change government policy. It might claim that covert influence had rendered some new Conservative government laws less homophobic than they might otherwise have been; but a full ten years after its foundation, and two years into the life-time of a Labour Government, Stonewall had yet to be able to point to a single major legislative reform which it had achieved. Only in late 1999 did the Labour government promise to deliver on its election manifesto promises to abolish Section 28 and to introduce an equal age of consent at sixteen years. Two previous attempts at equalising the age of consent – one in February 1994 on a Private Member's Bill supported by Stonewall and the second in February 1999 on a Labour government-backed Bill – had failed. The first fell when the Conservatives voted it down and settled for a reduced (but still unequal and discriminatory) age of consent for gay men and the second when the

House of Commons approved the measure but Conservatives in the House of Lords defeated it.

Stonewall found itself accused of toothlessness by activists who failed to see what quiet and respectable lobbying was actually achieving. Worse, it was accused of elitism, a lack of accountability to the wider lesbian and gay communities, and of being in tow to a basically homophobic political establishment. These simmering resentments on the part of radical activists boiled over when Ian McKellen accepted a knighthood from a Conservative prime minister (Major) who had done nothing to repeal homophobic laws or to move against discrimination and prejudice. McKellen found himself accused of simply allowing Major to project a softer and more 'liberal' image for the Conservatives without actually delivering any change.

In the mid-1990s Stonewall faced a stiff challenge for the heart and soul of lesbian, gay and bisexual politics from 'direct action' activists who aimed at focusing public attention on homophobic discrimination. Media attention was focused on homophobia within the mainstream religions when some activists publicly proclaimed the homosexuality or bisexuality of ten bishops of the Church of England. The practice of forcing out of the closet public figures who are known or rumoured to be lesbian, gay or bisexual – but who have never publicly acknowledged it and may even have denied it – has been called 'outing'. In 1996 threats were also made – but not carried out – to expose the identity of closeted homosexual MPs in the Conservative Party if they continued to vote for anti-gay measures such as an unequal age of consent. The tactic of 'outing' – condemned by Stonewall – was defended on the grounds that those in positions of power who hide their own homosexuality whilst promoting homophobia and hypocrisy are guilty of reinforcing an oppression and invisibility which every year claims lives. Against this, others argued that to deny someone the right to choose the moment and manner of their own 'coming out' was not merely an invasion of privacy but an authoritarian act. The issue proved very divisive within lesbian, gay and bisexual politics, exacerbating an always-present divide between 'radicals' and 'reformists'.

The arrival of this new wave activism touched many nerves within the media and the establishment, leading to bitter exchanges over privacy and accountability, and between liberalism and radicalism. As the tactic is directly linked to the development of so-called queer politics, it is worth exploring the background of this phenomenon.

Queer politics first developed in the USA, growing out of radical AIDS activism, with direct action groups such as Queer Nation. It arrived in the UK around 1990–91, where queer groups such as OutRage! and HomoCult propagated the new ideas. Although involving relatively few activists, queer groups captured the headlines with activities such as kiss-ins, mass queer weddings, the forcible 'outing' of allegedly gay public figures (some of it spurious and contrived) and, on occasion, highly polemical attacks upon the established lesbian and gay community. 'Stuff the lesbian and gay community' and 'Smash McKellen and Stonewall' were prominent queer slogans on demonstrations in the early 1990s. The Manchester-based HomoCult group rapidly established a reputation as amongst the most extreme and hard-core of such groups. They circulated posters and leaflets which proclaimed slogans such as 'Paki poof' (allegedly, to confront racism and homophobia head on), with leaflets inciting fire bomb attacks on 'capitalist' gay and lesbian clubs. They also ran a vigorous campaign to disrupt the 1992 gay and lesbian EuroPride mass rally – on the grounds that the concept of EuroPride was fascistic and racist. This rather missed the point that the rally was about gay and lesbian pride, not about taking pride in being European or white. HomoCult rejected that distinction.

Direct-action, 'in your face' radicalism became a hallmark of queer politics – as did the attack on the lesbian and gay 'establishment', on reformist political activism, and on the majority of existing lesbian and gay organisations, denounced as too respectable, middle class, male-dominated, white and smug. Particular vilification was reserved for the lesbian and gay press (seen as being in the hands of commercial interests, which of course it largely is) and for 'respectable' groups such as Stonewall (accused of assimilation into bourgeois politics). In 1994–5, there were indications that the biggest lesbian and gay weekly newspaper in the UK – the *Pink Paper* – was aligning itself with aspects of queer politics. It published repeated attacks on Stonewall. By 1996 the *Pink Paper* had modified its position (perhaps fearing that it risked too close an identification with what was probably a minority position), and by 1998 something of a truce had been called between the largest of the queer groups – OutRage! – and Stonewall. OutRage!, significantly, agreed to join the campaign for an equal age of consent for both homosexuals and heterosexuals at sixteen; it had previously veered between advocating an age of consent at fourteen and questioning such reformist demands. OutRage!'s willingness, by the late 1990s, to join with Stonewall in campaigning for reforms – without prejudice to its continuing use of direct-action tactics to highlight homophobic discrimination – underlined what some saw as a growing moderation (or loss of radicalism) on the part of most queer activists. This is unfair. OutRage! remains a unique and highly vocal presence on the radical sexual politics scene, vilified by the press but forcing the agenda forward and challenging the patronising liberal notion that non-heterosexuals ought to be 'grateful' for any concessions which come their way. Ian Lucas, who has penned the best inside history of OutRage!, expresses this succinctly: 'there are signs that some of the measures we campaigned for are at last likely to become reality, which is fine. If and when equality comes, I'll laugh, dance, weep and drink; in the morning, I'll wake up, smell the coffee and demand something better' (Lucas 1998: 229). This encapsulates perfectly the OutRage! refusal to settle for crumbs from the liberal table. Its response to Labour's announcement of an imminent equalisation of the age of consent and imminent abolition of Section 28 at the end of 1999 was to welcome both announcements, but to denounce the fact that young people are not being empowered to control their own sexuality through better sex education, and to demand compulsory outlawing of homophobic bigotry in schools.

Yet queer groups such as OutRage! have also exhibited their contradictions and failings. To begin with, as we saw in Chapter 1, 'queer' was not synonymous with 'homosexual' or with 'gay'. The queer movement has always denounced sexual definitions based on the gender of the people one sleeps with, and insisted that it is possible to be a 'straight Queer'. Denial of the importance of the gender or sex of one's partner(s) as a defining characteristic of either the relationship(s) or of one's identity (so-called gender-fucking) was an important aspect of queer politics, and endeared the movement to postfeminists such as Camille Paglia. But this has been an endless source of embarrassing contradictions, for the overwhelming majority of both activists and writers are of course non-heterosexual; and self-proclaimed queers, such as the late Derek Jarman and Peter Tatchell (of OutRage!), have invariably lapsed into using the label as a substitute for gay or lesbian.

Moreover, queer sloganising had already by the mid-1990s lost much of its shock potential and was well on the way to becoming as academic, commercial and bourgeois as the lesbian and gay identities it set out to attack. Even the term became something of a fashion accessory – queer tee-shirts were marketed amongst the young and trendy on the lesbian and gay scene at designer prices – perhaps the ultimate sign of revolutionary waning.

Queer politics began life by attacking what it saw as the racism, sexism and middle-class affluence characteristic of much of lesbian and gay (especially gay) life in the USA. Films such as the AIDS movie, *Long Time Companion*, provoked fury for their portrayal of gay life as middle class, white and 'normal' (according to the dominant construction of the latter). Queer activists picketed AIDS benefit performances of the musical *Miss Saigon*, in protest against the racism and sexism of the show, and attacked the gay establishment's alleged suppression of the fact that women, African-Americans and the poor were suffering from the AIDS crisis, not only white gay men who could afford to pay for health care (Signorile 1994).

The polarisation of 'homo' and 'hetero' identities was rigorously attacked and the gay 'establishment' accused of creating a ghetto from which they benefited commercially and in terms of career and class power. Queer proclaimed itself radically opposed to liberalism and reformism and to any assimilation into established norms of sexuality. It was determined, instead, to build common fronts between 'sexual rebels' or 'deviants' across the usual gay-straight divide. It was also more tolerant of groups spanning this divide, such as consenting sado-masochists or transsexuals, who are normally marginalised (it was claimed) by the reformist gay and lesbian culture, keen on establishing its claim to equality and acceptance. (In fact, the commercialised and capitalistic concerns which queer politics attacked have long been hard at work in the gay and lesbian and heterosexual press, attempting to create a consumer market for sado-masochism and other practices which involve the profitable sale of expensive sex toys. There is a hefty profit return on whips, hand-cuffs and dildos, after all – not to mention the lucrative rip-off of telephone sex-lines.) A queer manifesto puts it thus:

> It's time to smash once and for all the myth of the 'gay' community which allows fools like Stonewall and *Capital Gay* to sell us out . . . Liberate yourself from the lie that we're all lesbians and gay men. Free yourself from the lie that we're all the same . . . Queer means to fuck with gender . . . Queer is not about gay or lesbian. It's about sex . . . (quoted in Jarman 1993: 144)

Demands for legal reforms to accord everyone equality before the law might be accepted as a necessary first step, but the perceived limitations to such reformism were emphasised. Instead of extending existing legislation, embodying an often repressive regulation of heterosexuality, to lesbians and gay men, queer politics demanded an end to all controls on sexual expression between consenting adults. Thus, although Tatchell and OutRage! came round to supporting an equal age of consent at sixteen as an interim measure, other queer activists denounced the gay and lesbian campaign for equality here altogether, instead demanding an end to any age of consent at all (to be replaced by safeguards against abuse of children). Here, queer politics finds common ground with those academics who have questioned whether seeking equal rights means accepting heterosexual norms or seeking to join gay men with straight men in the benefits of masculine privilege. We have already encountered Stevi Jackson's arguments in this respect (Jackson 1996b). Momin Rahman (1996: 5–6) also questions whether an equal rights strategy is the best way forward for lesbian and gay politics, arguing that equality legislation has a limited capacity to deliver real cultural change and that 'many of the freedoms enjoyed by heterosexuals are not . . . encoded in formal rights. For example, heterosexuals can flaunt their sexuality in public . . .'. Equal rights legislation may protect against legal and police harassment and violence but it won't solve the problem of prejudice, because 'abstract formal equality has little effect in a society where inequality is perpetuated, both materially and ideologically, at a social level'.

Perhaps the most radical aspect of queer politics was its claim not only to transcend the homo/hetero boundary but to do so in such a way as to challenge the sexual regulation and repression of heterosexual desire, above all female desire. Queer politics, it was claimed, had a lot to teach those accustomed to the narrow confines of 'male' and 'female' heterosexual roles in relationships. The re-working of notions of monogamy and the send-up of marriage through queer weddings, the greater sexual adventurism, the rejection of the concept of gay men and lesbians as 'victims' in favour of assertiveness and redefinition, and the emphasis on the creation of more egalitarian relationships in the domestic, sexual and social spheres, were all cited as examples of how queer could contribute to a new sexual agenda of empowerment.

Critics would reply that all these themes were present in the old feminist and gay agendas of the late 1960s and early 1970s: now they were served up in a manner which denied the specificities and historical context of gay and lesbian experiences, not to mention the struggles of the feminist movement.

The advent of queer politics certainly provoked furious discussion and debate within the lesbian and gay communities. Whilst many activists across the spectrum have regarded the queer critique of the sexism, racism, cult of beauty and of money, class bias, and disablism present in so much of the gay commercial scene as necessary and well-taken, queer politics has been criticised on theoretical, organisational, and tactical and strategic grounds.

On theoretical grounds, queer politics has been criticised for being less radical or subversive than it claims. Parnaby (1993) argues that, by denying the existence of historically defined sexual identities and suppressing the social antagonisms caused by patriarchy, it leads us back into the arms of heterosexuality as an institution. It has also been argued that activism that relies on sound-bites and media-zapping lends itself readily to appropriation by capitalism as a designer fashion-accessory – with a shelf-life as long as that implies.

On organisational grounds, critics have pointed out that the move-ment's heavy-handed methods have assumed a distinctly 'macho' flavour, leading many of the women involved to break away and form their own groups. Certainly queer politics is a lot less cross-gender and cross-race now than it was when the movement started. It is also smaller, and has lost some of its shock appeal. Moreover, the claim that groups such as Stonewall are elitist and unrepresentative sits uneasily with the reality that many queer groups are scarcely any less so. It is certainly true that OutRage! is open to anyone and seeks to 'report back' to the lesbian and gay communities through public forums. But it is also an intensely metropolitan phenomenon – con-fined to a few big cities, primarily London and Manchester. Whether queer politics expresses the political orientation (as opposed to being a trendy label) of hundreds of thousands of lesbians, gay men, bisexuals and heterosexuals outside its own milieu is open to question.

On tactical and strategic grounds, critics have maintained that the methods of queer politics may make it more intimidating and difficult for those still 'in the closet' to come out; that its attacks on other lesbian, gay and bisexual groups are sectarian and undermine the very sexual diversity it claims to advocate; and that it leaves many non-heterosexuals suspicious and alienated. It could be argued, for example, that the tendency of many queer activists to denounce any non-heterosexual who chooses to remain 'in the closet' as guilty of a homophobic act has parallels with the 'blame the battered woman' mentality of some postfeminist writers.

My own view is that queer politics was a necessary and cathartic jolt to a subculture which had sunk into political apathy during the late 1970s, only to be re-radicalised and politicised by the twin impact of AIDS and anti-gay government legislation during the 1980s; and that it represented a search by a younger generation to define its own agenda. But I would also argue that the movement suffers from the same heady mixture of iconoclasm, political confusion and mystification of sexual pleasure (as in Derek Jarman's claim that 'every orgasm is its own revolution') as the Camille Paglia school of postfeminism. That said, lesbian, gay and bisexual political activism needs both covert lobbying to 'win friends and influence people' and 'in your face' direct action to combat invisibility and force the pace of events, both short-term, realisable, reformist goals and a healthy radical suspicion of the liberal concentration on formal legal rights. There is a real danger that when a few reformist measures have been passed – such as repeal of Section 28, an equal age of consent, and perhaps a version of the 'don't ask, don't tell' policy in the British armed forces – the British liberal political elite will consider the 'homosexual question' solved. They may reckon that there aren't many votes to be won in a more radical attack on hetero-sexist prejudice and privileges, and will simply go silent on homo-phobic discrimination for another generation. That is why both Stonewall and OutRage! have their role and why the dialectic between different forms of activism and understandings of sexual identities and politics is healthy and necessary. It is also why those who are com-mitted to a progressive sexual politics, whether gay or queer, would do well to resist what Anna Marie Smith (1997) calls the 'new homopho-bia' – the attempt by the establishment to draw a dividing line between the 'good homosexual' who is acceptable and the 'dangerous queer' who is not.

The different strategies and visions of 'reformists' and 'radicals' are not the only subject of major debate within lesbian, gay, bisexual and queer politics. The fact is that only a tiny minority of non-hetero-sexuals are involved in any sort of political activism. Various writers and activists have noted with rising alarm an almost mass depoliticisa-tion of lesbian and gay communities in the 1990s. The crass commer-cialism of the gay scene and the rise of the so-called pink pound and of 'lifestyle' as a signifier of sexual identity (and human worth) has allowed huge profits to be reaped. Playing on the insecurities of people sells 'packages' which can include everything from 'gay apartments' to 'gay holidays' and 'gay clothes' to designer drugs. As Chris Woods (1995) points out, there is now a huge problem of alcohol and drug abuse on the gay commercial scene and the long-term effects on the health of the emerging generation of young non-heterosexuals are frightening to contemplate. Paul Burston (1999) has penned an hilar-ious but also deeply moving account of the costs (financial, emotional and physical) of adopting a 'gay lifestyle' and of gaining acceptance in one of the metropolitan commercial gay ghettoes in contemporary Britain. Needless to say, this rampant consumerism constructs those who don't have the necessary 'sexual resources' to gain acceptance (good looks, health, youth, designer clothes and toiletries, drugs, expensive accessories and so on) as beyond the possibilities of the proper 'gay lifestyle'. The most recent and striking example of the triumph of commercial exploitation over political solidarity was the 're-branding' of the annual London lesbian, gay and bisexual Pride March as 'Mardi Gras' – although the efforts of organisers and business sponsors to depoliticise the march and to discourage banners and placards, met (in 1999 at least) with only limited success.

Once again, we have an example of the power of capitalism to assimilate sexuality and to regulate people's most intimate identities in exploitative ways. And many young non-heterosexual men and women, far from being the bold sexual radicals and dangerous deviants which the marketing slogans may flatter them into thinking themselves, are actually amongst capitalism's most slavish and self-destructive devotees. They pose a danger to no one but themselves. This is surely the most pressing challenge which confronts those who strive to keep alive the dream of a more just and less exploitative future, whether gay, lesbian, bisexual or queer.

The emergence of men's politics

The feminist movement and the lesbian and gay movement have been around now for a generation or more and have helped to change significantly attitudes towards both women's role in society and gay people. There has been no remotely comparable sustained critical re-evaluation of gender and sexuality from within male heterosexuality. That is not to say that heterosexual men have not changed and are not changing. What it means to be a heterosexual man in our society – and how male heterosexuality is experienced and lived – has certainly changed in recent decades in many complex ways. But more often than not these changes have been in reaction to changes in employment patterns, to feminism and to women's demands, or in response to social and legal changes which themselves have been provoked by feminism (for example, greater awareness of, and intolerance of, partner abuse or domestic violence).

The result, arguably, is that though the meanings attached to being a heterosexual man are changing, change is slow, contradictory, full of uncertainty and sometimes hidden resentment and fears. Many heterosexual men are defensive about the nature of sexual politics – feeling that change through desirable and inevitable, is being forced upon them through a series of 'unreasonable' demands by feminists and gay activists. Certainly a progressive men's movement is very recent and is very small. In academia it appears as men's studies, in society it takes the form of men's consciousness groups, and there are also some men's groups within political parties and trade unions which address issues of masculinity and power. It would probably be laughed at with derision by many heterosexual men, and indeed its growth is inhibited by those fears of derision and of being branded a wimp or a poof with which, we have seen, masculinity polices itself even as it is changing. Nevertheless, this progressive men's movement does have an effect, for example in the influence its politics have had on male counsellors working with young male offenders or drug abusers – especially those convicted of violent crimes against women and children – and by working also to change attitudes within the police force. Arguably, such unglamorous and invisible work may do much more to change masculinity in the long run than the so-called gender-blurring advertising images of the fashion world which have targeted the male body beautiful in order to sell products and make a profit.

This progressive men's politics has recently faced stiff competition from a wing of the men's movement – strong in the USA and now appearing in the UK – which hankers after a nostalgia for traditional masculinity and is explicitly or implicitly hostile to change.

The conservative and unashamedly patriarchal nature of the men's rights lobby – which might more accurately be called the men's power lobby – is well illustrated by some statements by one of its self-proclaimed spokesmen in the UK, Roger Whitcomb. He told a 1993 men's conference in the USA that men in the UK were beginning to fight back against 'the growing feminist tidal wave [which is responsible for] a sustained and remorseless attack against the institution of marriage and the patriarchal family based on it'. Like some government ministers, Whitcomb blamed 'lone-mother pseudo-families' for most social ills but he reserved particular anger for the House of Lords ruling on marital rape in 1991 ('a long-standing feminist dream') and for the Child Support Act which 'reduces fathers to cheque-signing machines without rights' (all quotes from Baker 1994).

His belief that 'the establishment is now totally under the thumb of the feminist lobby' is reflected by a small but growing body of men who have sought to organise themselves into an effective political lobby under the banner of the 'UK Men's Movement'. Another militant fathers' rights group, Dads After Divorce, soon proposed a link-up with the UK Men's Movement.

There are considerable grounds for confusion here for, until the late 1980s, the phrase 'men's movement' was widely deployed to refer to men who were motivated by sympathy with feminism and a belief that dismantling patriarchal privilege and oppression was as much in men's own long-term interests as in the interests of women. As Baker points out, the first such pro-feminist men's group in Britain was founded in Brighton in 1971 and a Men against Sexism conference was held in 1973. A magazine, *Achilles Heel*, was launched in 1978. 'However, anti-sexist men have generally been too suspicious of traditional male forms of organising and politicking to be able to create a coherent movement' (Baker 1994). This movement has been overwhelmed by severe divisions over whether it should be primarily devoted to actions supporting women – such as campaigning for abortion rights, raising money for rape crisis centres, and so on – or whether it should be prioritising consciousness-raising and personal change. In the UK, the movement is perhaps reduced to a few hundred activists throughout the country and consists mainly of campaigns against violence against women, including support by an active Edinburgh group for the Zero Tolerance campaign in the mid-1990s, some consciousness-raising groups, programmes of counselling for men who are violent to women and children, and academic research and publishing.

The men's rights lobby is different. These men are quite clear about the need to create a social and political movement and have sought to target and paralyse the Equal Opportunities Commission by bombarding it with complaints about 'discrimination' against men and to use the courts to reverse what they see as the gains of feminism. In so doing they construct men in the UK as 'emotionally hurt and economically disadvantaged' and as the victims of feminism's perverse demands (Baker 1994; Millar 1997). They seek to represent heterosexual men who feel threatened by women who are able to lead more independent lives and they present men as victimised by divorce laws and child maintenance arrangements.

By the end of 1993, as Baker reports, the main activities of this UK Men's Movement, still in embryonic form, was the establishment of a letter-writing network of several hundred activists to attack feminism in the letter columns of national newspapers and to chronicle alleged incidences of 'man-bashing', the establishment of a conservative men's quarterly magazine known as *Male View (The pro-Family Magazine Positively For Men)*, and the announcement of plans to establish a 24–hour telephone helpline for men who were 'victims' of harassment by women. Attacks on feminism in the columns of *Male View* included the frankly ridiculous assertion that feminism was comparable to Nazism as both were ideologies of 'a section of the human race proclaiming itself born with all manner of rights, qualities and privileges denied to the rest of us' (quoted in Baker 1994). Similar sentiments were repeated several years later by the UKMM's Scottish chairman, George McAulay, who declared that 'much of feminism is Hitlerian and Nazi' (quoted in Millar 1997). Incidentally, this sort of 'big lie' rhetoric has parallels with some of the over-the-top pronouncements of postfeminist guru Camille Paglia, who has also denounced the women's movement as 'feminazis'.

By 1997, the UKMM had assumed a more organised form. As well as attacking the Equal Opportunities Commission, the UKMM now sought the repeal of all equal rights legislation and the criminalisation of abortion (denounced as 'the female holocaust'), and directed attacks on rape crisis centres and even the National Lotteries Board for helping women's causes (Millar, 1997). As the 1990s ended, the UKMM was seeking to find unmarried fathers willing to take the UK Government to the European Court of Human Rights. As Millar points out, it represented an uneasy coalition of various men – out-and-out misogynists who resented women because of messy divorce cases or because of competition from women in the labour market, angry young hetero-sexuals – some of them urged on by the misogynistic culture of 'laddish' magazines – who seemed to derive pleasure from 'woman-baiting' (invading women-only classes at gyms and swimming pools and challenging women-only spaces in universities, for example), and some men who had genuine concerns about the lack of paternal rights, for example. In this respect, a survey by the Joseph Rowntree Foundation (reported in *The Guardian*, 22 September 1999) found that many unmarried British fathers were surprised and shocked to learn that they have no automatic legal rights in respect of their children, parental responsibility resting solely with the mother unless both parents go to court to make parental responsibility arrangements by which the father acquires the rights of a married man. Not surprisingly, the operations of the Child Support Agency have fuelled the sense of grievance upon which the UKMM feeds and have perhaps proven its best recruiting sergeant in the 1990s.

Conservative men's rights groups have also enlisted academic sup-port from a number of sources. Neil Lyndon's book *No More Sex War: the Failures of Feminism*, published in 1992, was a defining moment for the UK men's rights lobby. Warren Farrell, the American men's rights activist, later toured the UK addressing public meetings to promote his 1993 book, *The Myth of Male Power: Why Men are the Disposable Sex*, which sought to provide a coherent theoretical framework for an anti-feminist men's politics. In this work Farrell – a former supporter of feminism turned revisionist – asks a number of pertinent questions, as Grant (1994) notes: why the gap between male and female life ex-pectancy has widened as the twentieth century has passed; why men's health issues are ignored and male suicide rates are higher than female rates, and so on. But the answers he provides – that men are now powerless, the victims of women's advances, and united in their suffering by 'the wound of their disposability' – surely overstates the 'powerlessness' of Western men enormously. Incidentally, Farrell is able to arrive at his conclusion because he 'carefully redefined power by shifting from the public world to the inner world of emotion. Men did not *feel* emotionally in control of their lives therefore they lacked power' (Connell 1995: 208). However, when we examine differentials in earning power, the division of domestic labour, exposure to crimes of sexual violence and abuse, or a host of other relevant variables, the evidence is clear that the notion of men as victims and women (egged on by feminism) as the new power-holders is a perverse and absurd one. Many of the men's rights writers are in effect blaming women, and making feminism the scapegoat, for the fragmentation of male certainties and securities which have resulted from processes of de-industrialisation and the casualisation of labour.

These are amongst the factors attracting some men to men's rights politics and its attempt to re-establish an unquestioned male supremacy. The changing nature of work has disrupted the traditional notion of the male as breadwinner. Women's demands for more emotionally mature and equal relationships has challenged many heterosexual men's fears of commitment and unwillingness to shoulder their fair share of domestic labour. Male heterosexuality, as Baker (1994) argues, may feel threatened by the new concepts of sexual harassment and date rape, the greater visibility of homosexuality, and the much greater public attention given to male sexual abuse of children which has left some of those involved in the men's rights movement arguing that child sex abuse is being deliberately exaggerated by feminists in order to undermine fathers' rights to get close to their children. Hence the easy recourse to woman-blaming and woman-baiting even though men's real social and political power remains firmly entrenched. As Connell argues with great insight:

> Men continue to draw a patriarchal dividend, in the metropole as well as the periphery . . . In almost all regions of the world in the 1990s, men virtually monopolize the elite levels of corporate and state power. Heterosexual men of all classes are in a position to command sexual services from women, through purchase, custom, force or pressure. Men still virtually monopolize weapons, and mostly control heavy machinery and new technology. It is clear that massive inequalities of resources, and asymmetries in practice, persist . . .
> So the 'change' of which there is so much awareness is not the crumbling of the material and institutional structures of patriarchy. What has crumbled, in the industrialised countries, is the *legitimation* of patriarchy. (Connell 1995: 226)

This, undoubtedly, takes us to the heart of the appeal of the men's rights lobby: it expresses the anger and resentment of numbers of heterosexual men at having to account for their masculinity in an era of unprecedented social and economic change. Such men resent having to defend sexist and homophobic attitudes which a previous generation could simply express without fear of contradiction, having to take women seriously and having to defend against the charge of male privilege those social and economic advantages which their fathers' generation assumed were part of men's 'natural' birthright.

Women's ability to respond to those men seeking to label them the new gender oppressors, particularly if such men can rely on support from postfeminists such as Paglia, may well depend on their own self-confidence and on the internal strength of feminism. While feminism currently appears under siege, it is also, as we have seen, being refreshed by other activists and theorists even if some of the younger generation of British feminists have adopted a pragmatic and almost apologetic tone which, in the eyes of a veteran thinker such as Germaine Greer, does not best equip them to fight the arguments of the growing and powerful anti-feminist and anti-women's rights lobby. Feminism is certainly not an ideology in retreat. This brief discussion of both postfeminism and the men's rights lobby illustrates some of the new political challenges facing the women's and other progressive sexual politics movements.

Chapter 5

Selling sex:
the commercialisation
of sex and sexuality

Introduction

We have seen that a recurring theme in debates within contemporary sexual politics is the extent and implications of the commercialisation of sex and sexuality within the mass consumerist society that is typical of late capitalism. For example, we have commented on debates within lesbian and gay politics over the onset of 'lifestyle' politics and the growth of the so-called pink pound. In this chapter we build upon this theme by extending our discussion of the political implications of the commercialisation of sex and sexuality. We shall first examine the impact of the (mainly televisual) media and commercial advertising. We shall then briefly survey some of the debates which have taken place about prostitution and pornography.

The media and commercial advertising

Recent years have witnessed a flourishing of research which examines representations of gender behaviour and sexuality in popular culture. Much of this work reflects a growing tendency to treat culture as playing a key role in constructing what we understand by reality, and not simply acting as a reflection of it. The range of topics pertaining to gender and sexuality within cultural studies is very broad. Liesbet van Zoonen (1994: 148) points out that they include gender stereotypes, pornography, ideology, journalism, advertising, film and television, masculinity, ethnicity and aspects of popular culture. Sean Nixon (1996) concentrates on retailing practices and market research driven by gendered images, designer wear, fashion photography, and men's magazines. Helen Baehr and Ann Gray (1996) include the questions of class and gender in images of women, family ideology, soaps, pop music, women's and teenage girls' magazines, constructions of the housewife, daytime television, and talk shows. Mark Simpson (1994 and 1996) examines sport, advertising, and cinema. The range of methods and theories deployed is also diverse and includes feminist studies, lesbian and gay studies, queer theory, psychoanalysis, and semiology. However, most of these writers would agree that culture is a key part of the construction of meanings of gender. Or, as van Zoonen puts it, that 'the relation between gender and communication is primarily – although not only – a cultural one, concerning a negotiation of meanings and values that inform whole ways of life and which is vice versa informed by existing ways of life, with configurations of power and economic inequities being a key element within them' (1994: 148). That is, all media are part of the cultural struggle and the material struggle against constructions of gender and sexuality which impose inequalities, exclusions or marginalisations.

There is no agreement about how separate the cultural is from the economic, but a common point of departure is that culture can be a powerful source of inequality, as well as a rationalisation of it. In other words, the ways in which gender and sexuality are represented on television and radio, in newspapers, magazines and books, and in films and advertising, do not simply reflect and rationalise the inequalities which already exist in society. They can also inform and construct our view of what is normal and so not only reproduce inequality but contribute to it.

Most of those who have carried out studies of representations of gender and sexuality in popular media would, probably, agree on three things at least. First, media texts can never be characterised in terms of a single, settled meaning. These texts – be they films, novels, advertisements or soaps – may well, as van Zoonen puts it, convey 'stereotypical, degrading, humiliating and violating representations of women and femininity' (1994: 149) but they are also culturally and historically specific and therefore open to varying interpretations. They are never free of ambiguity. For instance, we might reflect on how a movie made forty years ago, and showing a woman sinking demurely into the heterosexual embrace of a leading man might be enjoyed ironically and even subversively today – particularly if the male actor was, say, Rock Hudson or Montgomery Clift. The meaning of gender and sexuality in media representations also changes depending on the viewer or receiver of the images. A generation ago John Berger (1972) wrote of the 'male gaze' in popular culture, referring to the ways in which women are often constructed as visual objects for the male spectator. And while this is still true – witness the countless ways in which women's bodies are used to sell cars and machines to men – feminist writers have also tried to identify niches in the dominant culture which allow the female gaze to operate. Feminist film makers, for example, have reworked traditional themes – such as the road buddy theme in *Thelma and Louise* – with this in mind. Advertisers have begun to identify a female gaze niche in the market (a recent example being the Diet Coke window cleaner advertisement). However, it is probably still the case that the great majority of female-centred readings need to be 'against the grain' of what is intended. Mark Simpson (1996) has also illustrated the point that images are never unambiguous by re-reading, from a gay perspective, traditional performances of masculinity, from the 'queering' of football matches to his reinterpretation of Laurel and Hardy as a sublimated gay couple.

Second, most writers would agree that an analysis of those forces involved in the production of media texts – the film producers, advertising executives, commissioners of market research, television producers and controllers of programmes, editors of newspapers and magazines – is important to negotiations over meaning. As far back as the early 1960s, Betty Friedan (in *The Feminine Mystique*, 1963) argued that the post-war 'evacuation' of women from positions of control within American magazines paved the way for the resurrection of traditional cultural discourses on femininity. Today, writers point not only to the gender division of labour within media production, but also to organisational practices and cultures. It is not simply a question of who edits magazines, but of the nature of the organisational culture that guides their hand. Is it a 'laddish' culture, for example? Advertisers will commission market research to tell them which images will maximise profit; but what matters is not only who carries out the research or designs the subsequent advertising campaigns, but the nature of the assumptions which underpin the questions they ask. When Pepsi commissioned research that told them that men considered a concern with dieting to be feminine and were more likely to buy Diet Pepsi if it could be sold to them under a different label were they reflecting male worries about masculinity or helping to construct them? The outcome was Pepsi Max, backed by an advertising campaign which associated it with sport and energy and 'living life to the max' rather than with dieting.

Third, some feminist writers have stressed the importance of no longer regarding the audience of media images as passive receptacles but as active negotiators of meaning. Women are no longer viewed within feminist cultural studies as passively consuming degrading images of women in romantic novels, soaps and advertisements for household goods. Rather, there is the possibility of a more diverse range of experiences and interpretations. It can still be argued, for example, that the sort of 'fantasies which make life at present acceptable' (van Zoonen 1994: 151) and which are offered to women in Mills and Boon novels, women's magazines and films, 'reconcile women to patriarchy' and thus hinder women's liberation. But such texts can also offer pleasure in allowing patriarchal stereotypes to be held up for ridicule and critical 'rubbishing'. Context and the diverse backgrounds of the consumers of images are obviously important.

Queer theory and associated forms of postmodernism are often accused of a tendency to divorce the study of cultural representations of gender and sexuality from any critical analysis of the economy. We sometimes find a celebration of style, fashion, and changes in advertising forms and consumer habits as heralding the dawn of a new era of gender equality and sexual democracy. It is as if the androgenous images in, for example, Calvin Klein advertising, the cross-over from gay sub-culture into the straight mainstream in fashion, music, or media sponsorship during the early 1990s, of the so-called 'new man' phenomenon (depicted in advertisements as cleaning the kitchen floor, doing the shopping or preparing dinner for his female partner) and the greater consumer expenditure on men's clothes and personal hygiene products somehow constitute a gender revolution. Of course, a more cynical view of the 'new man' and a more critical appraisal of the advertising and film industries is possible. It would be a mistake to neglect the fact that the popular culture media, while representing gender and sexuality to us in different ways, are also selling us packages and seeking to make a profit. This raises the question of the relationship of cultural representation to the demands of mass consumerist capitalism.

Once we begin to examine ways in which gender and sexuality are constructed as consumables, we question what we are being asked to consume, and why. We have become consumers of images and myths of gender and sexuality, through which we are sold products, encouraged to think and act in certain ways, adorn our bodies and even change our appearances. All this costs money. We are sold lifestyles. In the process, the most personal aspects of life, our concerns about our looks and our relationships, are commodified and marketed. Thus, in a Foucauldian sense, we might reflect on how mass consumerist discourses are deployed to regulate our sexual and gender behaviour in new ways – ways that reinforce the powers and profitability of big business.

This once again raises the question of power. Who benefits and who loses from the representation of certain images of gender and sexuality and the suppression or marginalisation of others? How does the profit motive operate to bring about certain outcomes? What are the processes involved? There are not always straightforward answers to these questions. For example, when several years ago a number of big companies such as Absolut Vodka started advertising in lesbian and gay publications, was this a sign of growing acceptance of the lesbian and gay communities? Or was it simply evidence that a big company recognised that homophobia should not stand in the way of possible increased profits, particularly as research evidence exists to suggest a big problem of alcohol abuse, fuelled by low self-esteem, within the lesbian and gay communities?

The question of context is also important in evaluating media representations of gender and sexuality. We need to question the role of context in giving meaning or significance to content. For example, does the fact that some women might find a naked Claudia Schiffer being used to sell cars harmless, or even enjoyable, render the image any less degrading or harmful to other women (or to women in general)? Does the revival of sexist language and imagery in 'laddish' magazines herald post-modern irony or a re-run of misogyny? If representations are contradictory and open to different interpretations, does this necessarily mean that they are therefore open to subversion, or that the differing interpretations enjoy equal weighting or equal power as cultural idioms?

Conversely, representations of gender and sexuality which challenge the dominant messages – for example from a feminist or gay-friendly perspective – may be open to reinterpretation or assimilation by traditional patriarchal or heterosexist discourses. One example might be the movie *The Accused*, starring Jodie Foster. This powerful and moving indictment of rape and of rape trials has, according to some reports, been sold as titillation in shops specialising in pornography. Foster's movie, *The Silence of the Lambs*, serves as another example. Made by Jonathan Demme, a liberal known for his pro-feminist and gay-friendly views, it caused a furore in the USA when it was first shown and was picketed by gay and lesbian groups. Far from being interpreted or received as a feminist film, with a strong female lead character fighting violence against women, audiences of young men clearly received it as a homophobic movie and were reported in the press as screaming at the cinema screen 'kill the faggot' each time the serial killer was shown (Signorile 1994). So the question arises as to whether representations of gender and sexuality that set out to challenge traditional discourses are not also open to co-option, and taming, by the marketplace. Do they cease to pose a challenge to patriarchy once they enter the commercial mainstream or have a designer label attached? Is the so-called style-led sexual politics of the 1980s and 1990s vacuous, and the 'new man' just a marketing device?

How much really has changed in media representations of masculinity or femininity and of sexuality in recent decades? For example, Myra MacDonald suggests that '. . . within advertising discourses, the range of what it means to be feminine has been surprisingly stagnant throughout the century, despite the profound cultural and social changes, and despite the commercial advantages to be gained from brand-differentiating the consumer as much as the product', although she does suggest that advertising campaigns of the postmodern era are more willing to cast women as the heroes of their plots (1995: 100). However, advertisers have long been willing to evoke the theme of women's self-determination in order to sell their goods. The television documentary *Tobacco Wars*, broadcast by the BBC in July 1999, demonstrates how cigarette manufacturers in the 1920s denounced the social taboo on women smoking in public as an example of man's inhumanity to woman and, claiming that cigarettes help women lose weight by suppressing the appetite, encouraged women to take up these 'torches of freedom'.

This challenges us to consider whether the way in which mass consumerism identifies and targets new groups for certain products – men for beauty or household products, or women for cars – actually changes in any significant way the construction of gender or sexual identities in our society? Which groups remain 'untapped'? Is it the economically weak groups – such as lone parents or ethnic minorities – whose spending power is not such as to attract the advertisers and who therefore remain alienated from the representations of gender and sexuality on our screens and in our magazines? There may also be groups who have considerable spending power – such as middle-class gay men – but to whom the advertisers' appeal remains heavily coded and sublimated. Representations of their sexuality in films or television programmes remains circumscribed, because advertisers or film-makers fear to offend dominant moral codes by giving too explicit a recognition.

Bocock and Thompson (1992) argue that gender has been an important variable influencing consumption over the past forty years or so. In targeting women as the major consumers of jewellery, clothes, personal hygiene products, baby products, and food and furniture, advertisers have represented certain clear images, associating femininity with domesticity, motherhood and looking and smelling good – often explicitly for the benefit of men. Such representations have also informed our perceptions of what should constitute a 'natural' sexual division of domestic labour, perpetuating the myth of male domestic helplessness and female wiliness. This continues today. Examples of such advertisements on British television during the 1990s include the

Persil advertisement showing a youth who doesn't know how a washing machine works; he cannot even hold the packet of washing powder the right way up. He succeeds in the end, but the viewer is left with little hope that this is the beginning of a new long-term relationship between man and washing machine. Another example might be advertisements showing men going shopping but needing the children's advice on what 'mum' usually buys – making it clear that this shopping trip is an exception and emphasising male helplessness in the face of matters domestic. Then there is the advertisement for Flash which shows a man fooling his wife into believing he has worn his back out washing the floor when the ease and convenience of the product is responsible for the result. Interestingly, these last two advertisements – like those for Lean Cuisine ready-made meals – point to an emergent theme: manufacturers have discovered that they can target men as shoppers for the weekly groceries without in any way challenging traditional sexist assumptions about domestic labour. The key seems to be to address the male shopper in ways which reassure him that his feelings of being ill at ease in a supermarket are perfectly understandable. In the Lean Cuisine and Flash advertisements the appeal to the male consumer seems to rest on the speed and convenience of the product, reflecting (and reinforcing?) traditional assumptions about the undomesticated state of men.

Recently, men have been targeted as consumers of beauty and personal hygiene products, clothes and fashion accessories as never before. This appears to be a trend across Europe and North America. Manufacturers of such products have tapped into the greater male spending power. In entering this potentially huge market advertisers have certainly sought to portray eroticised or sexualised images of men and masculinity – including, in some measure, homoerotic images – to a far greater extent than a generation or two ago. But whether this alleged sexual objectification of men in any way changes the gender power balance in society (for example by encouraging men to respond more to the erotic desires of women, or by constructing men as well as women as sex objects), or whether it simply reinforces gender inequality (by appealing to and underlining the greater wealth of men) is very much open to debate.

At any rate, alongside the traditional identification of masculinity with cars, technology, and electronics – status objects with associations of wealth and power – we have a new emphasis on male grooming and style. Above all, we have the advent of the designer label aimed at adolescents and young men in particular. The key ideological device used to sell these gendered images to men and youths has been the invocation of the cult of individuality. The message is that through creating their own image, with a particular aftershave, way of dressing, or hygiene products, men assert their individual personality. And this association of individuality with masculinity evokes traditional masculinist themes – of being competitive, aggressive, ahead of the crowd, first with the new idea – as well as appealing to very deep-rooted fears, especially in adolescent males, of peer disapproval if you fall behind. In such ways, products which are mass-produced and standardised – from Gillette razors to Nike sports wear – address the male as a fashion-conscious, individual consumer, without in any way challenging certain fundamental myths of masculinity.

Is the emergence of a greater postmodernist diversity of images of gendered consumption a step forward for gender equality? Many feminists would dispute that. Does the portrayal of women who drive fast cars challenge sexist assumptions, or does it merely make a fetish of consumption and wealth? Does it leave most women unrepresented and force upon us the idea of a successful woman as one who competes with masculinity on its terms? Does the greater attention paid to men's hygiene and appearance involve an eroticisation of men which is both pleasurable for straight women (and men) and marks a move away from women's portrayal as sex objects, or is it merely the discovery of narcissism by those who still have most money and power in our society?

There was a tendency towards the end of the 1980s to see the 'new man as consumer' as subversive and progressive. To a great extent this approach also influences the writings of Mark Simpson who sees a greater variety of performances of gender in popular culture as undermining the dichotomies upon which heterosexuality in its hegemonic form has rested. But it could also be argued that the variety of performances of gender has been exaggerated and that the 'new man' phenomenon is a busted flush, a product of the Thatcherite years which identified sexual attractiveness with the ability to purchase, and consequently with wealth, thus reinforcing traditional masculinist identification of money, sex and power.

Power can work in subtle ways. It is not necessarily a case of men – or some women imbued with masculinist values – holding positions of power within the media and using these positions to conspire to keep women in general down. It may also be that, having identified as good for business marketing strategies which represent and reproduce or even create gender inequalities, they then approve those strategies. Within the patriarchal system of values which predominates in mass culture, the pursuit of profit is paramount.

The profit motive plays a large part in determining which images of gender and sexuality are represented to us and which will be marginalised or silenced. Michelangelo Signorile (1994) has charted how the movie industry in the USA has been obsessed with profit to the extent of actively censoring, until very recently, virtually all positive por-trayals of gay or lesbian sexuality for fear of frightening off advertisers or losing customers. In an interesting linking of homophobia with misogyny, this also affected portrayals of strong, independent women. In its early days, Hollywood portrayed strong women – Bette Davis, Joan Crawford, Katharine Hepburn and Barbara Stanwyck. However, in the Cold War atmosphere of the 1950s 'deviant' actors and actresses were targeted and sacked and powerful gender stereotyping took over again. The hysteria unleashed by McCarthyism – and targeted at Hollywood in particular and the media in general – included not only anti-communism but also panic at the alleged moral decline of Amer-ica. In this message, anti-communism was not the only example of 'un-American activities'. Indeed, fear of communism, fear of homosexu-ality, and fear of non-traditional representations of gender roles, were all fused. Hollywood and the media were told that they had a duty not only to root out alleged communists, but to root out sexual 'deviants' and to reinforce the bedrock of American society – the all-American family.

Against this background, Hollywood, which has had such a powerful influence on much of the world, policed itself. Even after the McCarthyite witch-hunts passed, the fear remained that non-stereo-typical portrayals of gender and sexuality would offend advertisers and lose financial backers as well as audiences. Powerful Christian funda-mentalist lobbies targeted advertisers and financial backers, urging them to boycott programme- and film-makers whose work they dis-approved of.

Signorile recounts how, in the 1960s, it was a condition of the employment of gay and lesbian actors that they kept their sexuality hidden. The popular television show of the early 1960s, *The Zelda Gilroy Show*, was axed because the central female character was considered too strong, too butch, not sufficiently feminine, and was accused of giving bad ideas to women. Signorile also charts how the television show *Cagney and Lacey* was first dropped because the television moguls thought that the portrayal of two strong, independent women had dangerous associations with lesbianism and would offend the Christian Right. It was reinstated under the pressure of public demand. Finally, having failed to persuade the actress Sharon Gleeson to make her character more 'feminine', they dropped it again. (Ironically, the programme was also criticised by some feminists because Cagney and Lacey tended to be shown dealing with 'feminine' issues such as domestic violence and child pornography.)

Signorile cites numerous examples of ways in which the images of gender and sexuality we receive are censored and moulded by power and the fear of losing power, by money and the fear of unprofitability. Against the background of complex power games and the pursuit of profit, movies and television have repeatedly re-worked and re-presented 'reality' to reflect values and prejudices which the movie-makers attribute to their putative audiences or backers, invoking the need for profitability as their alibi, and have then sold this re-worked reality to the public.

Signorile also documents how, in the USA, only relentless campaigning by gay and feminist groups eventually led to a change in atmosphere in Hollywood in the late 1980s and early 1990s. This campaigning had to convince movie producers of three things: (a) that audiences are not as turned off by challenges to traditional gender roles as they might suppose; (b) that there are profits to be made by appealing to the so-called pink dollar and the spending power of (predominantly young and single) women; (c) that gay and feminist groups are capable of using modern technology, such as the internet, to launch a lobbying campaign to rival if not surpass that of the religious fundamentalists.

In the early 1990s films, appeared such as *Philadelphia*, which deals sympathetically with AIDS, and *Thelma and Louise*, which celebrates female friendship and solidarity between women, after years of women being portrayed as deadly rivals in the battle for male affection and approval. In the UK the fear of losing viewers through outraging 'public opinion', or offending powerful groups including the government, has continued to weigh upon programme makers. This has ensured that positive portrayals of sexual minorities tend to be banished to the less-watched BBC 2 or Channel 4, or are pulled from the schedules after a nervous testing of the waters. Clearly, what is presented to us is often not 'reality' – or at least not the rich diversity of experience which constitutes gendered and sexualised reality in a society such as ours today – but rather what producers feel is acceptable, or what will sell by courting controversy. There is a complex power relationship between the film and television industry, its viewers, its advertisers and power-holders, and 'public opinion' (itself constructed by television, newspapers and lobby groups).

In *Ways of Seeing* John Berger challenges us to 're-view' images by changing the gender of the 'watched' – that is, to consider how image, representation and 'seeing' are gendered. For example, he argues that the full power implications of certain typical representations of women become obvious when we mentally substitute men for women in those representations. By extension, this should alert us to the ever-present tendency in the mass televisual media to 'un-represent' or streamline for consumption sexualities in all their diversity.

Prostitution

'Prostitution', writes Priscilla Alexander (1996: 342),'has been a difficult issue for feminists both in the current wave of the feminist movement, which began in the late 1960s, and in the earlier wave which began in the 1860s'. Alexander goes on to explain that feminists have naturally deplored the exploitation of women's sexuality and women's bodies by profiteers and have tended to see prostitution as a means by which men keep women trapped in the old whore/madonna dichotomy. However, many contemporary feminists have come to the conclusion that laws against prostitution and the stigma which attaches to the selling of sex do regulate and control women's sexual behaviour and deny women self-determination. After all, such laws are enforced by a patriarchal state and reflect patriarchal assumptions about 'good' and 'bad' female sexuality. A lively debate has thus developed about exactly what power relationships are involved in prostitution, what should be the stance of those involved in progressive sexual politics towards women and men who sell sex, and what the role (if any) of the state should be.

One of the first issues requiring clarification concerns the circumstances of those involved in prostitution, or sex work. Numerous studies of prostitution have revealed that there is an enormous diversity of background experiences of both prostitutes and their clients. Many women become involved in prostitution through economic necessity. As Alexander writes, 'for a long period in history, women had only three options for economic survival: getting married, becoming a nun (earlier, a priestess), or becoming a prostitute' (1996: 343). In our own century, it is probably true that the overwhelming majority of women who have become prostitutes have done so through poverty, or because they had no choice in the matter. This is most obviously true of women in the so-called Third World and the former communist countries of eastern Europe, where large numbers of women have been trapped in vicious poverty and have been vulnerable to sexual exploitation by rich foreigners or organised crime. But in a society such as the UK, too, many women have been forced into prostitution because they are homeless, poor, addicted to drugs, or desperate for some means of providing for their children. Throughout the twentieth century, many single mothers were disowned by their families and left with little option – if they wished to support their children – but to resort to prostitution.

This is not the whole story, although it is probably the most typical one. Some prostitutes have freely chosen an occupation which they feel pays well, empowers them, and increases their range of choices in life. This is true of the subject of O'Connell Davidson's 1996 study, 'Desiree'. 'Desiree' is a self-employed female prostitute who makes a good living, chooses which clients she will have sex with and what sexual acts she will engage in, and feels in control of her life. Her lifestyle resembles that of a middle-class businesswomen in many ways. As O'Connell Davidson argues, 'where the voluntary, contractual character of the prostitute-client exchange is emphasised, a view of prostitution is constructed which diametrically opposes that produced by radical feminists. It is argued that, unlike wives whose legal right to refuse sexual access to their husbands was only even formally established in Britain in 1991, prostitutes actually exercise a great deal of power and control over their sexuality' (1996: 181). So the case of women like Desiree may be cited by those who wish to argue that selling sex is a form of labour contract like any other – not intrinsically more degrading or exploitative than agreeing to clean toilets or working on a factory assembly line – and usually a lot better paid.

But, of course, the self-confident, self-employed prostitutes who enter voluntarily into the 'profession' and remain in control of their working hours and conditions are far from typical. Quite apart from economic necessity or forced enslavement, surveys – such as that carried out by Jennifer James in Seattle (and quoted in Alexander 1996: 344) – reveal that a considerable number of those involved in prostitution have been sexually abused as children. In James' survey, as many as fifty per cent of adult prostitutes and between seventy-five and eighty per cent of juvenile prostitutes had histories of child sex abuse. This finding is supported by the work of Barbara Gibson amongst teenage male prostitutes in Britain. Gibson, a health worker with the Streetwise Youth charity, paints a heart-breaking picture of youngsters who have suffered abuse, rejection, and unhappy childhoods; and who, in many cases, turn to prostitution through a mixture of economic need and emotional need – hoping to find love and affection from the adult men who use their sexual 'services'. Needless to say, any sense that prostitution confers power – either in the form of money, or that of control over one's body – is usually illusionary in these cases; and many of these young people end up alone, abused, and lacking in self-worth (Gibson 1995). Again, 'rent boys' are a long way removed from the confident, self-employed male prostitute, complete with inner city apartment and mobile 'phone business, who may advertise in the pages of gay publications.

When we consider the issues raised by prostitution we need to bear in mind the diversity of prostitutes' experiences. Are we dealing with prostitutes who are desperately poor, homeless and vulnerable or with those who have a comfortable lifestyle and feel free to make choices? With individuals who are self-employed and able to control who they sleep with and what they do sexually, or those who work for pimps or organised crime, are forced into degrading sex acts and exposed to disease and HIV infection? With individuals who are emotionally well-balanced and strong, or those who are victims of child sex abuse and of continuing abuse and humiliation as adults? With adults or with children? With people who are ostensibly 'free' to make choices as adults, or with drug addicts, for example, who have little real choice?

The experiences of clients of prostitutes also reveal considerable diversity, as various studies have shown (Gibson 1995, O'Connell Davidson 1996, Hoigard and Finstad 1992 and 1996, McKeganey and Barnard 1996). Clients may well be men (although some women use the services of prostitutes, clients are overwhelmingly men) who abuse the prostitute and get sexual fulfilment through acts of sadism. Or they may be masochistic men who pay the prostitute in return for being ritually humiliated and abused (conveying upon the prostitute, as many women sex workers report, a sense of power). Or they may simply pay in return for voyeurism or even simple conversation or companionship, without any sexual contact being involved. Finally, there are those men who even entertain romantic fantasies of 'rescuing' the prostitute and setting him/her on a different path in life, paying for his/her education, and so on. Robin Lloyd (1979), in his study of adolescent male prostitutes, reports several such cases.

Such diversity of backgrounds and of power relationships has led some feminists to re-examine radical feminist critiques of prostitution, and has led some theorists into dialogue with prostitutes' organisations. What is fundamentally at issue here is whether prostitution is inherently and intrinsically degrading to women (and to male prostitutes presumably), and should therefore be condemned and measures taken to discourage and eliminate it. Or whether it is intrinsically no more degrading than many other forms of work but has been rendered 'dishonourable', dangerous, vulnerable and soul-destroying by a combination of social stigma (encouraged by moralising agendas) and state suppression or regulation. The description of prostitution as 'sex work' can sometimes reflect the latter position – a tendency to treat the selling of sex in much the same way as the selling of any other aspect of one's labour or personal skills.

Mary McIntosh (1996: 195) summarises the 'contractarian' view of prostitution as a type of labour contract like any other: prostitutes or sex workers sell their labour power in exchange for money and need 'trade union rights and a degree of control over their working situation just as other workers do'. The idea that sex in itself is dirty or degrading is part of the hypocrisy of patriarchy. Against this, McIntosh quotes Carole Pateman's argument that prostitution is not just another capitalist market transaction but is part of the exercise of men's right of access to women's bodies. Selling one's body is not the same as selling one's labour in, say, a factory; part of one's most intimate being is 'alienated' through the selling of sex – the experience is dehumanising. However, it can be argued against Pateman that women working in low-paid, monotonous, dangerous, back-breaking jobs are not necessarily involved in any less alienating and dehumanising activity than all sex workers. McIntosh certainly argues that, superficially at least, the dissimilarities are not great. She concludes that 'prostitution is a deeply paradoxical issue for feminism . . . [it] implies at once a challenge and an acceptance of the double standard of the *status quo*. As such, it can neither be condemned nor embraced wholeheartedly' (McIntosh 1996: 201). McIntosh does believe that it is important for feminists to move away from a blanket condemnation of prostitutes as willingly involved in propping up patriarchy, towards a real engagement with the voices of prostitutes increasingly heard nowadays through prostitutes' lobby groups. Many of these groups would argue that the label 'whore' affects all women and is used to regulate and control women in general, and that lifting the stigma from prostitution and demystifying sex work would unmask much patriarchal hypocrisy and covert male power.

Building on this idea, Alexander (1996) argues that late nineteenth-century and early twentieth-century middle-class feminists who joined with moral and religious crusaders against prostitution, by framing the issue in moralising tones, often helped to obscure the economic exploitation which their class inflicted upon working-class women whose sexuality was targeted by state regulation. Drawing a parallel with the present day, she argues that 'crackdowns, and arrests in general, tend to reinforce the dependence of prostitutes on pimps', many of whom extend their control over prostitutes when the latter are first imprisoned (Alexander 1996: 348). Moreover, attempts at legal suppression leads to many other problems. Prostitutes can actually end up servicing even more clients than they would otherwise do in order to pay fines. It has been argued that the UK's Imprisonment of Prostitutes (Abolition) Bill 1983 which imposes heavy fines if custodial sentences are to be avoided had precisely this effect (Sharpe 1998: 200). The police and other state authorities can sometimes extract bribes. The state as an institution – in the case of state regulation of prostitution through state-registered brothels, for example – can constrict women's freedom to control who they sleep with, and can actually perform the role of pimp. Moreover, state suppression or criminalisation can make it more difficult for women and boys involved in prostitution, in particular, to get access to safe sex information and proper health care, and make it almost impossible for them to report violent attacks and rapes which have been perpetrated against them. A very common attitude within western police forces is that it is not possible for a prostitute to be raped – that rape by a client simply 'comes with the job'. In addition, there is much evidence to suggest that there is sexual bias in the differential arrest rates, since police forces find prostitutes softer targets than their clients, and many clients are treated more leniently by the judicial system.

These concerns lead us to the debate about what exactly the role of the state should be, and what sort of reforms feminists and others involved in progressive sexual politics should campaign for. Many writers have argued that the state's criminalisation of sex workers simply punishes further those who are most vulnerable and most deserving of help. Criminalisation sets these sex workers outside the bounds of 'respectable' society and contributes to their dehumanisation, depriving them of dignity and rights.

A crucial distinction is usually drawn between legalisation and decriminalisation of prostitution, although confusion can be caused by the fact that these terms are not always used consistently. 'Legalisation' usually refers to various forms of state regulation or state control of prostitution. This can involve the state in controlling prostitutes' behaviour through compulsory health checks (which do not of course, apply to clients), compulsory registration with the police, systems of taxation, and even state-run brothels. Apart from the political and moral problems involved in a patriarchal state acting in effect as an institutional pimp, taking away what little control prostitutes might have over their lives, there are practical problems associated with legalisation. Most significantly it concentrates a great deal of power in the hands of state regulatory authorities, and prostitutes' attempts to evade these powers may force many into illegal back-street prostitution which is often highly dangerous. For example, state-run brothels in the US state of Nevada deprive the women of the right to refuse customers or to control the pace of their work. Groups such as the English Collective of Prostitutes oppose legalisation as 'state pimping'. Feminists also tend to argue that legalisation 'assume[s] that prostitution is here to stay. State brothels means institutionalizing women's poverty and degradation' (Hoigard and Finstad 1992: 178).

'Decriminalisation' by contrast usually refers to the simple removal of criminal laws governing prostitution. This may or may not involve government regulation of some specific aspects of prostitution; where it does, the difference from legalisation is often one of emphasis. In England and Wales, prostitution is not actually illegal, but pimping, pandering, procuring, advertising, soliciting, and renting or running a house for prostitution involving two or more women are all illegal. Often, local police practice and local by-laws mean that patterns of arrest can be quite arbitrary, and prostitutes are encouraged to negotiate with clients and enter their cars quickly. This increases threats to their safety. Decriminalisation without any form of regulation would end such restrictions. However, it can be argued that this would encourage further exploitation of women involved in prostitution by encouraging a sexual 'free for all' on the part of punters. Karen Sharpe suggests that the police might be even more unwilling to protect prostitutes, taking a 'you want your freedom so suffer the consequence' attitude (Sharpe 1998: 160–1). Alexander and others argue that decriminalisation with some kind of regulation – for example, recognition of prostitution as a legitimate occupation subject to taxation and social and health insurance – may be the best way to destigmatise and 'rehumanise' sex workers. Such a move was introduced in the Netherlands in October 1999, when the Dutch parliament removed the ban on (privately owned) brothels; prostitution itself had never been illegal in the Netherlands. Under the new Dutch law, brothels have to meet certain health and safety standards, prostitutes are guaranteed better working conditions with shorter hours, cannot be forced to have sex with someone against their will, and are entitled to pay taxes and receive welfare payments, health insurance, sick pay, maternity leave and holiday pay. The move was welcomed by the Dutch prostitutes' collective *Rode Draad* (Red Thread) as removing a stigma and encouraging the police to target real abuse, as opposed to voluntary sex work.

Ultimately, such moves might serve to expose the hypocrisy and indifference to abuse of sex workers which underpins adult male power over women and adolescent boys in our society. 'It would make it easier to prosecute those who abuse prostitutes, either physically or economically, because the voluntary, non-abusive situations would be left alone' (Alexander 1996: 354), and prostitutes' lives would become less dangerous as they were enabled to join unions and collectives and campaign for better working conditions. Certainly, the whole history of prostitution – and of patriarchal abuse of power in general – teaches us one lesson above all: that applying the double standard to the selling of sex and sweeping the uncomfortable issues raised by prostitution under the carpet only exacerbates problems of exploitation and inequality. The onus is on those who refuse to contemplate reforms of the laws on prostitution to specify how moralising and condemnation will solve these problems.

Pornography: the commodification of sex

Within Feminism, battles over pornography have become the wars
without end. (Segal 1998: 43)

Pornography is now big business. As a documentary series (*Pornography:
the Secret History of Civilisation*) broadcast on the UK's Channel 4 in
autumn 1999 argued, the invention of the home video cassette means
that the pornographic industry is now a huge transnational conglom-
erate with a turnover of countless billions of US dollars per annum.
Moreover, the mass availability of camcorders means that many millions of people are able to make their own, 'amateur', home-produced
pornographic videos, and research suggests that this is far from being
an unusual or exceptional occurrence. The Internet, flooded with
countless millions of pornographic images which can be easily down-
loaded by anyone with access to a computer and a modem, further
underlines the fact that we have come a long way from even the days of
the 1970s when, for most people in Western societies, pornography
involved 'top shelf' magazines or videos obtainable only in highly
restricted specialised 'sex shops'. Indeed, more than any other technological development in history the Internet has changed the nature
of pornography. A documentary broadcast on the UK's Channel 5 in
December 1999, *www.sex*, pointed out that an estimated thirty-six
million people – one-sixth of all Internet users – view pornography
sites on the Internet at least once a day and as many as forty per cent of
Internet users viewing pornography at least once a week. This business,
it is estimated, may have a turnover in excess of one hundred billion
dollars within a few years. Internet pornography is so decentralised that
it is almost impossible to legislate against. For example, it is illegal in
the UK to run an Internet site featuring hard-core pornography but this
does not prevent people accessing such sites based in other countries.
And Internet pornography completely undermines attempts to control
access in another important respect; although it is relatively easy (in
theory) to prevent children and teenagers buying top-shelf magazines
or pornographic videos, it is almost impossible to prevent them accessing images through the Internet. Devices which block pornography
sites – such as *net nanny* and *surf watch* – are available; but how many
parents are more adept at using Internet technology than their teenage
children?

The new technologies also raise other important questions. For
example, the advent of so-called virtual reality sex (where the technology now exists to allow people to experience the physical sensations of

a range of sexual activities, including rape and sadistic abuse, via sensor-pads) raises new political and moral issues. The question of who has access to the new technologies is rapidly becoming a gendered issue. It has been estimated that sixty-five per cent of Internet users in the UK are currently men, and that men may spend up to eight times longer on it than women, in the home, at work, in university and school computer labs and so on. This may reflect not only greater male access but also perhaps the male fascination with machines, with speed (computer games) and with depersonalised communication. Obviously, questions of access and of who controls the agenda in debates over computer pornography, will have a strong gender dimension in the future.

The power of pornographic representations to inform and shape our understanding of sexualities cannot be overlooked. Research carried out by Lambevski (1999) provides a fascinating example of how access to US pornographic gay videos has permitted middle-class homosexual men in Macedonia to imagine reciprocal and more equal sexual relationships between men which transgress the he-who-is-fucked-is-feminine-and-therefore-homosexual *versus* he-who-fucks-is-masculine-and-therefore-heterosexual dichotomy which remains so entrenched in Balkan and Mediterranean culture.

As Segal argues, rival schools of feminist thought and practice have been engaged in heated exchanges about pornography since at least the end of the 1970s. The best known statements of the anti-pornography and pro-censorship feminist position are those offered by Andrea Dworkin (1981) and Catharine MacKinnon (1987 and 1993) in the USA and by Diana Russell (1993 and 1998) and Catherine Itzen (1992) in the UK. Building on the notion that 'pornography is the theory, rape is the practice', Dworkin (1981) argues that male sexuality is violent and abusive and that male supremacy is sustained by a system of sexual terror against women; pornography lies at the heart of this male supremacy. The struggle against pornography is therefore a *sine qua non* of the struggle against patriarchy. Moreover, she argues that pornography should not be understood as merely representation of abstract fantasy, but rather that it constitutes literal torture, abuse, and domination of women by men. Pornography, from this perspective, both involves the actual torture and abuse of real women involved in its making, and functions to convince men that women in general are inferior, do not deserve full human rights, and are sexually available for abuse. As such, it constitutes an infringement of women's basic human rights.

MacKinnon, a feminist legal expert, joined with Dworkin in formulating the now famous Model Ordinance in the 1980s which classified pornography as a violation of civil liberties and as sex discrimination and argued that women should have the right to seek damages through the courts in the USA by suing anyone involved in manufacturing, selling, or distributing pornography, in public or in private. Their anti-pornography movement forged a powerful alliance with right-wing moralistic groups in the USA and they succeeded in having legislation passed in the state of Minneapolis (although they later suffered defeats in other US states) and in having the Canadian Supreme Court adopt a modified version of the Ordinance in 1992 which expressly accepted a link between 'obscenity' and harm to women (Segal 1998: 52). There have been campaigns for the implementation of the Ordinance in the UK, supported by Itzen and Russell and by feminist groups such as Women Against Violence Against Women (WAVAW) (Assiter 1989: 143–4). Diana Russell has clearly stated the case for censorship as follows:

> My theory, in a nutshell, is that pornography (1) predisposes some men to want to rape women or intensifies the predisposition in other men already so predisposed, (2) undermines some men's internal inhibitions against acting out their desire to rape, and (3) undermines some men's social inhibitions against acting out their desire to rape. (quoted in McIntosh 1996: 336)

Many other feminists have reached very different conclusions, whilst agreeing that pornography in our society often reflects misogynistic views and eroticisation of male abuse of power. It would be wrong to refer to such feminist writers and activists as 'pro-pornography', although the labels 'pro-sex' and 'anti-censorship' have been adopted on occasion. Amongst the main writings are Assiter (1989), Assiter and Avedon (1993), McIntosh (1996), Rodgerson and Wilson (1991), Segal and McIntosh (1994), and Segal (1998). Though it may be erroneous to describe him as a feminist, Thompson (1994) also shares some of the intellectual and political positions of these writers. The critiques they offer centre on the methodology and underlying assumptions behind the anti-pornography campaigners' work. They look at the nature of male and female sexuality, the nature of sexual fantasy, and the practical difficulties of formulating a satisfactory definition of pornography or obscenity which, in the hands of sexist and homophobic state institutions, is not going to be deployed to repress alternatives to the pervading heterosexist and patriarchal 'norms' of sexuality.

The anti-censorship lobby tend to agree on the following points. First, it is argued that the anti-pornography campaigners have a very simplistic view of male and female sexuality. Segal (1998) claims that such campaigners have allied themselves with the most reductionist behaviouristic psychology to give credence to a model in which women are always passive and abused and men are immoral, abusive, and driven by the irrepressible demands of their penises. Indeed, men are sometimes portrayed as having an almost Pavlovian dog-style reaction to pornography. Not only, argues Segal, is this a wholly false depiction of reality; it also masks the fact that men often use pornography because they are, for example, frightened by actual sex or worried by problems of impotence. Moreover, women can and do enjoy pornography – some surveys suggest that up to forty per cent of consumers of some leading titles are female. There is also the question of pornography or erotica produced by women for women. Dworkin has argued that the fact of some women enjoying pornography does not detract from the reality that pornography degrades and abuses all women. For example, she dismisses the view that the Ordinance drafted by herself and MacKinnon would criminalise lesbian erotica by arguing that lesbian erotica is simply heterosexual pornography with no man present, the camera constituting the male presence: 'the male defines and controls the idea of the lesbian in the composition of the photograph. In viewing it, he possesses her' (Dworkin 1981: 47). Segal argues that this sort of argument simply denies the possibilities of female sexuality and denies the possibility of changing the significances of sexual scripts. She goes on to say that the relentless emphasis on male sadism and female powerlessness in the writings of anti-pornography campaigners actually reproduces some of the most objectionable sado-masochistic glorification of sexual inequality.

Second, Dworkin, MacKinnon and others are accused of faulty methodology. There is simply inadequate evidence to establish a causal link between the free availability of pornographic or erotic materials and the level of crimes of rape and sexual abuse against women. Some surveys have suggested that pornography does indeed desensitise men to sexual violence. Segal (1998) argues, however, that the context in which images are viewed and consumed is very important. Other surveys, from Scandinavia, the USA and elsewhere, deny any such link. As is often cited, the rate of sex crimes in Denmark actually fell after the legalisation of pornography. Some writers have even argued that it may be possible to wean sex offenders away from their criminal activities through the use of pornography – with pornography acting as a substitute for sexual acts rather than a stimulant. This ties in with the argument that the pro-censorship lobby fails to distinguish between fantasy and reality, and to recognise that many people – including feminists! – can behave in perfectly decent, moral and non-abusive ways whilst enjoying 'politically incorrect' sexual fantasies. The as-

sumption that fantasy leads to crimes of abuse is both highly contentious and inevitably seems to 'criminalise' sexual fantasy. Moreover,
the argument that exposure to pornography *causes* men to act in a
violent or abusive way towards women is surely undermined by even a
casual look at human history and at the contemporary world. Pornography is strictly prohibited in the Islamic Republic of Iran and in
Afghanistan under the Taliban, for example; yet does any Western
feminist seriously wish to argue that women are freer, safer from crimes
of sexual violence, and more able to seek and obtain justice if they are
victims of violence in such societies? Thus pornography should be seen
as only one form of discourse and the view that by banning it or driving
it underground one thereby deals a 'knock-out blow' to misogyny may
be hopelessly utopian and misplaced.

Third, the anti-pornography lobby is accused of grossly exaggerating
the extent of really violent and disturbing images in pornography.
Feminists (and most sane people) would agree that materials depicting
the sexual abuse of children or crimes of sadistic violence against
women (or men), for example, are immensely disturbing and morally
indefensible. But the pro-censorship lobby is accused by groups such
as Feminists Against Censorship of presenting almost all pornographic
or erotic material in this light. Segal (1998: 51) argues that surveys
have consistently found that explicitly violent imagery in pornography has been decreasing since 1977. Thompson (1994: 266–7) accuses
the pro-censorship lobby of practically inventing certain urban le-
gends such as 'snuff movies' in order to harness tabloid sensationalism
to their cause.

A fourth important criticism of anti-pornography campaigns is that
they simplify the complex power relationships involved in an issue
such as pornography. McIntosh argues that pornography is not just a
weapon in the hands of men which is used against women. It is also
'banned, seized, burned, kept shamefully under the bed . . . by men'
(1996: 336). McIntosh believes that the internal contradiction of
pornography may lie in this fact – that representations of sexuality
have been stigmatised until very recently (and still are in many
societies). This means that much of the appeal and attraction of certain
types of pornography may reside in their illicit nature; thus banning
and prohibition, far from removing the problem, may increase it.
Moreover, the moral crusades and legal campaigns against pornography may very well increase the power of patriarchy in new ways; it is,
after all, male police officers, judges, politicians and clerics who frequently see their powers enhanced by such crusades. For McIntosh, the
internal contradiction of patriarchy revealed here 'calls for a politics of
subversion, not of reform' (1996: 340). Acts of subversion might

include transgressive cultural politics and the production of pro-feminist erotica which confidently asserts women's sexuality.

Fifth, the anti-pornography campaigners have been accused of forming explicit alliances with right-wing, conservative and religious 'anti-sex' groups in their fight for censorship. This is clearly linked to the highly paradoxical fact – for most feminists – that any increase in censorship represents an increase in the powers of the (patriarchal) state. For whatever definition of 'pornography' we wish to enshrine in law, ultimately it will be for the male-dominated institutions of the state – police, judiciary, customs and excise, film censors – to interpret that definition and translate it into legally binding decisions. At present, the UK has amongst the most restrictive anti-pornography laws in Europe, if not the Western world. Under the Obscene Publications Act 1959, 'an article shall be deemed to be obscene if its effect . . . is . . . such as to tend to deprave and corrupt persons who are likely, having regard to all relevant circumstances, to read, see or hear the matter contained or embodied within it'. Although this has tended to be interpreted in a more liberal fashion in the 1990s than in previous decades, it should be clear that, potentially, it could be interpreted as offering grounds for a blanket ban on all gay or lesbian literature and sexual representations, for example. Any more restrictive legal ruling is likewise open to repressive and authoritarian interpretation by sexist and homophobic judges and other state officials. Indeed, when Dworkin and MacKinnon's Ordinance was incorporated into Canadian law, it was not 'offensive' heterosexual pornography which was amongst the primary targets of the state. Rather, gay and lesbian book-shops were raided, lesbian feminist magazines seized and, in a richly ironic twist, Andrea Dworkin's own writings were temporarily banned because they contained quotations from pornographic texts. Censorship is thus a double-edged sword, and censorship which increases the power of a sexist and heterosexist state is a very dangerous weapon for feminists and other sexual democrats to wield.

These brief comments on the problematic nature of state power and the sometimes paradoxical nature of state regulation of gender and sexual behaviour lead us on to the final part of our discussion of contemporary sexual politics: the role of the state and of public policy.

Chapter 6

Regulating gender and sexuality: the state and the public policy agenda

Introduction

This chapter explores some aspects of state regulation of gender and sexual behaviour in the UK over the past two decades in particular. It examines how state policy has sought to encourage and promote certain forms of behaviour, and discourage, penalise, repress or stigmatise others. Space restricts the discussion to three case studies which, it is hoped, will illustrate some of the main contours of state policy. The promotion of heterosexuality explores how the heterosexist state has sought to promote discrimination and cast non-heterosexuals in the role of second-class citizens. Family policy examines how a particular model of the family informed state policy under the Conservative governments of the 1980s and 1990s to the detriment of other family types, and the significant changes to family policy which have occurred since the election of a Labour government in May 1997. Public policy on sexual violence (including so-called domestic violence) examines police and judicial responses to sexual violence and asks whether state initiatives are adequate.

The Thatcher government came to power in 1979. In common with so-called New Right governments elsewhere (for example, the Reagan administration in the USA), it demonised the 1960s as a decade of permissiveness and the breakdown of order, tradition and morality, leading to social decay and substantial economic costs. Rising crime, the growing burden of the welfare state, and the growth of what was called a culture of dependency were all attributed in part – sometimes in large part – to the crisis of the traditional two-parent heterosexual family. The rise of single-parent families, and the manifold changes in male and female gender roles within the family and within society, were singled out for attack, and feminism and homosexuality identified as the enemy within.

Central to the agenda of the conservative backlash against the 1960s, and against the ideologies of socialism and feminism which were accused of having dominated the intellectual and political agenda of the 1960s, were discourses aimed at reversing the advances of the 'sexual revolution'. These gave comfort to those who felt undermined or threatened, and invoked a rhetoric of moral restoration, even whilst further drastic social and economic changes were effected through the economic policies of the New Right. State discourses throughout the 1980s seemed to have been aimed at placing those who felt empowered by the changes achieved in the 1960s on the defensive, whilst rallying as broad a constituency as possible behind the populist clarion call to moral certainty and restoration of a hierarchy of sexualities and gender roles which had felt itself threatened.

Of course, not all the New Right – never mind all of the Conservative or US Republican parties as a whole – shared this agenda, nor did all on the centre-left in the UK and USA consistently oppose it. Even amongst those we generally regard as the New Right there are divisions between those who apparently see a natural link between Victorian economics and Victorian moral values, and those moral libertarians, such as ex-Tory MP Edwina Currie, who believe with J. S. Mill that the state should mind its own business where private consensual relationships between adults are concerned.

Some writers question how far-reaching in practice the sexual agenda of Thatcherism has been. Martin Durham (1991 and 1997) argues that the rhetoric often outstripped the performance. Mrs Mary Whitehouse and her supporters did not succeed in having rigid censorship laws reimposed. The Society for the Protection of the Unborn Child and other such groups did not succeed in having abortion outlawed, although this is currently heating up in the UK as a political issue once more – doubtless influenced by events in the USA where abortion clinics have been bombed and doctors actually killed by 'pro-life' extremists. Prominent heterosexist Conservative MPs of the 1980s such as Elaine Kellet-Bowman and Jill Knight did not succeed in having male homosexuality completely recriminalised. However, before we conclude that the sexual agenda of Thatcherism was just so much 'hot air', we need to reflect on those progressive social and legislative changes, not to mention health initiatives, which were blocked or neglected, as well as the negative measures which were implemented. The virtual absence of legal reforms or other political measures aimed at promoting greater gender and sexual equality marks the UK out from many other European Union countries during this period. This is especially true of the position of gay men and lesbians, who have been one of the principal targets of government attacks, both legislative and rhetorical, in recent decades.

The three main themes in Conservative government discourses on sexuality and gender from 1979 to 1997 were the restoration of 'family values', the need to control 'anarchic' male sexuality in the interests of societal stability, and the need to discourage homosexuality and promote heterosexuality. Although Durham may have a point in arguing that the first two, involving perceived financial savings to the Treasury, were taken more seriously, all three are intrinsically linked. It can be argued that the regulation (and, in part, repression) of lesbian and gay sexuality by the state has a far broader significance and relevance and tells us much about concerns over heterosexuality, male and female gender roles and behaviour, and family patterns.

It is perhaps not surprising in retrospect that in times of far-reaching economic and social change, and perceived national decline, gender and sexuality should become the focus of so much political attention. So it has been throughout history. It has often been noted, as Grant (1993) points out, that the erotic is the place where different classes, races and generations meet and as such it has always been the focus for anxieties about the collapse of the existing economic and social order. It is a place where barriers are broken down and passions, loves and lusts lead those who 'should know better' in the eyes of authority to 'betray' their class, or country, or masculinity, or femininity, by falling in love inappropriately. It is a place where dreams of a future where they do things differently can take root dangerously; in other words, the erotic can be seen as the great leveller. Throughout history, seemingly intelligent people – usually men – have written earnestly about how the collapse of great empires and civilisations was due to sexual degeneracy.

Promoting heterosexuality: the state and the enforcement of discrimination

Perhaps an obvious place to begin any discussion of the role of the British state in promoting heterosexuality and enforcing discrimination in recent decades is with a brief overview of state responses to the arrival of HIV and AIDS in the early 1980s. Various writers have noted how, in the 1980s, the British media promoted the view that AIDS was a 'gay plague' which sexual deviants had brought upon themselves (Davenport-Hines 1991, Garfield 1994, and King 1993). Whilst gay men's health groups and charitable organisations such as the Terrence Higgins Trust (founded in 1982) set about organising health education and caring for those who were ill, the responses of the Thatcher governments were characterised by widespread indifference. Weeks

(1992: 118) argues that the Conservative government saw AIDS as affecting only a small and politically embarrassing minority. No government policy was formulated until 1986.

In some ways, AIDS was welcomed by the moralising right as a vindication of their message of discrimination against sexual minorities and calls for abstinence from sex outside marriage. During the phase which Weeks (1992: 119) calls 'moral panic' (roughly 1982–5), propaganda attacked 'sexual promiscuity' and 'permissive lifestyles'; prejudice was whipped up against those with HIV and AIDS, especially gay men; and discrimination in access to services, health care and education became widespread. Government rhetoric drew a distinction between 'innocent' and 'guilty' sufferers, the latter usually being gay men. As Weeks et al (1996) point out, government members on occasion spoke of AIDS as a self-inflicted 'disease of the diseased'. This rhetoric sought to pathologise all same-sex relationships and to draw a *cordon sanitaire* around the 'normal', that is, heterosexual, population.

A turning-point came in 1985–6 when either rising public awareness of the disease (with the deaths of celebrities such as Rock Hudson), or fears that it might spiral out of control imposing unmanageable costs on the exchequer, led to measures such as the compulsory detention in hospital of those thought to put others at risk. Such an authoritarian 'solution' further whipped up public hysteria. In 1986, the government finally set aside the princely sum of thirteen million pounds to prevent the spread into the heterosexual population. The clear message that this sent to lesbian and gay citizens was, of course, that gay lives (and deaths) did not matter. The distinction between 'innocent' and 'guilty' sufferers was further underlined by financial awards to haemophiliacs who had contracted the virus through infected blood supplies, justified by one national newspaper on the grounds that 'they have led blameless lives and it could never be said that they have brought the tragedy on themselves' (the *Daily Express*, quoted in Garfield, 1994: 211). Nevertheless government ministers, when faced with the task of belatedly drawing up a strategy to tackle the problem, found themselves relying in part on the expertise amassed by lesbian and gay organisations such as the Terrence Higgins Trust which had pioneered the fight against HIV and AIDS. Government funding of these organisations, in turn, was to lead to charges from the mid-1980s that they were being 'de-gayed' and encouraged to turn their attention towards heterosexuals. This 'covert' alliance was not particularly publicised by either side, particularly as it coincided (as we will see) with renewed attacks by the Conservative government upon gay men and lesbians. From the government's point of view, 'covert' work alongside organisations such as the Terrence Higgins Trust has one big advantage. Directly addressing the sexual health needs of gay and bisexual men was seen as morally distasteful and politically undesirable. Yet simply allowing gay and bisexual men to die in ever larger numbers, with the risk of 'contamination' of the heterosexual population, was risky. The government therefore took the option of allowing voluntary sector bodies to undertake specifically gay education and health-risk-reduction work in relation to safer sex practice whilst retaining control of the purse strings (and thus of the power to veto 'offensive' material). The National AIDS Trust, launched in May 1987 as an independent organisation (but reliant on state funding) also concentrated on the general population, failing to establish a good relationship with the non-heterosexual communities.

In the 1990s, the danger of a mass outbreak of HIV amongst the heterosexual population seemed to diminish – and so, too, did the amount of time and money which the government was prepared to devote to the problem. The relatively low number of heterosexuals infected was heralded as a triumph by the government. The fact that gay men continued to be the group most affected was taken as evidence that the crisis was over, and could be ignored. As Watney (1994: 20) argues, if any other social group had been affected by a deadly virus in this way, government action would have been swift and publicly supported. The early 1990s saw the right-wing press call for a complete ban on funding of the Terrence Higgins Trust, accused of 'promoting homosexuality' (the *Daily Telegraph*, 7 May 1991) and in fact the government announced in 1992 that its grant to the Trust would be cut by two-thirds over three years. The Trust itself was placed in a very difficult position. As its former chief executive Naomi Wayne said in 1991, 'As long as AIDS is ghettoised as gay, it will not be taken seriously.' The financial incentive – or even financial imperative – to down-grade emphasis on the very section of the community most at risk and to emphasise instead the danger to heterosexuals, resulted in no new initiatives aimed at gay men being undertaken by the Trust in the period from 1987 to 1991. In June 1996 the government finally announced that it would make two million pounds available to the Trust to undertake a national prevention strategy. However, fears were rife in the lesbian and gay community that the homophobia which had at every stage marked Conservative government responses to the crisis would again mean that the health needs of non-heterosexuals would be ignored or treated as of secondary importance.

The election of a Labour government in May 1997 brought new initiatives but also initial disappointment. In 1998, the government committed itself to a new national strategy on every aspect of AIDS and HIV prevention, treatment and care. However, speaking to a conference of HIV experts in October 1998 the Health Minister, Tessa Jowell, mentioned gay men only once, sparking fears of further 'de-gaying' of the disease, and she refused to guarantee that local authority funds for HIV prevention would be targeted at gay men. Despite the fact that more than sixty per cent of new HIV infections in the UK are still of gay and bisexual men, the Minister announced that priorities for prevention work were now mother-to-baby infection and cutting new infections amongst African women in the UK. This prompted one gay activist to argue that 'when it comes to the crunch, the politicians will always talk about 'good AIDS' – heterosexuals and babies' (quoted in National AIDS Trust 1998). Moreover, the Labour government was reluctant to commit itself to a thorough programme of repeal of all anti-gay discriminatory laws despite a plea from the National AIDS Trust that such discrimination makes it more difficult to get the safer sex message across, especially to young gay and bisexual men.

This brief discussion of how the state has dealt with the realities of HIV and AIDS highlights the continuing inability (or unwillingness) of the state to let go of a pathologising model of homosexuality, to accept moral diversity when it comes to sexual relationships, and to cherish all citizens equally. Indeed, the moral and ideological constructions which the state, media and churches have given to HIV and AIDS in the 1980s and 1990s have contributed to a climate in which anti-gay discrimination (until very recently at least) appeared to enjoy a new lease of state approval. It was against the background of media hysteria over gay 'promiscuity' and 'disease' that the Conservative government introduced Section 28 of the Local Government Act 1988 prohibiting local authorities from 'promoting homosexuality' or teaching its 'acceptability as a pretended family relationship'. This was the first major legislative move in nearly twenty years aimed at actually reinforcing discrimination against non-heterosexuals. But it did not occur in a vacuum. The broader legal, social and political context must not be overlooked. It can be seen as an attempt by a heterosexist state to reinstate the very limited and begrudging 'settlement' implied by partial decriminalisation of male homosexuality in 1967, whereby certain forms of same-sex activity would be 'tolerated' (but never accepted) within carefully drawn boundaries but same-sex relationships would neither be socially sanctioned or accorded anything like the same respect that heterosexual relationships received. We need to explore that broader context.

Until 1967 in England and Wales, 1980 in Scotland and 1982 in Northern Ireland, the relationships of homosexual men were completely criminalised. Since those dates, a partial legal tolerance has been extended. Until 1994, relationships continued to be criminalised where one or both partners was under the age of twenty-one. In no other area of law was the age of majority still fixed at twenty-one. With the passage of the Criminal Justice Act of 1994, the age of consent for gay men was lowered to eighteen. The age of consent for heterosexuals is sixteen, and there is no age of consent at all for lesbians, although they can be prosecuted under different legislation for indecent behaviour.

At the start of 2000, sexual acts between men remained a criminal offence, even over the age of eighteen, if more than two people are involved or if they were conducted other than in private. In England, Wales and Northern Ireland, 'in private' means in the domestic dwelling of one partner with no one else present in the same house or flat. Consensual sex between men over eighteen remained a criminal offence if it took place in an hotel, or if another person was staying overnight in the dwelling place. In Scotland, these provisions did not apply. (Although these aspects of the law were virtually impossible to enforce, the fact that they remained on the statute book reinforces the social and legal inferiority of same-sex relationships).

The armed forces were exempted from even this partial reform. Until June 1992, consensual sex between gay or lesbian soldiers, even if off-duty and in private, remained punishable by court martial, imprisonment of up to two years in a military prison, and subsequent dishonourable discharge. Between 1982 and 1992, on average, ten men per year were sent to military prison for an average period of eighteen months; lesbians tended to be threatened with imprisonment. Although, in the broader context, lesbian relationships are not criminalised, within the armed forces they are – under a military ordinance covering 'disgraceful conduct of an indecent kind'. From June 1992, imprisonment for consensual sex between gay or lesbian soldiers was dropped, but all gay or lesbian soldiers still faced dishonourable discharge from the armed forces. Moreover, it was and remains the policy of the UK government through the Ministry of Defence to discharge any member of the armed forces who admits to homosexual thoughts or feelings, whether the individual is sexually active or entirely celibate. Thus private letters, diaries and conversations wherein an individual might have admitted to homosexual or lesbian thoughts or feelings may suffice as evidence in deciding to end a soldier's, sailor's or airperson's career. Between 1991 and 1994 around 260 servicemen and women were discharged for homosexuality. This figure does not include those who resigned out of fear of being discharged. A challenge to the legality of this policy failed in June 1995, despite the judges declaring their sympathy with the four discharged service people who brought the case against the Ministry of Defence, and the policy was upheld by 188 votes to 120 in the House of Commons debate on the Armed Forces Bill in May 1996. In September 1999, the European Court of Human Rights unanimously ruled that the Ministry of Defence's ban on homosexuals serving in the armed forces was unlawful and a breach of human rights. The court upheld the case brought before it by the same four service personnel who had earlier challenged the policy in the UK courts. Despite this ruling, and with Conservative Party spokespersons demanding a UK 'opt-out' from the judgement, the Labour government showed little sign of moving quickly to implement the decision. One government minister indicated that a new code of conduct was unlikely before 2001 and another suggested that a Clinton-style 'don't ask, don't tell' compromise might be introduced (*The Guardian*, 28 September 1999).

Back in civilian life, convictions for consensual sex with men aged between sixteen and twenty-one, and since 1994 between sixteen and eighteen (sixteen being the heterosexual age of consent) have been punishable by up to five years imprisonment. In 1989, thirty-two men were imprisoned in the UK for this offence, for which there is no heterosexual equivalent, and in 1995 – that is, after partial reform – this number rose to 130: further evidence that partial reform tends to be followed by more vigorous police enforcement of what are still discriminatory laws. In Scotland, however, the legal position is again more liberal. *Crown Office circular 2051/1* instructed the police not to proceed with prosecutions on grounds of consensual sex involving men aged sixteen to twenty-one unless 'corruption or breach of trust' – for example between a school teacher and a pupil – was involved. Since the passage of the Criminal Justice Act of 1994, and despite the insistence of the then Home Secretary Michael Howard that young gay men aged sixteen to eighteen would face prosecution, the Lord Advocate in Scotland has repeated his instruction that police are not to bring charges unless there are very special circumstances; that any decision to bring charges must be cleared at a more senior level in Edinburgh; and that chasing after young gay men or their lovers, if the relationship is based on consent, is not to be regarded as a police priority.

The offence of gross indecency applies, only by definition, to consenting sex between men: there is no heterosexual equivalent. This covers having sex in a public place – for example on a beach or in a wood, or a park or public toilet, or in one's own back garden for that matter. But it should be remembered that where sex between men is concerned, 'in a public place' in the UK apart from Scotland can also mean in a hotel or even in a domestic dwelling if someone else is present. Moreover, the specifically gay offence of "gross indecency" is often treated much more harshly by the courts than equivalent heterosexual offences. For example, 'in 1991, 28 men arrested for "gross indecency" after police went searching woodlands in Surrey were fined up to £1,000. Yet, a year later, a heterosexual couple who had sex on a train in full view of other passengers were fined £50 each' (Stonewall 1998). In Scotland, the offence of 'shameless indecency' exists in law. Although this is a relatively minor offence, which is not in the nature of an assault, it is also a broad offence used to cover many acts including urinating in public, displaying indecent materials, or having sex in a public place. The Public Order Act 1986 and numerous local by-laws have also been used to criminalise public displays of affection between men – for example kissing or holding hands in public. In addition, it is a criminal offence for a man to make contact with another man in a public place for the purposes of having sex: theoretically, this includes chatting someone up in a gay pub.

Quite apart from these measures, the state enforces heterosexist discrimination in numerous other ways which touch directly on the social construction of heterosexuality and the social construction of the family. Some of these measures are so commonplace that many people don't stop to think about how they affect and inform heterosexuality as the only form of state-sanctioned and institutionalised sexuality in our society.

The law does not recognise long-term lesbian or gay relationships. Lesbian and gay couples do not have any rights of inheritance, taxation benefits, tenancy rights (although, as we shall see, a recent House of Lords decision has changed this), next-of-kin visiting rights in hospitals or prisons, insurance or pension rights. Nor, in the event of a gay or lesbian person's death, does his or her partner have the legal right to bury them, unless a Will has been made to this effect. In the absence of a Will, the biological family of the deceased may take legal control of burial arrangements. With the impact of AIDS, many hundreds of gay men have found themselves barred from even attending the funeral of their lover or friend.

In early 2000, there were signs that significant changes to family law were possible in Scotland. In the context of consideration of an incapable adults bill, which grants rights to the nearest relatives of someone who becomes incapable of making significant decisions for themselves, the Scottish Justice Minister, Jim Wallace, pledged to eliminate discrimination against same-sex couples and ensure equal treatment. A move to give same-sex couples the same rights as un-married heterosexual couples was condemned by MSPs as unfair to same-sex couples and the Scottish Parliament's equal opportunities committee pledged to oppose discriminatory legislation. In an atmo-sphere of renewed public homophobia whipped up by religious groups and tabloid newspapers (see below), the Conservative Party and 'family values' campaigners in Scotland pledged to fight against any new rights for same-sex couples. Nevertheless, in early 2000 it seemed likely that Scotland might set an example for the rest of the United Kingdom in extending the legal definition of the family, if not marriage itself.

Another area of discrimination is that the foreign (that is, non-European Union) partners of UK lesbians and gay men have no right of residence. This situation forces many gay men or lesbians in love with a non-EU national to advertise in lesbian and gay publications for others in similar situations interested in 'mutually beneficial arrangements' – a code for marriages of convenience. In April 1999, the Labour Home Secretary Jack Straw moved to change this situation somewhat. He recognised same-sex couples in immigration policy but then partially undermined this potentially landmark decision by introducing very strict conditions including a four-year test (requiring proof that the couple have been together for four years) (*Independent on Sunday*, 25 April 1999). However, after intense pressure from lobby groups such as Stonewall, Straw agreed in June 1999 to reduce this waiting period to two years.

Judges have frequently ruled that a 'normal family life' is preferable for a child involved in a divorce case where one parent is gay or lesbian. Custody is then awarded to the other parent. However, 1994 saw a landmark legal case when the Law Lords awarded a lesbian mother custody of her child, declaring her to be a fit mother, despite an outcry both from the tabloids and from some Conservative MPs. In 1997, the Court of Appeal upheld the adoption of an eleven-year-old girl by a lesbian and held that homosexuality should not be an absolute bar to adoption. Another significant step forward was taken in October 1999 when England's top family law judge, Dame Elizabeth Butler-Sloss, ruled that children could be brought up successfully by gay or lesbian couples, thus attacking the anomaly by which only married couples or single people could adopt or foster children. Dame Elizabeth Butler-Sloss argued that 'over the years research has shown that for some children, that is the best that is available for them . . . We should not close our minds to suitable families who are clearly not within the old fashioned approach' (*The Guardian*, 16 October 1999). Yet gay fathers fighting for custody still face enormous prejudice; and many councils are afraid of allowing gay men or lesbians to adopt or foster in case they are attacked in the press.

In October 1999, the Law Lords handed down another important judgement. In the case of Martin Fitzpatrick, a gay man who had been evicted from his Housing Association home after the death of his lifelong partner whom he had cared for through years of illness, and in whose name the tenancy agreement had been, the Law Lords ruled by three votes to two that Mr Fitzpatrick and his partner constituted a family and that he was entitled to be treated as such. This historic ruling was the first ever by the state which did not deal with male homosexuality in terms of 'sexual acts' but rather in terms of loving relationships. It clearly reflects a significant change in public opinion which had been building up throughout the 1990s. There is still a very long way to go in the UK, however. Six European states now recognise same-sex partnerships in law (Stonewall 1998). In the UK, the fight for equal pensions rights, inheritance rights and a right to civil marriage is just beginning.

Things are changing somewhat. Yet it has too often been left to the courts, either in the UK or in Europe, to suggest change to a political elite which often appears timid and uninterested in challenging heterosexist privilege, when not actually clamouring for the reinforcement of that privilege. It is also much too early to speak of the demise of state-sponsored heterosexism or of 'gays entering the mainstream', as some newspaper headlines proclaimed at the end of the 1990s, although it is perhaps true to say that the introduction of the Scottish Parliament added a new dimension to the fight for equality. Many of the areas of legal competence devolved to the Scottish Parliament include the type of reforms which might encourage greater sexual equality, and the Scotland Act (establishing the Parliament) contains a definition of equal opportunities which specifically mentions sexual orientation. This has raised the hopes of groups such as the Edinburgh-based Equality Network that the Scottish Parliament may take a lead (in the UK context) in tackling legal discrimination and promoting equality before the law for all citizens.

The law in the UK still does not protect against discrimination on the grounds of sexuality in the provision of services such as housing, education or policing or in employment – as the law does in some EU countries, including Ireland, where an Equal Status Act exists. It is not unlawful to decide not to employ someone because they are gay or lesbian, or to treat someone less favourably (by denying them promotion, for example), or to harass an employee or to allow others to harass them on homophobic grounds. It is not unlawful to pay a gay or lesbian employee less (by refusing them partnership benefits, for example), or in some cases to make that employee redundant because of their sexual orientation. No protection is extended to non-heterosexuals remotely equivalent to that which exists to prevent discrimination on grounds, for example, of sex or race. There is no legal protection against incitement to hatred on grounds of sexuality (again, there is in Ireland). Under the Conservative governments of the late 1980s and early 1990s, the Department of Education issued guidelines instructing schools that sex education lessons must have 'due regard to moral considerations and family life', which former Education Secretary John Patten explained as meaning that teachers have an obligation to teach the superiority of heterosexuality over homosexuality.

Section 28 of the Local Government Act 1988, as we have seen, prohibits the 'promotion of homosexuality' by local authorities and prohibits also the 'teaching in any maintained school of the acceptability of homosexuality as a pretended family relationship'. The phrase 'pretended family relationship' is an interesting one; it makes it clear that the Conservative government of the day thought it was 'protecting' the social and cultural hegemony and moral monopoly enjoyed by the traditional two-parent, heterosexual family against any claim by same-sex couples to be treated as loving, mutually caring units (or building blocks) of society – rather than 'deviants' driven by sex. It is a nonsense to suggest that gay relationships are anti-family; it is closer to the truth to say that many families are anti-gay! But Section 28 was clearly intended as part of the ideological struggle to bolster the fading allure of the traditional two-parent heterosexual family as a tranquil, harmonious and natural haven – ordained by God and by the state – against the social reality of rapidly increasing diversity of family forms and marital break-down.

At one level, Section 28 might be said to be almost meaningless legally as there is no agreement on whether one can promote any form of sexuality. However, it has succeeded in frightening some councils, and has been invoked by others as justification for banning gay and lesbian books from local-authority-funded libraries, and withdrawing or withholding funding from lesbian and gay switchboards and other voluntary organisations. That said, the measure has probably had far less impact than had been feared or hoped at the time, and in retrospect did not turn out to be the beginning of a drive by the state to recriminalise homosexuality. The main impact of Section 28 has probably been in legitimising homophobia within schools – frightening into silence those teachers who may have been inclined to speak about different sexualities in a non-condemnatory manner or to speak out against homophobic bullying. An academic survey commissioned by Stonewall and by the Terrence Higgins Trust in the late 1990s, *Playing It Safe*, found that eighty-two per cent of teachers were aware of verbal homophobic bullying and twenty-six per cent aware of anti-gay physical attacks on students, but only six per cent said that their schools had policies which made reference to homophobic bullying. Moreover, many teachers felt that Section 28 made it 'dangerous or wrong' to discuss the needs of gay, lesbian or bisexual students.

The last years of Conservative rule (circa 1994–7) were a period of increasing disarray on government benches over the Conservative Party's sexual agenda. Prime Minister Major's 'back to basics' campaign – an ill-considered attempt to whip up public support by invoking 'Victorian' moralism and traditional family values – collapsed in the wake of the sexually compromising death of Conservative MP Stephen Milligan. At the same time, widespread public cynicism over the private lives of other Conservative MPs coincided with renewed disagreement between the libertarian right and the moralistic or moralising right over what, if any, should be the state's role in regulating sexuality. This came to the fore during the unsuccessful attempt by libertarian Conservative MP Edwina Currie to introduce an equal age of sexual consent at sixteen years for all. Moreover, the Criminal Justice Act 1994, which became law on 3 November 1994, represents a further partial retreat from state criminalisation of alleged sexual deviance.

This important piece of legislation was widely condemned by civil liberties groups as authoritarian. It increased sentences for young offenders, reduced the right to bail, abolished the requirement for judges to warn juries against convicting on uncorroborated evidence, restricted the right to silence for accused persons, increased police powers to take intimate body samples, increased police powers of search and arrest. It also increased police powers to arrest trespassers, ban raves or any other form of outdoor music and to arrest people travelling to outdoor concerts, contained new measures aimed at hunt saboteurs, travelling people and squatters and created a new offence of 'causing intentional harassment, alarm or distress' which could make many forms of peaceful demonstration illegal. Indeed, some senior police chiefs warned at the time that their powers under the Act were so great that they might alienate the police from middle-class communities.

In some respects, however, the Act was less illiberal in effect, despite government efforts to defeat amendments introduced by individual MPs and the House of Lords. Part XI on Sexual Offences (sections 142 to 148) is the relevant section. Three types of change were introduced: those applying to the whole of the UK, those applying to Scotland only, and those applying to England and Wales only. (The Act was subsequently enforced in Northern Ireland under 'an Order in Council' – the device used to transport English law to Northern Ireland.)

Changes across the UK: (1) the age of consent for gay men was reduced from twenty-one to eighteen, although equality was denied. The law remains blatantly discriminatory in another way. In the case of consensual sex between a man over the age of eighteen and a fifteen-year-old girl, say, it is only the man who commits a criminal offence.

But in the case of consensual sex between a man over the age of eighteen and a seventeen-year-old youth, both can be prosecuted. (2) The Act formalised the decriminalisation of gay sex by men and women in the armed forces and merchant navy. However, as already mentioned, they still face dishonourable discharge from the services – it is still not permitted to be gay in the armed forces. The reform meant that gay men and lesbians would no longer be sent to military prison. Even this was somewhat undermined by a late government amendment in the House of Lords which states that gay service personnel can still face criminal prosecution if a sexual act 'occurs in conjunction with other acts or circumstances'. No one is yet quite sure what that means and it remains to be thoroughly tested. The government claimed it covered sexual harassment by senior officers, for example. Others have suggested it could be used by the military police to cover just about everything.

Changes in Scotland only: The old Scottish offence of 'shameless indecency' which had been used in Scotland to prosecute displays of same-sex affection in public, such as kissing, is no longer to be used against consensual homosexual acts between men over eighteen years of age.

Changes in England and Wales only: (1) the Act extends the definition of rape to include anal rape of a woman or a man. This was not applied to Scotland because in Scotland rape is a common law offence, not a statutory offence, and the maximum penalties for rape of a man (prosecuted as 'indecent assault') and of a woman are already the same. (2) Consensual anal sex between a man and a woman is decriminalised with an age of consent for heterosexual anal intercourse of eighteen years. This had previously been completely illegal in England and Wales: consensual anal intercourse between a man and a woman was already legal in Scotland with an age of consent of sixteen. (3) The Act reduces maximum penalties for some consensual gay sex acts from five years to two years. This does not apply, however, to consenting sex between a man over twenty-one and a man aged sixteen or seventeen which remains at five years. This provision was not relevant to Scotland where the maximum penalty for all specifically gay sex offences where consent of both parties is present was already two years.

The election of a Labour government in 1997 raised hopes amongst lesbian and gay activists of real legal change, away from state-sponsored discrimination and towards sexual equality and acceptance of diversity. There was evidence of a significant change in public opinion, a good working relationship had been built up over several years between the Labour Party and Stonewall, Labour had committed itself to a repeal of Section 28 and the introduction of an equal age of consent (but to few other specific reforms), there was a huge Labour majority in parliament, and the presence after 1997 of at least eight 'out' gay and lesbian MPs, including several cabinet ministers. Yet Labour's paper commitment to sexual equality soon came into conflict with its reluctance to risk losing the support of former Conservative voters and, perhaps, a socially authoritarian streak in parts of the party leadership – ever anxious to distance themselves from the perceived social liberalism of the Labour Party in the past.

One of the first measures introduced by the new Home Secretary, Jack Straw, was a Sexual Offenders Act which established a Sex Offenders' Register and required people who have been convicted of one of a range of specified offences to register their names and addresses with the police. The stated aim of this measure was to provide the police with a valuable tool in their fight against serious sex offenders, especially child abusers. The problem with the measure relates to the existing inequalities in law between homosexuals and heterosexuals. For example, one of the categories of offence requiring registration is 'indecent assaults and related offences against people under 18, or against people over 18 if the sentence on conviction was at least 30 months imprisonment'. But this means that a man sent to prison for two years for an indecent assault on a woman would not be required to register, whereas a man sentenced to three years for consensual sex with a seventeen-year-old man (which would not be an offence at all if it were a seventeen-year-old woman, given the differential ages of consent) would have to register. The inclusion in Scotland of a range of minor offences in the list of offences requiring registration has created an anomaly whereby two twenty-year-old men found guilty of 'indecency between men' for having consensual sex in a parked car and fined, say fifty pounds, would be forced to register as serious sex offenders. These discriminatory and dangerous provisions have infuriated equal rights campaigners.

At the beginning of 2000, and half-way through Labour's first term of office, nothing very concrete had been achieved by way of pro-equality reforms although action on both Section 28 and an equal age of consent appeared imminent. The Labour government fought at the European Court of Human Rights to retain the ban on gay and lesbian personnel in the armed forces and, having lost that battle, seemed in no hurry to introduce full equality of treatment. Labour killed off Baroness Turner's proposed Sexual Orientation Discrimination Bill (backed by Stonewall) which would have outlawed incitement to hatred and discrimination against gay people. Labour even refused to repeal laws which are blatantly discriminatory, such as the offence of gross indecency.

The government did support a private member's Bill which would have equalised the age of consent for all at sixteen. When this was blocked in the House of Lords, the government announced in the Queen's Speech at the end of 1999 its intention to introduce a Sexual Offences Bill in 2000 which would deal with the issue. This measure was welcomed by lesbian and gay campaigners, as was the assurance that it would no longer be the case that the younger same-sex partner would be criminalised along with the older. However, both Stonewall and OutRage! expressed dismay at the government's handling of this issue, in particular its decision to appease homophobic opinion by including in the proposed new bill a new measure criminalising sex between teachers and sixth formers, and between carers and young people aged sixteen to eighteen. Although this might seem laudable – and it does apply to all, gay and straight – the fact that it is to be introduced only now, to coincide with the promised equal age of consent, sends a rather nasty subliminal message, conflating gay sexuality with a threat to young people. OutRage! also opposed this move on the grounds that it could leave a twenty-two-year-old teacher who had a consensual relationship with a seventeen-year-old sixth-former facing five years' imprisonment.

The government also moved in late 1999 and early 2000 to repeal Section 28. The devolved Scottish Executive had earlier announced its decision to repeal the legislation in Scotland, denouncing it as discriminatory and as promoting bullying in schools. This decision was met with a well-financed and at times hysterical campaign by religious and self-appointed 'family values' groups, backed by several tabloid newspapers, which sought to cajole politicians into abandoning or watering down their commitment to repeal. Full page advertisements and cut-out petitions in newspapers sought to unleash the full weight of homophobic prejudice. Amongst the most ridiculous arguments promoted by the 'Keep the Clause' campaign were that repeal of this discriminatory legislation would lead to teachers trying to 'convert' children to homosexuality, and that schools would suddenly be flooded by gay pornography. The obvious response to the first argument is that teachers have been trying to 'convert' children to heterosexuality for years by promoting heterosexual lifestyles, with little effect on gay or lesbian teenagers other than loneliness, isolation, self-hatred, and unhappy marriages. The answer to the second argument is that the onus on teachers to promote heterosexuality has not exactly led to classrooms being flooded with heterosexual pornographic materials. But reason had little place in the arsenal of arguments deployed by those who regard every aspect of same-sex love and affection, and every piece of evidence that gay men and lesbians can live happy, fulfilled lives, as 'pornographic'.

Although the Scottish Executive stuck to its pledge to proceed with the repeal of Section 28, the success of the homophobic lobby in polarising Scottish society around the issues and in tapping into pent-up anger at the erosion of heterosexist privilege sent a warning shot across the bows of the more cautious and conservative Labour administration at Westminster. Ever anxious to retain the votes of 'middle England' and to remain on good terms with the British establishment, the Blair government reacted to defeat in the House of Lords in February 2000 on Section 28 reform (in England and Wales) with a pledge to combine repeal of the Section with the introduction of new guidelines on sex education which would emphasise the importance of marriage. At the time of going to press, it was still unclear whether such guidelines would give privilege to heterosexual marriage over same-sex (and unmarried other-sex) relationships, and whether they would have statutory force. (The Scottish Executive had earlier disregarded statutory guidelines as Scotland does not have a single national curriculum in the same way as England and Wales.) If the answer to both these questions is in the affirmative then such guidelines would clearly constitute a new form of heterosexist discrimination.

The Sexual Offences Bill was opposed in the House of Lords in February 2000, but Home Secretary Jack Straw was now able to invoke the Parliament Act, over-riding the opposition of the Lords without the need for another vote in the House of Commons. This effectively guaranteed that an equal age of consent would be introduced later in 2000.

In Chapter 4 we saw that it can be argued that formal rights are meaningless without measures to tackle social prejudice and discrimination; rights which are guaranteed on paper can be easily undermined in practice. This is undoubtedly true; nevertheless, the establishment of equal rights before the law would appear to be a *sine qua non* of further progress towards sexual equality. It will not remove the problem of heterosexism but it would create a climate in which arguments for real equality and campaigns against exclusion could be taken to a new level. There is still the danger, that once a few token measures have been implemented, politicians will back away from pro-active measures needed to tackle bigotry, discrimination and bullying. Given the prevailing climate of depoliticisation within the lesbian and gay communities (examined in Chapter 4), and the reluctance of politicians to risk votes on 'minority' issues, there will be intense pressure on the relatively small number of committed lesbian, gay and bisexual activists to ensure that the heterosexist state does not attempt to impose a new version of the 1967 compromise: greater tolerance of difference but not acceptance of diversity.

Family policy and changing family realities

Weeks (1992) argues that legislation such as Section 28 was rooted in anxiety about the family. We have seen that this 'sacred institution' was seen by some conservative politicians and thinkers and their supporters as being under attack from rising divorce rates, single parentage, and 'alternative lifestyles'. The state, according to Weeks, was unwilling to concede the right of gay men and lesbians to assert the equal validity of their relationships with heterosexual relationships. Instead of being 'grateful' for the limited liberal tolerance conceded to date, gay men and lesbians had the audacity to push for equal citizenship rights. The coupling of sexuality with a claim to equal citizenship rights in this way is crucial, for it was seen as challenging the hegemony or dominance of one, proper, way of living: the married, two-parent heterosexual nuclear family. Section 28, from this perspective, can be seen as an attempt to restate that heterosexuality and marriage are socially necessary and moreover 'natural', 'God-given', and should be bolstered by state policy, and that homosexuality, within rigidly defined boundaries, may be tolerated but never accepted.

Weeks suggests that the family as an institution has been suffering from a crisis of identity and self-confidence. He identifies three processes: (1) demands made upon the family, and especially women, in times of rapid social change; these include an increasing burden of care on women; and increasing strain on married heterosexual relationships, partly the result of changes in society and the labour market, partly from the challenge of feminism; (2) the increased emotional pressure on the nuclear family, due to the decline in extended families and in the importance of the community. Many young couples move away from their parents' home, resulting in greater emotional demands on each other and concern over the security of the relationship. For policy-makers this has been reflected in a mounting concern over the behaviour of men; (3) increased diversity of family forms, which raises the question of value. What ought to change? What ought to be the ideal family? Should there be an ideal? This confusion creates moral panic. The greater the social change and social diversity, the more many people and policy-makers look to the family for resolution of otherwise intractable problems – social, political and personal. Indeed, the struggle over the family becomes in itself a fourth source of pressure on the family. As the state perceives a reinvention of the so-called 'normal' family – women staying at home, caring for the sick, and the elderly and the children – as a solution to the dilemma of how to reduce public spending on health and social security and how to reduce crime rates, so pressures on women mount. They are increasingly being forced to 'carry the can' for society's problems, and single mothers in particular find themselves stigmatised.

The changing role of women in society, the growth in the numbers of single mothers, and the existence of gay or lesbian relationships are seen by some conservative thinkers as threatening the social dominance of the 'normal family'. Such views influenced government policy during the Thatcher years. As Abbott and Wallace (1992: 117) point out, Thatcher did not develop an explicit and coherent family policy 'but did endorse a particular image of "the family"'. This was the notion of a family based on marriage with a strong father figure and a mother who looks after her children as her primary vocation. The Conservatives argued in their 1987 election that 'the origins of crime lie deep in society: in families where parents do not support or control their children' (quoted in Abbott and Wallace 1992: 117). In particular, lone parents were singled out for attack as the Conservative governments of the 1980s and early 1990s sought to reduce public spending on welfare and to 'remoralise' society. As Laws (1996: 60–1) argues, 'lone parents have been presented as a threat to others, either through competition for resources, or as a cause of various social problems'. In a much-quoted speech in 1993, government minister John Redwood accused some young women of getting pregnant 'with no apparent intention of even trying a marriage or stable relationship with the father of the child' and argued that in such cases it would be right to pursue the father for child maintenance. The speech invoked the spectre of anarchic and irresponsible male sexuality – the 'promiscuous male' who, for Roger Scruton, Ferdinand Mount, and other Conservative thinkers, must be constrained by marital law and custom, for the foundations of society will be undermined if he is let loose.

This was followed, as Laws points out, by a blitz of articles in the popular press accusing lone parents – more precisely, single mothers – of imposing an impossible financial burden on the country. This media campaign helped to create a climate in which, for example, it was widely believed (despite lack of clear evidence) that many young women deliberately get pregnant in order to skip the housing queue. The governmental response to this was the Housing Act (1996), which sought to reduce access to permanent housing for homeless families. Such families would henceforth have their needs met by temporary housing while allocation of permanent housing was solely via the local authority's waiting list. One of the effects, of course, was to make victims of abuse especially vulnerable.

Public opinion had been well prepared for the introduction of the Child Support Act (1991), perhaps the Conservatives' biggest contribution to family policy. This established a Child Support Agency (CSA) within the Department of Social Security, charged with the task of saving the Treasury money by pursuing absent parents (usually fathers) for payments which would then be deducted from the welfare benefits of the parents (usually mothers) bringing up the children. The CSA was to prove an extremely unpopular institution. Lone mothers benefited much less financially than had initially been hoped and were made financially dependent (to a degree) on the fathers of their children, from whom in many cases they had separated for very good reasons. Moreover, 'those in receipt of family credit supplemented by maintenance payments are especially vulnerable to maintenance shortfalls or cessation, since they cannot adjust the amounts of their family credit awards for up to six months' (Ford and Millar 1998: 16). Many fathers who had remarried and started second families found themselves facing heavy financial demands. By the mid-1990s, the CSA faced a barrage of criticism for administrative incompetence and stories of several suicides of men pursued for payments which they could not afford had appeared in the same newspapers which had clamoured for such an agency in the first place.

The Conservative Family Policy Group pressed for measures, including adjustments to the taxation system, to persuade married mothers to leave the workforce and stay at home. It was also urged that 'the family' should be 'encouraged' to take more responsibility for the care of the elderly (as well as the young). The NHS and Community Care Act (1990) effectively imposed a huge additional burden of care on many women. As Harding argues, 'Women have been assumed to be the dependents of males, to be out of the labour market – or easily able to leave it – and therefore available for caring duties at home. There is also evidence that female carers receive less support from the formal services than do male carers. In this sense the assumptions are patriarchal' (Harding 1996: 159).

The first years of the Labour government were clearly marked by debate and tensions within the cabinet over priorities where family policy is concerned. Journalists, commentators and feminist critics of New Labour identified a number of so-called 'Christian crusaders' within the cabinet, including Tony Blair, Jack Straw and junior Home Office minister Paul Boateng, whom Beatrix Campbell has referred to as 'pilots' of 'the marriage movement'. These ministers have been seen as pioneering a number of proposed changes which have presented marriage as a morally desirable state, and divorce or singlehood as of secondary moral worth.

For example, Home Secretary Jack Straw declared in July 1998 that strengthening the institution of marriage as a basis for bringing up children was a cornerstone of Labour's family policy. He claimed that couples who chose to get married were more likely to stay together and provide stability for children than couples who chose to cohabit. He made it clear that the Government saw the crisis of the traditional family – married heterosexual couples bringing up children – as a fundamental cause of social malaise and set out a series of proposals aimed unapologetically at strengthening the bonds of marriage. These included the establishment of a National Family and Parenting Institute with the power to accredit parenting groups throughout Britain, which in turn will organise parenting classes. Straw claimed that the intention was not to stigmatise single parents; indeed he acknowledged the good work done by many single parents and cohabiting couples in bringing up children. Yet critics certainly saw in his assertion that government policy would be based on a presumption that the stability which children needed was best provided by strengthening marriage an implicit view that single parenthood was very much a second-best option. When the National Family and Parenting Institute was finally launched in November 1999, its first chief executive, Mary MacLeod, was keen to stress that 'there are lots of different ways in all kinds of families to raise happy children who become decent adults' (*The Guardian*, 24 November 1999). But much will depend on the Institute's relationship with its paymaster, the Home Office.

Straw, despite his support for measures such as an equal age of consent for gay and straight people, certainly made no effort to hide his conservative approach to gay and lesbian families. He expressed his personal opposition to gay adoptions and to lesbian couples receiving IVF treatment when he launched the government consultation paper on the family in November 1998. His decision to spell out his personal limits as to acceptable family forms greatly angered gay and lesbian groups and lone parents groups. Stonewall, for example, accused him of being out of line with stated Labour Party commitments, and stigmatising parents or potential adoptive or foster parents solely on the grounds of their sexuality. The lone parents group *Gingerbread* warned Straw that it was not possible to give a privileged position to heterosexual marriage without stigmatising lone parents or alternative families (*The Guardian*, 5 November 1998). The Liberal Democrats also warned against stigmatising children who are not brought up in 'Government approved relationships' (*The Guardian*, 5 November 1998).

The November 1998 consultation paper, objectionable as certain of its aspects and Straw's rhetoric were to lone parents and gay groups, did not go as far as a proposal from one senior New Labour figure – for the introduction of state dowries for heterosexual couples getting married. This proposal was that taxpayers' money should be used to support heterosexuality and support marriage by giving several thousands of pounds to heterosexual couples who agree to embark on married life. This piece of social engineering – which would go beyond anything the previous Conservative administration contemplated – would clearly discriminate against both lesbian and gay people and unmarried heterosexual couples. Ironically, its author was reported to be Peter Mandelson.

Tensions within the cabinet – or at least clear differences in approach and emphasis – were evident from the fact that within a week of the launch of the consultation paper by Jack Straw and Paul Boateng in November 1998, the newly appointed Ministers for Women, Baroness Jay and Tessa Jowell, launched new research evidence showing how far behind women still are in terms of the gender pay gap. The key point is that the women's ministers had no comforting rhetoric about how marriage and family values would solve social problems; instead they placed the emphasis squarely on equal pay and fighting sexism. Feminist journalist Polly Toynbee urged them to 'snatch back the entire family policy' from the 'ill-judged' pro-marriage moralising of 'those Christian ministers, Straw, Boateng and Blair, who see marriage as a sacrament' (*The Guardian*, 9 November 1998).

A new Modernisation of Justice Bill proposes reforms to the Family Law Act which should come into effect in 2000. The reforms will require couples seeking divorce to attend an information meeting, then wait three months before filing for divorce, then be required to attend further meetings aimed at mediation, reconciliation and saving the marriage. Most couples with children will have to wait eighteen months. The proposals have been criticised by lawyers and others as prolonging the agony of divorce proceedings, wasting public money, and extending the nanny state by lecturing to couples who have already made their minds up about what is best for them.

In Scotland a document, Improving Scottish Family Law, was issued on 24 March 1999 and invited input from the public on a wide range of issues including the law concerning single parents, the rights and responsibilities of unmarried fathers, and domestic violence. Perhaps the most central proposal concerned reform of the divorce law in Scotland. The document proposed cutting to one year the time taken for couples consenting to a divorce, and reducing from five years to two the time taken where one party does not consent. The document was, however, presented in the sort of moralising and pro-marriage language which has become characteristic of New Labour. The Scottish Office briefed journalists on its release that 'this is not to make divorce easier' and that couples seeking divorce would be offered counselling and mediation as in England and Wales (*The Guardian*, 24 March 1999).

As regards the Child Support Agency, the government clearly recognises the need for reform, but has rejected calls for the CSA's abolition. Media reports in January 1998 that the CSA was to be scrapped and replaced 'by a new organisation with special powers to investigate the incomes of absent fathers and fine them a flat rate "child levy"' (*Scotland on Sunday*, 25 January 1998) proved premature. In July 1998 the government published plans to force absent fathers to pay up to twenty-five per cent of their take-home pay in child maintenance. The number of families expected to be covered will reach one million in 2001. Mothers on benefits will be given a financial incentive to cooperate with the CSA – seventy per cent of lone mothers at present do not cooperate – by being allowed to keep an additional ten pounds of the maintenance per week. A new formula will see absent parents pay on a sliding scale, according to the number of children involved in both first and second families, instead of paying a flat rate. The proposed reforms – which are supposed to simplify the system and make it fairer – are scheduled to come into effect in 2001. Some problems clearly remain. About one in four mothers will be worse off. Of the thirty per cent of absent parents due to pay more, a disproportionate number are less well-off (*The Guardian*, 7 July 1998). The government announced a further change in late 1999 – fines of £1,000 for parents who fail to pay maintenance.

Partly in response to these findings, further changes were announced in March 1999. The Government announced that the CSA would be relieved of more than 180,000 cases – more than a fifth of its workload – as lone parents receiving a state top-up of low earnings will no longer be required to cooperate with the Agency. The lone parents affected are to be allowed to keep all child maintenance paid by a former partner (*The Guardian*, 8 March 1999). These changes were warmly welcomed by welfare groups and by the Scottish and the National Councils for One Parent Families. At the same time, the CSA is to receive the power to access confidential tax files of absent parents and to deduct monies which they owe directly from their pay packets (*Independent on Sunday*, 21 March 1999).

Concern with reducing the costs of welfare has continued to influence the thinking of the Labour government. Labour in office has demonstrated its belief that 'policy should encourage, but not compel, mothers into employment where possible' (Ford and Millar 1998: 14).

However, the forms of 'encouragement' included cuts to lone parent benefits in December 1997, which brought allegations that the government was targeting one of the poorest and most vulnerable groups in society. The measure reduced the benefit entitlement of new claimants amongst lone parents. Forty-seven Labour MPs rebelled against the cut.

Since then, the government has sought to reassure its supporters that it is committed to targeting poverty, not hitting the poor, and it has cited measures designed to help lone parents out of the poverty trap, such as paying seventy per cent of child care costs for families whose annual income is under £20,000, to enable people to return to work. The success of this measure will depend on whether adequate child care is available, and on whether work is available. In any case, more than six million families with children earn less than £20,000 and in theory stand to benefit from the measure which poverty campaigners acclaimed as one of the most significant redistributive measures in recent decades. A 'new deal for lone parents' was launched in October 1998 with the task of assisting lone parents back into work through providing advice and training yet, in the first year of its operation, only 18,000 out of almost two million lone parents had found work in this way.

In 1998–9 the Chancellor of the Exchequer, Gordon Brown – one of the senior cabinet ministers who has consistently stayed clear of moralising rhetoric about family values and concentrated on practical help to the poorest families – introduced many measures designed to help low-income families. These include a Working Families Tax Credit which incorporates a childcare credit worth seventy per cent of eligible registered childcare costs up to a ceiling of £100 for one child and £120 for two or more, and rises in child benefit. In general these measures have been warmly welcomed by charities and campaigners for lone parents and the poor.

In a highly significant move, the Chancellor also announced the abolition of the married couple's tax allowance from April 2000. Making it clear that his priority was children, and not marriage *per se*, Gordon Brown announced its replacement by a children's tax credit which will redirect resources to families with children. The identification of poverty as the main social problem which needs to be tackled – and not the fact that people choose not to get married – and the fact that resources are to be directed towards children in general and not heterosexual marriage *per se* is important. It suggests that, despite the rhetoric of several of his cabinet colleagues, budgetary policy under Chancellor Brown is not determined by the sort of pro-marriage moralising which many lone parents and cohabiting couples find offensive and threatening.

Labour also introduced an Employment Relations Act 1999 which raises paid maternity leave from fourteen to eighteen weeks. In addition, unpaid parental leave of three months for both biological and adopting parents, spread over several years, became law. The government hailed these measures as 'family friendly'. However, the measures were described by feminist commentator Yvonne Roberts as 'little more than a lick of paint on the sweatshop privy – attractive but insufficient' (*The Guardian*, 26 January 1999). She pointed out that research in the EU shows that, without pay, there is low take-up of such leave and almost none amongst fathers. Poverty campaigners pointed out that unpaid leave effectively excludes low earners (*The Guardian*, 28 January 1999).

The carrot-and-stick combination of practical assistance and moralising, penalising measures continues. In October 1998 the Social Security secretary Alastair Darling announced measures to compel lone parents to attend job centres for interviews by threatening to withdraw their benefits. The threat brought accusations from the Liberal Democrats that the government was seeking to 'punish children and families' and from others that the government was resorting to bully-boy tactics which penalised those least able to fight back (*The Guardian*, 27 October 1998).

Although the Labour government demonstrates significant differences in emphasis and direction of family policy from its Conservative predecessor, a clear and consistent message is hard to detect. The government seems divided between those who support full acceptance of the diverse range of families that characterise contemporary society and those who would like to emphasise a preference for traditional heterosexual marriage, between those who articulate family policy in religious-inspired and moralising language and those who prefer the language of secular humanism, and between a desire to tackle gendered poverty and gendered inequality and a reluctance to increase social welfare costs or to raise taxes.

State responses to sexual violence

According to Edwards (1996: 178), 'there is now extensive research showing that, in Western countries, the question of evidence and the role of the complainant, who is also the principal and often the only witness, are handled by police and the courts in cases of rape quite differently from other kinds of assault. A deep-seated belief that accusations of rape are easily made and often false seems to persist and this then justifies treating the woman (complainant/victim/survivor) as though it were she who were on trial'. The process of reporting and prosecuting a rape or serious sexual assault is fraught with myths and stereotypes about gendered sexual behaviour which can add to the trauma endured by the victim and often result in an acquittal if the case gets to court. The institutions of the state – the police and judiciary above all – are not only dominated by men numerically, but also often reflect masculinist assumptions about 'norms' of sexual behaviour. Sue Lees reports that 'the problem in part lies in the [police] force's failure to change its composition to reflect the community. Women still represent only fourteen per cent' (Lees 1999). Likewise, the judiciary is overwhelmingly male and tends to be drawn from very narrow social strata. As Lees argues, these men are predominantly white, upper-class, and educated in single-sex public schools which 'tend to foster extreme forms of masculinity' (Lees 1996: 246).

The problems which result from this patriarchal domination of key state institutions can be illustrated by considering some of the difficulties which victims of sexual violence face, first when they report the incident to the police and later, if a prosecution results (which in many cases it does not), at the hands of the judicial system.

Ward (1995: 26) argues that police procedure in cases of reported rapes and other crimes of sexual violence often add considerably to the pain of the victim. The police may refuse to believe that a rape or sexual assault has taken place unless there is physical evidence of severe violence; police officers and police surgeons have, on occasion, been accused of trivialising women's accounts of their ordeal. The police may also, in order to ensure that there is sufficient evidence to sustain a prosecution and that the victim will prove a credible witness in court, feel obliged to 'lean heavily' on the victim, tearing her story to shreds. As a result, many women in this situation feel dehumanised. One of those interviewed by Ward declared: 'the rape was probably the least traumatic incident of the whole evening. If I'm ever raped again I wouldn't report to the police because of all the degradation'.

Some British police forces have made significant changes to their practice, introducing, for example, special suites where victims of rape and sexual violence are received, examined and interviewed away from intimidating surroundings of ordinary police rooms. These facilities often include medical examination rooms and shower rooms. Such innovations are, however, limited by pressure on resources. Given such pressure, women who are the victims of sexual violence are not always seen as a top priority by a patriarchal institution.

There is also evidence from some police forces of changes in police attitudes and training. Some forces have developed interviewing skills and educate officers about the impact of crimes of sexual violence. Officers may also work alongside other services such as Rape Crisis

Centres and Victims' Support groups. However, responses to these initiatives have been mixed. Overwhelmingly the officers assigned to this sort of work are female and some surveys suggest that the message sent to male police officers is that sexual violence against women is marginal within police culture, and that dealing with such crimes is low status.

Similarly, police attitudes have often led to crimes of sexual violence or battering in the home – so-called domestic violence – being under-reported and under-prosecuted. Traditionally such crimes have been dismissed by many police officers as 'domestics', private affairs between husband and wife which require no further action. Women in such situations often end up isolated and unsupported. According to Kelly (1989: 67), '. . . studies of police response reveal that domestic violence is not seen as "serious" police duties, despite evidence that a high proportion of domestic homicides involve households known to the police for prior violence'. Only with a House of Lords ruling in 1991 did rape within marriage become a criminal offence in the UK. Masculinist assumptions that a man has the right to 'be the boss' in his own house – even if this involves beating, battering or sexually abusing his female partner (or children) – remain widespread. Kelly (1989: 148) points out for example that the police and judiciary are more likely to take seriously attacks by complete strangers and to regard non-stranger rape as not rape at all. Such is the strength of traditional assumptions and beliefs about a man's 'conjugal rights' that many women, also, may accept forced sex within marriage – or beatings – as part of the marital contract. Lees (1996: 216) cites research which shows that class differentials are important in explaining discrepancies in the reporting of rape within marriage. This research suggests that women from higher social classes are less likely to accept that forced sex within marriage is rape or to risk incurring stigma by reporting it to the police or other agencies.

The British Crime Survey in 1983 estimated that only seven per cent of sexual assaults were reported to the police. More recent figures show that the percentage of reported assaults resulting in a conviction is actually falling. Lees (1996: 237–8) quotes Home Office figures which show that the number of men convicted of rape in 1994 was lower than the number convicted in 1985, despite the fact that the number of reported rapes had trebled. Moreover, the number of rape cases dropped as 'unwinnable' had trebled between 1985 and 1994. Not surprisingly Lees concludes that '. . . the image conveyed by the judiciary is that . . . the main problem is to protect men from false allegations'.

It was only in 1994 that the offence of male rape was recognised in

English law; it is still not recognised in Scottish law. A man who has been raped by another man faces many disincentives when considering whether to report the attack to the police. He is likely to be interrogated as to why he didn't fight back, or fight hard enough. He may often be questioned about his sexuality – the masculinist assumption being that he must be gay and must have 'asked for it' by sexually propositioning the attacker. If he is gay, he may well struggle to have the attack taken seriously, and may feel that his private life and sexuality are under investigation, rather than the alleged attack.

Whenever a case of rape or sexual violence actually makes it to court, the alleged victim (usually a woman) faces what is often a gruelling ordeal at the hands of the defence counsel, and sometimes also the judge. The prosecution must prove the absence of consent, which can often be extremely difficult. A problem often arises between 'consent' and 'submission', where a woman submitted to sex because she feared the consequences of failing to do so. In such cases a judge may direct the jury but there are no clear guidelines on distinguishing those threats of pressures which would vitiate consent from those which would not. The whole concept of 'consent' is problematic for many feminist writers on gendered power relations. As both Edwards (1996) and Jamieson (1996) argue, the 'mistaken belief in consent' defence is common in rape trials and the use of binary oppositional categories – consent/non-consent, active/passive – tends to simplify and confuse. A woman's experience of sexual relations may well be very different from a man's, yet the masculinist assumption so often present in rape trials is that if she did not clearly and loudly say 'No', and 'actively' resist the sexual attack, then she can be presumed to have welcomed it. In this scenario, the woman's body is assumed to be 'available' to the man unless she can prove otherwise. Indeed, in the UK the courts have upheld a defence of *unreasonable* mistaken belief in consent – that is, men have walked free because they were found to have 'believed' the woman consented to sex even where this belief was held to be un-reasonable. In such cases, what the male defendant asserts to have been his state of mind carries more weight than the woman's experience. As Jamieson (1996: 70) argues, this complete denial of female will demon-strates clearly the patriarchal nature of the law in such cases.

Another problem is that the defence counsel in rape trials will inevitably seek to undermine the alleged victim's credibility by drag-ging her previous sexual history through the courtroom or by playing on the way she dresses or talks to suggest that she is of 'low sexual morals'. A man's previous sexual history – if, for example, he has previous convictions for rape or sexual assault – is not admissible as evidence. The introduction of an alleged victim's sexual history is left to the discretion of the trial judge; but if the judge refuses to allow such 'evidence' this can lead to the conviction being quashed at appeal. In such areas as this, Britain has fallen behind countries such as Australia where most states consider past sexual history to be inadmissible as evidence and where judges have to warn against prejudices against women who do not report the crime of rape immediately, introducing an appreciation of Rape Trauma Syndrome.

Such is the trauma which many women face in rape trials that the trial itself has sometimes been described as a 'second rape'. The woman in such a situation has to achieve the impossible: she has to relive the horrifying experience of assault and subject herself to intensive, personal and often humiliating cross-examination and yet retain her composure. She must not appear too calm or she risks being stereotyped as a 'hard-faced bitch', nor must she become too tearful or she risks being portrayed as 'hysterical' and therefore an unreliable witness.

Lees has suggested a number of reforms to judicial practice which might improve the situation for victims of crimes of sexual violence. These include: radical reform of the Court of Appeal, the introduction of a stringent definition of the grounds for appeal, and the introduction of a measure of accountability on the part of the judiciary, perhaps with the appointment of a Royal Commission which would, Lee proposes, work with representatives of Rape Crisis Centres, survivors' groups and so on. Better specialised training of trial judges, curtailment of judges' discretion in admitting women's past sexual histories as evidence, broadening the definition of corroboration, admitting victim impact evidence, clarifying judges' powers to give directions to juries, allowing alleged victims to give evidence without having to directly face their alleged attackers, and establishing an effective complaints procedure would also help. She also advocates reform of the Crown Prosecution Service to make it more accountable for its decisions in rape cases. Administrative reforms which would benefit victims of rape and sexual violence could include: better safeguards to prevent witness statements being used as pornography in prisons, improved medical services with pregnancy, HIV and STD counselling, better reception facilities for victims in courts, and monitoring of acquittal rates throughout the country. She also recommends a review of the definition of both 'rape' and 'consent' – 'one possibility is to use some external criteria such as whether the reasonable person should have known that the woman was not consenting, (Lees, 1996: 250–6).

There are some signs that the Labour government is listening. In February 1998 the government adopted a Violence Against Women strategy – the first such strategy in the UK. The first project commissioned as part of this strategy has been a national survey of women's refuges to establish whether provision for victims of domestic violence is adequate (*The Guardian*, 26 February 1998). A review of how domestic and sexual violence are dealt with by the Crown Prosecution Service, the Courts, prisons and the police has also been launched. And a review of women's safety in public spaces – addressing issues such as street lighting, safety on public transport and workplace harassment has been promised. In November 1998 the government launched the *Delivering for Women* strategy which amongst other measures promised a crackdown on domestic violence, including support for a Zero Tolerance advertising campaign. Moreover, the government introduced measures in late 1998 to remove the right of rape defendants to cross-examine their alleged victims personally, and to restrict the circumstances under which women can be cross-examined on their sexual history. Women's groups continue to call for a complete ban on the admissibility of such evidence. The government also commissioned work on service provision to women experiencing domestic violence in Scotland, allocating eight million pounds in Scotland, and supported initiatives in England and Wales which aimed at coordinating examples of best practice and planned government action.

These are piecemeal reforms and much will depend on how consistently they are followed through, how well initiatives are financed and resourced, and how serious politicians are at tackling the fundamental problem – the masculinist assumptions which permeate state institutions and the wholly unrepresentative nature of these institutions in gender terms.

Select bibliography

This guide to further reading is not intended to be exhaustive. The first section lists some general readers or texts, which cover a multitude of topics and issues, and the other sections follow the structure of the book.

Readers and general texts

Abbott, Pamela, and Wallace, Claire (eds) (1991), *Gender, Power and Sexuality*, Basingstoke: Macmillan.

Adkins, Lisa, and Holland, Janet (eds) (1996), *Sex, Sensibility and the Gendered Body*, Basingstoke: St Martin's Press.

Adkins, Lisa, and Merchant, Vicki (eds) (1996), *Sexualizing the Social: Power and the Organization of Sexuality*, Basingstoke: St Martin's Press.

Brook, Barbara (1999), *Feminist Perspectives on the Body*, London: Longman.

Bryson, Valerie (1992), *Feminist Political Theory: An Introduction*, Basingstoke: Macmillan.

Bryson, Valerie (1999), *Feminist Debates: Issues of Theory and Political Practice*, Basingstoke: Macmillan.

Campbell, Kate (ed.) (1992), *Critical Feminism: Arguments in the Discipline*, Buckingham: Open University Press.

Carver, Terrell, and Mottier, Veronique (1998), *The Politics of Sexuality*, London: Routledge.

Connell, Robert (1987), *Gender and Power: Society, the Person and Sexual Politics*, Cambridge: Polity Press/Blackwell.

Corrin, Chris (1999), *Feminist Perspectives on Politics*, London: Longman.

Crowley, Helen, and Himmelweit, Susan (eds) (1991), *Knowing Women: Feminism and Knowledge*, Cambridge: Open University Press/Polity Press.

de Lauretis, Teresa (1988), *Feminist Studies, Critical Studies*, Basingstoke: Macmillan.

Evans, Judith (1995), *Feminist Theory Today: an Introduction to Second Wave Feminism*, London: Sage Publications.

Feminist Review (1987), *Sexuality: a Reader*, London: Virago.

Hawkes, Gail (1996), *A Sociology of Sex and Sexuality*, Buckingham: Open University Press.

Humm, Maggie (1992), *Feminisms: a Reader*, London: Harvester Wheatsheaf.

Jackson, Stevi (ed.) (1993), *Women's Studies: a Reader*, London: Harvester Wheatsheaf.

Jackson, Stevi, and Scott, Sue (eds) (1996), *Feminism and Sexuality: a Reader*, Edinburgh: Edinburgh University Press.

Jackson, Stevi, and Jones, Jackie (eds) (1998), *Contemporary Feminist Theories*, Edinburgh: Edinburgh University Press.

Kemp, Sandra, and Squires, Judith (eds) (1997), *Feminisms*, Oxford: Oxford University Press.

Kirkup, Gill, and Smith Keller, Laurie (eds) (1992), *Inventing Women: Science, Technology and Gender*, Cambridge: Polity Press/Open University Press.

McDowell, Linda, and Pringle, Rosemary (eds) (1992), *Defining Women: Social Institutions and Gender Divisions*, Cambridge: Polity Press/Open University Press.

McLaren, Angus (1999), *Twentieth Century Sexuality: a History*, Oxford: Blackwell.

Nye, Robert (ed.) (1999), *Sexuality*, Oxford: Oxford University Press.

Parker, Richard and Aggleton, Peter (eds) (1999), *Culture, Society and Sexuality*, London: UCL Press.

Phillips, Anne (1998), *Feminism and Politics*, Oxford: Oxford University Press.

Porter, Elizabeth (1999), *Feminist Perspectives on Ethics*, London: Longman.

Price, Janet and Shildrick, Margrit (eds) (1999), *Feminist Theory and the Body*, Edinburgh: Edinburgh University Press.

Richardson, Diane, and Robinson, Victoria (1992), *Introducing Women's Studies*, London: Macmillan.

Segal, Lynne (1987), *Is the Future Female? Troubled Thoughts on Contemporary Feminism*, London: Virago.

Segal, Lynne (ed.) (1997), *New Sexual Agendas*, Basingstoke: Macmillan.

Weeks, Jeffrey (1994), *The Lesser Evil and the Greater Good: the Theory and Politics of Social Diversity*, London: Rivers Oram Press.

Weeks, Jeffrey, and Holland, Janet (eds) (1996), *Sexual Cultures: Communities, Values and Intimacy*, Basingstoke: St Martin's Press.

Part I Foundations
Chapter 1 Theoretical and historical foundations

General reading

Bland, Lucy, and Mort, Frank (1997), 'Thinking Sex Historically', in Segal (ed.), *New Sexual Agendas*, Basingstoke: Macmillan, pp. 17–31.

Connell, Robert (1997), 'Sexual Revolution', in Segal (ed.), *New Sexual Agendas*, Basingstoke: Macmillan, pp. 60–76.

Hall, Lesley (1997), 'Heroes or Villains? Reconsidering British *fin de siècle* Sexology', in Segal (ed.), *New Sexual Agendas*, Basingstoke: Macmillan, pp. 3–16.

Humphries, Steven (1988), *A Secret World of Sex; Forbidden fruit – the British experience*, London: Sidgwick and Jackson.
Lerner, Gerda (1986), *The Creation of Patriarchy*, Oxford: Oxford University Press.
Plummer, Ken (1994), *Telling Sexual Stories*, London: Routledge.
Spender, Dale (1980), *Man–Made Language*, London: Pandora.
Weeks, Jeffrey (1986), *Sexuality*, London: Routledge.
Weeks, Jeffrey (1989), *Sexuality and its Discontents*, London: Routledge.
Weeks, Jeffrey (1989), *Sex, Politics and Society*, second edition, London: Longman.
Weeks, Jeffrey (1991), *Against Nature: Essays on History, Sexuality and Identity*, London: Rivers Oram Press.
Weeks, Jeffrey (1997), 'Sexual Values Revisited', in Segal (ed.), *New Sexual Agendas*, Basingstoke: Macmillan, pp. 43–59.
Zeldin, Theodore (1995), *An Intimate History of Humanity*, London: Minerva.

Introduction

Evans, David (1993), *Sexual Citizenship: the Material Construction of Sexualities*, London: Routledge.
Tatchell, Peter (1996), 'It's Just a Phase: Why Homosexuality is Doomed', in Simpson (ed.), *Anti-Gay*, London: Cassell.

Social constructionism versus biology

Channel Four (1992), *Born That Way? The Biological Basis of Homosexuality*, London: Channel Four Publications.
Ellis, Havelock (1933), *The Psychology of Sex*, London: William Heinemann.
Ellis, Havelock (1934), *Man and Woman: a Study of Secondary and Tertiary Sexual Characteristics*, London: William Heinemann.
Fausto–Sterling, Anne (1992), *Myths of Gender: Biological Theories about Men and Women*, New York, NY: Basic Books.
Featherstone, Mike, Hepworth, Mike, and Turner, Bryan S. (eds) (1991), *The Body: Social Process and Cultural Theory*, London: Sage Publications.
Gazzaniga, Michael (1992), *Nature's Mind: the Biological Roots of Thinking. Emotions, Sexuality, Language and Intelligence*, Harmondsworth: Penguin Books.
Gould, Stephen Jay (1995), *Adam's Navel*, Harmondsworth: Penguin Books.
Hamer, Dean and Copeland, Peter (1995), *The Science of Desire: the Search for the Gay Gene and the Biology of Behavior*, New York, NY: Touchstone.
Jackson, Stevi (1996a), 'The Social Construction of Female Sexuality', in Jackson and Scott (eds), *Feminism and Sexuality*, Edinburgh: Edinburgh University Press.
Jacobus, Mary, Fox Keller, Evelyn, and Shuttleworth, Sally (1990), *Body Politics: Women and the Discourses of Science*, London: Routledge.
Laqueur, Thomas (1990), *Making Sex: Body and Gender from the Greeks to Freud*, Cambridge, MA: Harvard University Press.

Le Vay, Simon (1993), *The Sexual Brain*, London: MIT Press.

Maynard, Mary (ed.) (1997), *Science and the Construction of Women*, London: UCL Press.

McKnight, Jim (1997), *Straight Science? Homosexuality, Evolution and Adaptation*, London: Routledge.

Moir, Anne and Moir, Bill (1999), *Why Men Don't Iron*, London: HarperCollins.

Poovey, Mary (1987), 'Scenes of an Indelicate Character: the Medical "Treatment" of Victorian Women', in Gallagher, Catherine, and Laqueur, Thomas (eds), *The Making of the Modern Body: Sexuality and Society in the Nineteenth Century*, Berkeley: University of California Press.

Porter, Roy, and Teich, Mikulas (1994), *Sexual Knowledge, Sexual Science: the History of Attitudes to Sexuality*, Cambridge: Cambridge University Press.

Potts, Annie (1998), 'The science/fiction of sex: John Gray's Mars and Venus in the Bedroom', *Sexualities*, vol. 1, no. 2, May.

Rhode, Deborah L. (1990), Theoretical Perspectives on Sexual Difference, London: Yale University Press.

Rosario, Vernon (1997), *Science and Homosexualities*, London: Routledge.

Rose, Hilary (1996) 'Gay Brains, Gay Genes and Feminist Science Theory', in Weeks and Holland (eds), *Sexual Cultures: Communities, Values and Intimacy*, Basingstoke: Macmillan, pp. 53–72.

Scruton, Roger (1987), *Sexual Desire: a Philosophical Investigation*, London: The Free Press.

Stein, Edward (1993), *Forms of Desire: Sexual Orientation and the Social Constructionist Controversy*, London: Routledge.

Tiefer, Leonore (1993), *Sex is not a Natural Act*, Boulder, CO: Westview Press.

Vance, Carole (1992), 'Social Construction Theory', in Bocock & Thompson (eds), *Social and Cultural Forms of Modernity*, Oxford: Basil Blackwell, pp. 257–9.

Vines, Gail (1993), 'All in the Genes', *Everywoman*, November.

Weeks, Jeffrey (1995), *Invented Moralities: Sexual Values in an Age of Uncertainty*, Cambridge: Polity Press.

Weitz, Shirley (1977), *Sex Roles*, Oxford: Oxford University Press.

Wittig, Monique (1992), *The Straight Mind and Other Essays*, London: Harvester Wheatsheaf.

The work of Michel Foucault: tensions between Foucault and feminism

Acker, Joan (1989), 'The problem with patriarchy', *Sociology*, vol. 23, no. 2.

Assiter, Alison (1993), 'Essentially Sex: a New Look', in Assiter, Alison and Carol, Avedon (eds), *Bad Girls and Dirty Pictures*, London: Pluto Press, pp. 88–104.

Bristow, Joseph (1997), *Sexuality*, London: Routledge.

Foucault, Michel (1981), *The History of Sexuality: Volume One: an Introduction*, London: Pelican.

Foucault, Michel (1987), *The History of Sexuality: Volume Two: the Use of Pleasure*, London: Pelican.

Foucault, Michel (1988), *The History of Sexuality: Volume Three: the Care of the Self*, London: Pelican.

Grant, Linda (1993), *Sexing the Millennium: Women and the Sexual Revolution*, London: Grove Press.

Halperin, David M. (1995), *Saint Foucault: Towards a Gay Hagiography*, Oxford: Oxford University Press.

Hekman, Susan (ed.) (1996), *Feminist Interpretations of Michel Foucault*, Philadelphia, PA: Pennsylvania State University Press.

Jackson, Stevi (1996), 'Heterosexuality as a Problem for Feminist Theory', in Adkins and Merchant (eds), *Sexualizing the Social: Power and the Organization of Sexuality*, Basingstoke: Macmillan, pp. 15–34.

Jackson, Stevi (1996a), 'The Social Construction of Female Sexuality', in Jackson and Scott (eds), *Feminism and Sexuality*, Edinburgh: Edinburgh University Press.

McIntosh, Mary (1993), 'Queer Theory and the War of the Sexes', in Bristow and Wilson (eds), *Activating Theory: Lesbian, Gay, Bisexual Politics*, London: Lawrence and Wishart.

McNay, Lois (1992), *Foucault and Feminism*, Cambridge: Polity Press.

McNay, Lois (1994), *Foucault: a Critical Introduction*, Cambridge: Polity Press.

Ramazanoglu, Caroline (1993), *Up Against Foucault*, London: Routledge.

Sawicki, Jana (1991), *Disciplining Foucault: Feminism, Power and the Body*, London: Routledge.

Walby, Sylvia (1989), 'Theorising patriarchy', *Sociology*, vol. 23, no. 2.

Walby, Sylvia (1990), *Theorising Patriarchy*, Oxford: Blackwell.

Weeks, Jeffrey (1991), 'The Uses and Abuses of Michel Foucault' in Weeks, *Against Nature: Essays on History, Sexuality and Identity*, London: Rivers Oram Press, pp. 157–69.

Weeks, Jeffrey (1992), 'The Body and Sexuality', in Bocock and Thompson (eds), *Social and Cultural Forms of Modernity*, Cambridge: Polity Press, pp. 220–56.

Weeks, Jeffrey (1997), 'Sexual Values Revisited', in Segal (ed.), *New Sexual Agendas*, Basingstoke: Macmillan, pp. 43–59.

The impact and limits of 'queer theory'

Bristow, Joseph (1997), *Sexuality*, London: Routledge.

Butler, Judith (1990), *Gender Trouble: Feminism and the Subversion of Identity*, London: Routledge.

Butler, Judith (1993), *Bodies That Matter: on the Discursive Limits of "Sex"*, London: Routledge.

Butler, Judith (1997), *Excitable Speech: a Politics of the Performative*, London: Routledge.

de Lauretis, Teresa (ed.) (1991), *Queer Theory: Lesbian and Gay Sexualities*, Bloomington, IN: Indiana University Press.

Dollimore, Jonathan (1991), *Sexual Dissidence: Augustine to Wilde, Freud to Foucault*, Oxford: Oxford University Press.

Edwards, Tim (1998), 'Queer Fears: Against the Cultural Turn', *Sexualities*, 1, 4, November.

Hood–Williams, John, and Cealey Harrison, Wendy (1998), 'Trouble with Gender', *Sociological Review*, vol. 46, no. 1.

Humphrey, Jill (1999), 'To Queer or Not to Queer a Lesbian and Gay Group? Sexual and Gendered Politics at the Turn of the Century', *Sexualities*, 2, 2, May.

Jarman, Derek (1993), *At Your Own Risk*, London: Vintage Publishers.

Jackson, Stevi (1996a), 'The Social Construction of Female Sexuality', in Jackson and Scott (eds), *Feminism and Sexuality*, Edinburgh: Edinburgh University Press.

McIntosh, Mary (1993), 'Queer Theory and the War of the Sexes', in Bristow and Wilson (eds), *Activating Theory: Lesbian, Gay, Bisexual Politics*, London: Lawrence and Wishart, pp. 30–52.

Manning, Toby (1996), 'Gay Culture: Who Needs It?', in Simpson (ed.), *Anti-Gay*, London: Cassell, pp. 98–117.

Merck, Mandy (1997), 'Death Camp: Feminism vs Queer Theory', in Segal, (ed.), *New Sexual Agendas*, Basingstoke: Macmillan, pp. 232–7.

Parnaby, Julia (1993), 'Queer Straits', *Trouble and Strife: the Radical Feminist Magazine*, no. 26, Summer.

Phelan, Shane (1996), *Playing with Fire: Queer Politics, Queer Theories*, London: Routledge.

Sedgwick, Eve Kosofsky (1991), *Epistemology of the Closet*, Harmondsworth: Penguin Books.

Seidman, Steven (ed.) (1996), *Queer Theory/Sociology*, Oxford: Basil Blackwell.

Sinfield, Alan (1997), 'Queer Identities and the Ethnicity Model', in Segal, (ed.), *New Sexual Agendas*, Basingstoke: Macmillan, pp. 196–204.

Spargo, Tamsin (1999), *Foucault and Queer Theory*, Cambridge: Icon Books.

Tatchell, Peter (1992), 'Do us a favour, call us Queer', *The Independent*, 26 July.

Tatchell, Peter (1996), 'It's Just a Phase: Why Homosexuality is Doomed', in Simpson (ed.), *Anti-Gay*, London: Cassell, pp. 35–54.

Weed, Elizabeth and Schor, Naomi (eds) (1997), *Feminism Meets Queer Theory*, Bloomington: Indiana University Press.

Sex, gender, sexuality: terminology

Acker, Joan (1989), 'The problem with patriarchy', *Sociology*, vol. 23, no. 2.

Allen, Sheila and Leonard, Diana (1996), 'From Sexual Divisions to Sexualities: Changing Sociological Agendas', in Weeks and Holland (eds), *Sexual Cultures: Communities, Values and Intimacy*, Basingstoke: Macmillan, pp. 17–33.

Burkitt, Ian (1998), 'Sexuality and Gender: from a Discursive to a Relationship Analysis', *Sociological Review*, vol. 46, no. 3.

Carver, Terrell (1995), *Gender is Not a Synonym for Women*, New York, NY: Lynne Rienner Publishers.

Connell, Robert (1985), 'Theorising gender', *Sociology*, vol. 19, no. 2.

Hawkes, Gail (1996), *A Sociology of Sex and Sexuality*, Buckingham: Open University Press.

Hood–Williams, John (1996), 'Goodbye to Sex and Gender', *Sociological Review*, vol. 44, no. 1.

Hood–Williams, John (1997), 'Real Sex, Fake Gender: a Reply to Robert Willmott', *Sociological Review*, vol. 45, no. 1.

Jackson, Stevi, and Scott, Sue (eds) (1996), *Feminism and Sexuality: a Reader*, Edinburgh: Edinburgh University Press.

Laqueur, Thomas (1990), *Making Sex: Body and Gender from the Greeks to Freud*, Cambridge, MA: Harvard University Press.

Oakley, Ann (1972), *Sex, Gender and Society*, London: Maurice Temple Smith.

Walby, Sylvia (1988), 'Gender politics and social theory', *Sociology*, vol. 22, no. 2.

Walby, Sylvia (1989), 'Theorising patriarchy', *Sociology*, vol. 23, no. 2.

Walby, Sylvia (1990), *Theorising Patriarchy*, Oxford: Blackwell.

Willmott, Robert (1996), 'Resisting sex/gender conflation: a rejoinder to John Hood-Williams', *Sociological Review*, vol. 44, no. 2.

Part II Sexualities, genders
Chapter 2 Modern sexualities and their meanings

General reading

Caplan, Pat (ed.) (1987), *The Cultural Construction of Sexuality*, London: Routledge.

Davenport–Hines, R. T. P. (1991), *Sex, Death and Punishment: Attitudes to Sex and Sexuality in Britain Since the Renaissance*, London: Fontana.

Gallagher, Catherine, and Laqueur, Thomas (eds) (1987), *The Making of the Modern Body: Sexuality and Society in the Nineteenth Century*, Berkeley: University of California Press.

Hall, Lesley (1991), *Hidden Anxieties: Male Sexuality, 1900–1950*, Cambridge: Polity Press.

Haste, Helen (1993), *The Sexual Metaphor*, London: Harvester Wheatsheaf.

Heath, Stephen (1982), *The Sexual Fix*, Basingstoke: Macmillan.

Kinsey, Alfred, et al., (1948 and 1952), *Sexual Behaviour in the Human Male* and *Sexual Behaviour in the Human Female*, Bloomington: Indiana University Press.

McNeill, Pearlie, Freeman, Bea, and Newman, Jenny (eds) (1992), *Women Talk Sex: Autobiographical Writing on Sex, Sexuality and Sexual Identity*, London: Scarlet Press.

Mort, Frank (1998) *Dangerous Sexualities: Medico–Moral Politics in England since 1830*, second edition, London: Routledge.

Parker, Andrew, Russo, Mary, Sommer, Doris, and Yaegar, Patricia (1991), *Nationalisms and Sexualities*, London: Routledge.

Plummer, Ken (1996), 'Intimate Citizenship and the Culture of Sexual Story Telling', in Weeks and Holland (eds), *Sexual Cultures: Communities, Values and Intimacy*, Basingstoke: Macmillan, pp. 34–52.

Seidman, Steven (1998), 'The Brits are Coming . . . again: Sex Studies in the UK',
    Sexualities, 1, 1, February.

Introduction

Kinsey, Alfred, et al., (1948 and 1952), *Sexual Behaviour in the Human Male* and
    Sexual Behaviour in the Human Female, Bloomington: Indiana University
    Press.

Male homosexualities

Boswell, John (1980), *Christianity, Social Tolerance and Homosexuality*, Chicago:
    University of Chicago Press.
Cant, Bob (ed.) (1993), *Footsteps and Witnesses: Lesbian and Gay Life stories from
    Scotland*, Edinburgh: Polygon.
Carpenter, Edward (1984), *Selected Writings Vol. 1: Sex*, London: GMP Publish-
    ers.
David, Hugh (1997), *On Queer Street: a Social History of British Homosexuality
    1895–1995*, London: HarperCollins.
Duberman, Martin Bauml, et al. (eds) (1991), *Hidden From History: Reclaiming the
    Gay and Lesbian Past*, London: Penguin Books.
Edwards, Tim (1993), *Erotics and Politics: Gay Men, Masculinities and Feminism*,
    London: Routledge.
Greenberg, David F. (1988), *The Construction of Homosexuality*, Chicago, IL:
    Chicago University Press.
Hall Carpenter Archives (1989), *Walking After Midnight: Gay Men's Life Stories*,
    London: Routledge.
Herek, Gregory M. (ed.) (1998), *Stigma and Sexual Orientation: Understanding
    Prejudice against Lesbians, Gay Men and Bisexuals*, London: Sage Publications.
Highwater, Jamake (1997), *The Mythology of Transgression: Homosexuality as
    Metaphor*, Oxford: Oxford University Press.
Jeffery–Poulter, Stephen (1991), *Peers, Queers and Commons: the Struggle for Gay
    Law Reform from 1950 to the Present*, London: Routledge.
Jivani, Alkarim (1997), *It's Not Unusual: a History of Lesbian and Gay Britain in the
    Twentieth Century*, London: Michael O'Mara Books/BBC.
Kennedy, Hubert (1988), *Ulrichs: the Life and Works of Karl Heinrich Ulrichs,
    Pioneer of the Modern Gay Movement*, Boston: Alyson.
Krafft-Ebing, Richard von (1959), *The Psychopathia Sexualis*, London: Staples
    Press.
Lambevski, Sasho (1999), 'Suck My Nation – Masculinity, Ethnicity and the
    Politics of (Homo)Sex', *Sexualities*, vol. 2, no. 4.
Lofstrom, Jan (1997), 'The Birth of the Queen/the Modern Homosexual:
    Historical Explanations Revisited', *Sociological Review*, vol. 45, no. 1.
Mac an Ghaill, Máirtín (1996), 'Irish Masculinities and Sexualities in England',
    in Adkins and Merchant (eds), *Sexualizing the Social: Power and the Organiza-
    tion of Sexuality*, Basingstoke: Macmillan, pp. 122–44.

McIntosh, Mary (1997), 'Seeing the World from a Lesbian and Gay Standpoint', in Segal (ed.), *New Sexual Agendas*, Basingstoke: Macmillan, pp. 205–13.

Nardi, Peter M., Marmor, Judd, and Sanders, David (1994), *Growing Up Before Stonewall*, London: Routledge.

National Gay and Lesbian Survey (1993), *Proust, Cole Porter, Michelangelo, Marc Almond and Me*, London: Routledge.

Plummer, Kenneth (1975), *Sexual Stigma: An Interactionist Account*, London: Routledge and Kegan Paul.

Plummer, Kenneth (1981), *The Making of the Modern Homosexual*, London: Hutchinson.

Plummer, Kenneth (ed.) (1993), *Modern Homosexualities*, London: Routledge.

Porter, Kevin, and Weeks, Jeffrey (1990), *Between the Acts: Lives of Homosexual Men, 1885–1967*, London: Routledge.

Sanderson, Terry (1989), *How to be a Happy Homosexual*, London: Gay Men's Press.

Sanderson, Terry (1995), *Mediawatch: The Treatment of Male and Female Homosexuality in the British Media*, London: Cassell.

Weeks, Jeffrey (1990), *Coming Out: Homosexual Politics in Britain from the Nineteenth Century to the Present*, (revised ed), London: Quartet Books.

Weeks, Jeffrey (1998), 'The "homosexual role" after 30 years: an appreciation of the work of Mary McIntosh', *Sexualities*, vol. 1, no. 2, May.

Zeldin, Theodore (1995), *An Intimate History of Humanity*, London: Minerva.

Lesbianisms

Ainley, Rosa (1995), *What is She Like? Lesbian Identities from 1950s to 1990s*, London: Cassell.

Campbell, Beatrix (1987), 'A Feminist Sexual Politics: Now You See It, Now You Don't', in Feminist Review, *Sexuality: a Reader*, London: Virago, pp. 19–39.

Ettorre, Eliz (1980), *Lesbians, Women and Society*, London: Routledge & Kegan Paul.

Faderman, Lillian (1992), *Odd Girls and Twilight Lovers: a History of Lesbian Life in Twentieth Century America*, London: Penguin Books.

Hall Carpenter Archives (1989), *Inventing Ourselves: Lesbian Life Stories*, London: Routledge.

Hamer, Emily (1996), *Britannia's Glory: Lesbian Politics in the Twentieth Century*, London: Cassell.

Jackson, Stevi, and Scott, Sue (eds) (1996), *Feminism and Sexuality: a Reader*, Edinburgh: Edinburgh University Press.

Kitzinger, Celia (1987), *The Social Construction of Lesbianism*, London: Sage Publications.

Kitzinger, Celia, and Wilkinson, Sue (eds) (1993), *Heterosexuality: a Feminism and Psychology Reader*, London: Sage Publications.

Markowe, Laura (1996), *Redefining the Self: Coming Out as Lesbian*, Cambridge: Polity Press.

National Gay and Lesbian Survey (1992), *What a Lesbian Looks Like*, London: Routledge.

Rich, Adrienne (1996), 'Compulsory Heterosexuality and Lesbian Existence', in Jackson and Scott (eds), *Feminism and Sexuality*, Edinburgh: Edinburgh University Press, pp. 130–43.

Richardson, Diane (1996), 'Constructing Lesbian Sexualities', in Jackson and Scott (eds), *Feminism and Sexuality*, Edinburgh: Edinburgh University Press, pp. 276–86.

Roof, Judith (1993), *A Lure of Knowledge: Lesbian Sexuality and Theory*, New York, NY: Columbia University Press.

Schneider, Beth (1992), 'Lesbian Politics and AIDS Work', in Plummer, Ken (ed.), *Modern Homosexualities*, London: Routledge, pp. 160–74.

Smith, Anna Marie (1994), *New Right Discourse on Race and Sexuality: Britain, 1968–1990*, Cambridge: Cambridge University Press.

Sutcliffe, Lynn (1995), *There Must be 50 Ways to Tell Your Mother*, London: Mansell.

Weeks, Jeffrey (1987), 'Questions of Identity', in Caplan (ed.), *The Cultural Construction of Sexuality*, London: Routledge, pp. 31–51.

Weeks, Jeffrey (1990), *Coming Out: Homosexual Politics in Britain from the Nineteenth Century to the Present*, (revised ed), London: Quartet Books.

Wittig, Monique (1992), *The Straight Mind and Other Essays*, London: Harvester Wheatsheaf.

Heterosexualities

Campbell, Beatrix (1987), 'A Feminist Sexual Politics: Now You See It, Now You Don't', in Feminist Review, *Sexuality: a Reader*, London: Virago, pp. 19–39.

Chauncey, George (1999), 'The Invention of Heterosexuality', in Nye (ed.), *Sexuality*, Oxford: Oxford University Press, pp. 198–202.

Cohen, David (1990), *Being a Man*, London: Routledge.

Dallos, Rudi and Foreman, Sally (1997), *Couples, Sex and Power: the Politics of Desire*, Buckingham: Open University Press.

Dhavernas, Marie-Jo (1996), 'Hating Masculinity Not Men', in Jackson and Scott (eds), *Feminism and Sexuality*, Edinburgh: Edinburgh University Press, pp. 150–4.

Duncombe, Jean and Marsden, Dennis (1996), 'Whose Orgasm is this Anyway? "Sex Work" in Long-term Heterosexual Couple Relationships', in Weeks and Holland (eds), *Sexual Cultures: Communities, Values and Intimacy*, Basingstoke: Macmillan, pp. 220–38.

Formaini, Heather (1990), *Men: the Darker Continent*, London: Heinemann.

Gill, Rosalind, and Walker, Rebecca (1993), 'Heterosexuality, Feminism, Contradiction: On Being Young, White, Heterosexual Feminists in the 1990s', in Kitzinger, Celia, and Wilkinson, Sue (eds), *Heterosexuality: a Feminism and Psychology Reader*, London: Sage Publications, pp. 68–72.

Hanscombe, Gillian, and Humphries, Martin (eds) (1987), *Heterosexuality*, London: Gay Men's Press.

Hearn, Jeff, and Ford, David (1991), *Studying Men and Masculinity: a Sourcebook of Literature and Materials*, Bradford: University of Bradford.

Jackson, Stevi (1996), 'Heterosexuality as a Problem for Feminist Theory', in Adkins and Merchant (eds), *Sexualizing the Social: Power and the Organization of Sexuality*, Basingstoke: Macmillan, pp. 15–34.

Jackson, Stevi (1996a), 'The Social Construction of Female Sexuality', in Jackson and Scott (eds), *Feminism and Sexuality*, Edinburgh: Edinburgh University Press, pp. 62–73.

Jeffreys, Sheila (1996), 'Heterosexuality and the Desire for Gender', in Richardson, Diane (ed.), *Theorising Heterosexuality*, Buckingham: Open University Press, pp. 75–90.

Kitzinger, Celia, and Wilkinson, Sue (eds) (1993), *Heterosexuality: a Feminism and Psychology Reader*, London: Sage Publications.

Maynard, Mary, and Purvis, June (eds) (1995), *(Hetero)sexual Politics*, London: Taylor and Francis.

Morris, Larry (1997), *The Male Heterosexual: Lust in His Loins and Sin in His Soul?*, London: Sage Publications.

Nye, Robert (ed.) (1999), *Sexuality*, Oxford: Oxford University Press.

Prendergast, Shirley, and Forrest, Simon (1997), ' "Hieroglyphs of the Heterosexual": Learning about Gender in School', in Segal (ed.), *New Sexual Agendas*, Basingstoke: Macmillan, pp. 180–95.

Richardson, Diane (ed.) (1996), *Theorising Heterosexuality*, Buckingham: Open University Press.

Segal, Lynne (1994), *Straight Sex: the Politics of Pleasure*, London: Virago.

Segal, Lynne (1997), 'Feminist Sexual Politics and the Heterosexual Predicament', in Segal (ed.), *New Sexual Agendas*, Basingstoke: Macmillan, pp. 77–89.

Seidler, Victor (ed.) (1991), *The Achilles Heel Reader*, London: Routledge.

Smart, Carol (1996), 'Desperately Seeking Post-Heterosexual Woman', in Holland and Adkins (eds), *Sex, Sensibility and the Gendered Body*, Basingstoke: Macmillan, pp. 222–41.

VanEvery, Jo (1995), *Heterosexual Women Changing the Family: Refusing to be a 'Wife'!*, London: Taylor and Francis.

VanEvery, Jo (1996), 'Sinking into his arms . . . Arms in his Sink: Heterosexuality and Feminism Revisited', in Adkins and Merchant (eds), *Sexualizing the Social: Power and the Organization of Sexuality*, Basingstoke: Macmillan, pp. 35–54.

Vanwesenbeeck, Ine (1997), 'The Context of Women's Power[lessness] in Heterosexual Interactions', in Segal (ed.), *New Sexual Agendas*, Basingstoke: Macmillan, pp. 171–9.

Wight, Daniel (1996), 'Beyond the Predatory Male: The Diversity of Young Glaswegian Men's Discourses to Describe Heterosexual Relationships', in Adkins and Merchant (eds), *Sexualizing the Social: Power and the Organization of Sexuality*, Basingstoke: Macmillan, pp. 145–70.

Wilton, Tamsin (1996), 'Genital Identities: an Idiosyncratic Foray into the Gendering of Sexualities', in Adkins and Merchant (eds), *Sexualizing the Social: Power and the Organization of Sexuality*, Basingstoke: Macmillan, pp. 102–21.

Wittig, Monique (1992), *The Straight Mind and Other Essays*, London: Harvester Wheatsheaf.

Bisexualities

Eadie, Jo (1993), 'Activating Bisexuality: Towards a Bi/Sexual Politics', in Bristow, Joseph, and Wilson, Angelia (eds), *Activating Theory: Lesbian, Gay, Bisexual Politics*, London: Lawrence and Wishart, pp. 139–70.

Firestein, Beth (ed.) (1996), *Bisexuality: The Psychology and Politics of an Invisible Minority*, London: Sage Publications.

Garber, Marjorie (1995), *Vice Versa: Bisexuality and the Eroticism of Everyday Life*, Harmondsworth: Penguin Books.

George, Sue (1993), *Women and Bisexuality*, London: Scarlet Press.

Hemmings, Clare (1993), 'Resituating the Bisexual Body: From Identity to Difference', in Bristow and Wilson (eds), *Activating Theory: Lesbian, Gay, Bisexual Politics*, London: Lawrence and Wishart, pp. 118–38.

Humphrey, Jill (1999), 'To Queer or Not to Queer a Lesbian and Gay Group? Sexual and Gendered Politics at the Turn of the Century', *Sexualities*, 2, 2, May.

Hutchins, Loraine and Kaahumanu, Lani (eds) (1990), *Bi – Any Other Name: Bisexual People Speak Out*, London: Alyson Publications.

Rose, Sharon, and Stevens, Cris (1996), *Bisexual Horizons: Politics, Histories, Lives*, London: Lawrence and Wishart.

Rose, Sharon (1996), 'Introduction: What are Bisexual Politics?', in Rose and Stevens (eds), *Bisexual Horizons: Politics, Histories, Lives*, London: Lawrence and Wishart, pp. 215–18.

Storr, Merl (1999), 'Postmodern Bisexuality', *Sexualities*, vol. 2, no. 3, August.

Tiefer, Leonore (1993), *Sex is not a Natural Act*, Boulder, CO: Westview Press.

Udis-Kessler, Amanda (1996), 'Challenging the Stereotypes', in Rose and Stevens (eds), *Bisexual Horizons: Politics, Histories, Lives*, London: Lawrence and Wishart, pp. 45–57.

Weinberg, Martin S., Williams, Colin J., and Pryor, Douglas W. (1993), *Dual Attraction: Understanding Bisexuality*, Oxford: Oxford University Press.

Wilkinson, Sue (1996), 'Bisexuality a la mode', *Women's Studies International Forum*, vol. 19, no. 3.

Chapter 3 Gender ideologies and gender regulation

General reading

Connell, Robert (1985), 'Theorising gender', *Sociology*, vol. 19 no. 2.

de Beauvoir, Simone (1953), *The Second Sex*, London: Jonathan Cape.

Evans, Mary, and Ungerson, Clare (1983), *Sexual Divisions: Patterns and Processes*, London: Tavistock Publications.

French, Marilyn (1986), *Beyond Power: On Women, Men and Morals*, London: Abacus.

Friedan, Betty (1963), *The Feminine Mystique*, New York, NY: W.W. Norton.

Friedan, Betty (1981), *The Second Stage*, New York, NY: Summit.

Garrett, Stephanie (1987), *Gender*, London: Taylor and Francis.

Hammersley, Martyn (1995), *The Politics of Social Research*, London: Sage Publications.

Harding, Jenny (1998), *Sex Acts: Practices of Femininity and Masculinity*, London: Sage Publications.

Leonard, Diana, and Allen, Sheila (eds) (1991), *Sexual Divisions Revisited*, London: Macmillan.

Maynard, Mary (1990), 'The Re-Shaping of Sociology? Trends in the Study of Gender', *Sociology*, vol. 24, no. 2.

Mead, Margaret (1935), *Sex and Temperament in Three Primitive Societies*, New York, NY: Dell.

Millett, Kate (1970), *Sexual Politics*, London: Virago.

Pateman, Carole (1988), *The Sexual Contract*, Cambridge: Polity Press.

Ramazanoglu, Caroline (1989), 'Improving on sociology: problems in taking a feminist standpoint', *Sociology*, vol. 23, no. 3.

Rothblatt, Martine (1996), *The Apartheid of Sex: a Manifesto on the Freedom of Gender*, London: Pandora.

Schwartz, Pepper, and Rutter, Virginia (1998), *The Gender of Sexuality*, London: Sage Publications.

Shilling, Chris (1993), *The Body and Social Theory*, London: Sage Publications.

Squires, Judith (2000), *Gender in Political Theory*, Cambridge: Polity Press.

Tolleson Rinehart, Sue (1992), *Gender Consciousness and Politics*, London: Routledge.

Wilkinson, Sue, and Kitzinger, Celia (eds) (1996), *Representing the Other: a Feminism and Psychology Reader*, London: Sage Publications.

Intersecting identities: cultural constructions of gender

Bonvillain, Nancy (1995), *Women and Men: Cultural Constructions of Gender*, London: Prentice Hall.

Goddard, Victoria (1987), 'Honour and Shame: the Control of Women's Sexuality and Group Identity in Naples', in Caplan (ed.), *The Cultural Construction of Sexuality*, London: Routledge, pp. 166–92.

Hofstede, Geert (ed.) (1998), *Masculinity and Femininity: the Taboo Dimension of National Cultures*, London: Sage Publications.

hooks, bel (1996), 'Continued Devaluation of Black Womanhood', in Jackson and Scott (eds), *Feminism and Sexuality*, Edinburgh: Edinburgh University Press, pp. 216–23.

Roper, Michael, and Tosh, John (1991), *Manful Assertions*, London: Routledge.

Stockard, Jean, and Johnson, Miriam (1992), *Sex and Gender in Society*, London: Prentice Hall.

Tseelon, Efrat (1995), *The Masque of Femininity: the Presentation of Women in Everyday Life*, London: Sage Publications.

Ideologies of masculinity and of femininity: the critique of 'men's studies' and of feminism

Ardener, Shirley (ed.) (1993), *Defining Females: the Nature of Women in Society*, London: Berg Publishers.

Askew, Sue, and Ross, Carol (1988), *Boys Don't Cry: Boys and Sexism in Education*, Buckingham: Open University Press.

Bly, Robert (1990), *Iron John: a Book About Men*, Reading, MA: Addison-Wesley.

Bowker, Lee (1998), *Masculinities and Violence*, London: Sage Publications.

Brandth, Berit, and Kvande, Elin (1998), 'Masculinity and Child Care', *Sociological Review*, vol. 46, no. 2.

Brannen, Julia, and Moss, Peter (1993), 'Managing Mothers', in Jackson (ed.), *Women's Studies: a Reader*, London: Harvester Wheatsheaf, pp. 207–11.

Bristow, Joseph (1991), *Empire Boys: Adventures in a Man's World*, London: Unwin Hyman.

Brittan, Arthur (1989), *Masculinity and Power*, Oxford: Blackwell.

Brod, Harry (1987), *The Making of Masculinities: the New Men's Studies*, London: Allen and Unwin.

Brod, Harry, and Kaufman, Michael (eds) (1994), *Theorizing Masculinities*, London: Sage Publications.

Brownmiller, Susan (1986), *Femininity*, London: Paladin.

Bryan, Beverley, Dadzie, Stella, and Scafe, Suzanne (1985), *The Heart of the Race. Black women's lives in Britain*, London: Virago.

Carabine, Jean (1992), '"Constructing Women": Women's Sexuality and social policy', *Critical Social Policy*, vol. 12, no. 34.

Chapman, Rowena, and Rutherford, Jonathan (eds) (1996), *Male Order: Unwrapping Masculinity*, London: Lawrence and Wishart.

Cohen, David (1990), *Being a Man*, London: Routledge.

Connell, Robert (1995), *Masculinities*, Cambridge: Polity Press.

Coward, Ros (1984), *Female Desire*, London: Paladin.

de Beauvoir, Simone (1953), *The Second Sex*, London: Jonathan Cape.

Dworkin, Andrea (1981), *Pornography: Men Possessing Women*, London: The Women's Press.

Edley, Nigel, and Wetherell, Margaret (1995), *Men in Perspective: Practice, Power and Identity*, London: Prentice Hall.

Edwards, Tim (1993), *Erotics and Politics: Gay Men, Masculinities and Feminism*, London: Routledge.

Evans, Judith (1995), *Feminist Theory Today: an Introduction to Second Wave Feminism*, London: Sage Publications.

Evans, Mary (ed.) (1993), *The Woman Question*, second edition, London: Sage Publications.

Everingham, Christine (1994), *Motherhood and Modernity*, Buckingham: Open University Press.

Faludi, Susan (1999), *Stiffed: the Betrayal of the Modern Man*, London: Chatto and Windus.

Fillion, Kate (1997), *Lip Service: the Myth of Female Virtue in Love, Sex and Friendship*, London: Rivers Oram Press.

Formaini, Heather (1990), *Men: the Darker Continent*, London: Heinemann.

Forna, Aminatta (1999), *Mother of all Myths: How Society Moulds and Constrains Mothers*, London: HarperCollins.

Fransella, Fay, and Frost, Kay (1977), *On Being a Woman: A Review of Research of How Women See Themselves*, London: Tavistock Publications.

Friedan, Betty (1963), *The Feminine Mystique*, New York, NY: W.W. Norton.

Friedan, Betty (1981), *The Second Stage*, New York, NY: Summit.

Hall, Lesley (1991), *Hidden Anxieties: Male Sexuality, 1900–1950*, Cambridge: Polity Press.

Hammersley, Martyn (1995), *The Politics of Social Research*, London: Sage Publications.

Hearn, Jeff (1987), *The Gender of Oppression: Men, Masculinity and the Critique of Marxism*, Brighton: Wheatsheaf Books.

Hearn, Jeff, and Morgan, David (1990), *Men, Masculinities and Social Theory*, London: Unwin Hyman.

Hite, Shere (1989), *The Hite Report: A Nationwide Study of Female Sexuality*, London: Rivers Oram Press.

Hutter, Bridget, and Williams, Gillian (eds) (1981), *Controlling Women: The Normal and the Deviant*, London: Croom Helm.

Jackson, Stevi (1996), 'Heterosexuality as a Problem for Feminist Theory', in Adkins and Merchant (eds), *Sexualizing the Social: Power and the Organization of Sexuality*, Basingstoke: Macmillan, pp. 15–34.

Jeffreys, Sheila (1996), 'Sadomasochism', in Jackson and Scott (eds), *Feminism and Sexuality: a Reader*, Edinburgh: Edinburgh University Press, pp. 238–44.

Mac an Ghaill, Máirtín (1994), *The Making of Men: Masculinities, Sexualities and Schooling*, Buckingham: Open University Press.

Mac an Ghaill, Máirtín (1996a), *Understanding Masculinities: Social Relations and Cultural Arenas*, Buckingham: Open University Press.

Martin, Emily (1989), *The Woman in the Body: a Cultural Analysis of Reproduction*, London: Open University Press.

Nardi, Peter (ed.) (1992) *Men's Friendships*, London: Sage Publications.

Nixon, Sean (1996), *Hard Looks: Masculinities, Spectatorship and Contemporary Consumption*, London: UCL Press.

Oakley, Ann, and Mitchell, Juliet (eds) (1976), *The Rights and Wrongs of Women*, Harmondsworth: Penguin Books.

Oakley, Ann (1982), *Subject Women*, London: Fontana.

Petersen, Alan (1998), *Unmasking the Masculine: 'Men' and 'Identity' in a Sceptical Age*, London: Sage Publications.

Phoenix, Ann, Woollett, Anne, and Lloyd, Eva (1991), *Motherhood: Meanings, Practices and Ideologies*, London: Sage Publications.

Richardson, Diane (1993), *Women, Motherhood and Childbearing*, Basingstoke: Macmillan.

Rowbotham, Sheila (1993), 'To be or not to be: the Dilemmas of Mothering', in

Jackson (ed.), *Women's Studies: a Reader*, London: Harvester Wheatsheaf, pp. 204–7.

Rutherford, Jonathan (1992), *Men's Silences: Predicaments in Masculinity*, London: Routledge.

Salisbury, Jonathan, and Jackson, David (1996), *Challenging Macho Values: Practical Ways of Working with Adolescent Boys*, London: Falmer Press.

Segal, Lynne (1990), *Slow Motion: Changing Masculinities, Changing Men*, London: Virago.

Seidler, Victor (1997), *Man Enough: Embodying Masculinities*, London: Sage Publications.

Simpson, Mark (1994), *Male Impersonators: Men Performing Masculinity*, London: Cassell.

Simpson, Mark (ed.) (1996), *Anti–Gay*, London: Cassell.

Squires, Judith (2000), *Gender in Political Theory*, London: Sage Publications.

Stoltenberg, John (1990), *Refusing to Be a Man*, London: Fontana.

Tolson, Andrew (1977), *The Limits of Masculinity*, London: Tavistock Publications.

Vance, Carole (1993), *Pleasure and Danger: Exploring Female Sexuality*, London: HarperCollins.

Walkerdine, Valerie, and Lucey, Helen (1989), *Democracy in the Kitchen: Regulating Mothers and Socialising Daughters*, London: Virago.

Whelehan, Imelda (1995), *Modern Feminist Thought: From the Second Wave to "Post-Feminism"*, Edinburgh: Edinburgh University Press.

Whitelegg, Elizabeth (1982), *The Changing Experience of Women*, Oxford: Blackwell.

Wolf, Naomi (1991), *The Beauty Myth*, London: Vintage.

Woollet, Anne, and Phoenix, Ann (1993), 'Issues Related to Motherhood', in Jackson (ed.), *Women's Studies: a Reader*, London: Harvester Wheatsheaf, pp. 216–17.

Gender divisions and paid work: the 'public' sphere

Adkins, Lisa (1995), *Gendered Work: Sexuality, Family and the Labour Market*, Buckingham: Open University Press.

Adkins, Lisa and Lury, Celia (1996), 'The Cultural, the Sexual, and the Gendering of the Labour Market', in Adkins and Merchant (eds), *Sexualizing the Social: Power and the Organization of Sexuality*, Basingstoke: Macmillan, pp. 204–23.

Bradley, Harriet (1989), *Men's Work, Women's Work: a Sociological History of the Sexual Division of Labour*, Cambridge: Polity Press/Blackwell.

Cockburn, Cynthia (1991), *In the Way of Women: Men's Resistance to Sex Equality in Organisations*, Basingstoke: Macmillan.

Crompton, Rosemary (1996), 'Paid Employment and the Changing System of Gender Relations', *Sociology*, vol. 30, no. 3.

Crompton, Rosemary and Harris, Fiona (1998), 'Explaining Women's Employment Patterns', *British Journal of Sociology*, vol. 49, no. 1.

Crowley, Helen (1992), 'Women and the Domestic Sphere', in Bocock and Thompson (eds), *Social and Cultural Forms of Modernity*, Cambridge: Polity Press.

Dex, Shirley (1985), *The Sexual Division of Work: Conceptual Revolutions in the Social Sciences*, London: St Martin's Press.

Formaini, Heather (1990), *Men: the Darker Continent*, London: Heinemann.

Hearn, Jeff, and Parkin, Wendy (1983), 'Gender and Organizations', *Organization Studies*, vol. 4, no. 3.

Hearn, Jeff, and Parkin, Wendy (1987), *'Sex' at 'Work': the Power and Paradox of Organisation Sexuality*, Brighton: Wheatsheaf.

Hearn, Jeff (1989), *The Sexuality of Organisation*, London: Sage Publications.

Hearn, Jeff (1992), *Men in the Public Eye: The Construction and Deconstruction of Public Men and Public Patriarchies*, London: Routledge.

Hood, Jane C., (ed.) (1993), *Men, Work, and Family*, London: Sage Publications.

Itzin, Catherine, and Newman, Janet, (eds) (1995), *Gender, Culture and Organizational Change: Putting theory into practice*, London: Sage Publications.

Kelly, Rita Mae (1991), *The Gendered Economy: Work, Careers and Success*, London: Sage Publications.

Knights, David, and Willmott, Hugh (1986), *Gender and the Labour Process*, Aldershot: Gower.

Morgan, Glenn (1990), *Organizations in Society*, Basingstoke: Macmillan.

Nicholson, Paula (1996), *Gender, Power and Organisations*, London: Routledge.

Oakley, Ann (1974), *Housewife*, London: Penguin Books.

Piachaud, David (1984), *Round About Fifty Hours a Week: the Time Costs of Children*, London: Child Poverty Action Group.

Pringle, Rosemary (1992), 'What is a Secretary?', in McDowell and Pringle (eds), *Defining Women: Social Institutions and Gender Divisions*, Cambridge: Polity Press.

Seidler, Victor (ed.) (1991), *The Achilles Heel Reader*, London: Routledge.

Siltanen, Janet, and Stanworth, Michelle (eds) (1984), *Women and the Public Sphere: A Critique of Sociology and Politics*, London: Hutchinson.

Tilly, Louise A., and Scott, Joan W. (1988), *Women, Work, and Family*, London: Routledge.

Walby, Sylvia (1986), *Patriarchy at Work: Patriarchal and Capitalist Relations in Employment*, Cambridge: Polity Press.

Williams, Christine L. (1993), *Doing 'Women's Work': Men in Nontraditional Occupations*, London: Sage Publications.

Witz, Anne (1990), 'Patriarchy and professions: the gendered politics of occupational closure', *Sociology*, vol. 24, no. 4.

Witz, Anne (1992), *Professions and Patriarchy*, London: Routledge.

Witz, Anne, Halford, Susan and Savage, Mike (1996), 'Organized Bodies: Gender, Sexuality and Embodiment in Contemporary Organizations', in Adkins and Merchant (eds), *Sexualizing the Social: Power and the Organization of Sexuality*, Basingstoke: Macmillan, pp. 173–90.

Gender divisions and 'emotion–work': the 'private' sphere

Burkitt, Ian (1997), 'Social Relationships and Emotions', *Sociology*, vol. 31, no. 1.

Canary, Daniel, and Emmers–Sommer, Tara, with Faulkner, Sandra (1997), *Sex and Gender Differences in Personal Relationships*, London: Guiford Press.

Craib, Ian (1995), 'Some Comments on the Sociology of the Emotions', *Sociology*, vol. 29, no. 3.

Duncombe, Jean, and Marsden, Dennis (1993), 'Love and Intimacy: the Gender Division of Emotion and "Emotion Work": a Neglected Aspect of Sociological Discussion of Heterosexual Relationships', *Sociology*, vol. 27, no. 2.

Duncombe, Jean and Marsden, Dennis (1996), 'Extending the Social: a Response to Ian Craib', *Sociology*, vol. 30, no. 1.

Formaini, Heather (1990), *Men: the Darker Continent*, London: Heinemann.

Giddens, Anthony (1992), *The Transformation of Intimacy: Sexuality, Love and Eroticism in Modern Societies*, Cambridge: Polity Press.

Hansen, Karen (1992), '"Our Eyes Behold Each Other": Masculinity and Intimate Friendship in Antebellum New England', in Nardi, Peter M. (ed.), *Men's Friendships*, London: Sage Publications.

Jackson, Stevi (1993), 'Even Sociologists Fall in Love: an Exploration in the Sociology of Emotions', *Sociology*, vol. 27, no. 2.

Jackson, Stevi, and Scott, Sue (1997), 'Gut Reactions to Matters of the Heart: Reflections on Rationality, Irrationality and Sexuality', *Sociological Review*, vol. 45, no. 4.

Langford, Wendy (1999), *Revolutions of the Heart: Gender, Power and the Delusions of Love*, London: Routledge.

Nardi, Peter (ed.) (1992), *Men's Friendships*, London: Sage Publications.

Nardi, Peter (1992a), 'Sex, Friendship, and Gender Roles Among Gay Men', in Nardi (ed.), *Men's Friendships*, London: Sage Publications.

O'Connor, Pat (1991), 'Women's Confidants Outside Marriage: Shared or Competing Sources of Intimacy?', *Sociology*, vol. 25, no. 2.

O'Connor, Pat (1991a), *Friendships Between Women*, London: Guilford Press.

Risman, Barbara J., and Schwartz, Pepper (1989), *Gender in Intimate Relationships: A Microstructural Approach*, Belmont, CA: Wadsworth Publishing.

Seidler, Victor (ed.) (1991), *The Achilles Heel Reader*, London: Routledge.

Seidler, Victor (1992), 'Rejection, Vulnerability and Friendship', in Nardi, (ed.), *Men's Friendships*, London: Sage Publications.

Shilling, Chris (1997), 'Emotions, Embodiment and the Sensation of Society', *Sociological Review*, vol. 45, no. 2.

Tannen, Deborah (1991), *You Just Don't Understand: Women and Men in Conversation*, London: Virago.

Weston, Kath (1992), *Families We Choose: Lesbians, Gays, Kinship*, New York, NY: Columbia University Press.

Williams, Simon, and Bendelow, Gillian (1996), 'Emotions and "Sociological Imperialism": a Rejoinder to Craib', *Sociology*, vol. 30, no. 1.

Wood, Julia (1996), *Gendered Relationships*, Mountain View, CA: Mayfield Publishing.

Policing gender boundaries

Adam, Barry D. (1998), 'Theorizing Homophobia', *Sexualities*, 1, 4, November.

Dollimore, Jonathan (1991), *Sexual Dissidence: Augustine to Wilde, Freud to Foucault*, Oxford: Oxford University Press.

Epstein, Debbie (1996), 'Keeping them in their Place: Hetero/sexist Harassment, Gender and the Enforcement of Heterosexuality', in Holland and Adkins (eds), *Sex, Sensibility and the Gendered Body*, Basingstoke: Macmillan, pp. 202–21.

Epstein, Debbie, Steinberg, Deborah, and Johnson, Richard (eds) (1997), *Border Patrols: Policing the Boundaries of Heterosexuality*, London: Cassell.

Epstein, Julia, and Straub, Kristina (eds) (1991), *Body Guards: the Cultural Politics of Gender Ambiguity*, London: Routledge.

Hawkes, Gail (1995), 'Dressing–Up – Cross–dressing and Sexual Dissonance', *Journal of Gender Studies*, vol. 4, no. 3.

Holland, Janet, Ramazanoglu, Caroline, Sharpe, Sue, and Thomson, Rachel (1996), 'Reputations: Journeying into Gendered Power Relations', in Weeks and Holland (eds), *Sexual Cultures: Communities, Values and Intimacy*, Basingstoke: Macmillan, pp. 239–60.

Nayak, Anoop, and Kehily, Mary Jane (1996), 'Playing it Straight: Masculinities, Homophobias and Schooling', *Journal of Gender Studies*, vol. 5, no. 2.

Nayak, Anoop, and Kehily, Mary Jane (1997), 'Why are Young Men so Homophobic?', in Epstein, Steinberg and Johnson (eds), *Border Patrols: Policing the Boundaries of Heterosexuality*, London: Cassell, pp. 138–61.

Rothblum, Esther, and Bond, Lynne (1996), *Preventing Heterosexism and Homophobia*, London: Sage Publications.

Segal, Lynne (1990), *Slow Motion: Changing Masculinities, Changing Men*, London: Virago.

Woodhouse, Annie (1989), *Fantastic Women, Sex, Gender and Transvestism*, Basingstoke: Macmillan.

Part III Sexual politics
Chapter 4 Contemporary debates and challenges

General reading

Edwards, Tim (1993), *Erotics and Politics: Gay Men, Masculinities and Feminism*, London: Routledge.

Faulder, Carolyn (1985), *Whose Body is it? The Troubling Issue of Informed Consent*, London: Virago.

Harwood, Victoria, et al., (eds) (1993), *Pleasure Principles: Politics, Sexuality and Ethics*, London: Lawrence and Wishart.

Jacques, Trevor (1996), *On the Safe Edge: a Manual for SM Play*, Toronto: WholeSM Publishing.

Phillips, Eileen (ed.) (1983), *The Left and the Erotic*, London: Lawrence and Wishart.

Richardson, Diane (1998), 'Sexuality and Citizenship', *Sociology*, vol. 32, no. 1.
Snitow, Ann, Stansell, Christine, and Thompson, Sharon (1984), *Desire: The Politics of Sexuality*, London: Virago.
Thompson, Bill (1994), *Sadomasochism*, London: Cassell.

Introduction

Grant, Linda (1993), *Sexing the Millennium: Women and the Sexual Revolution*, London: Grove Press.
Weeks, Jeffrey (1995), *Invented Moralities: Sexual Values in an Age of Uncertainty*, Cambridge: Polity Press.

Debates between feminists and postfeminists

Brooks, Ann (1997), *Postfeminisms*, London: Routledge.
Coppock, Vicki, Haydon, Deena and Richter, Ingrid (1995), *The Illusions of 'Post–Feminism': New Women, Old Myths*, London: Taylor and Francis.
Coward, Rosalind (1999), *Sacred Cows*, London: HarperCollins.
Dworkin, Andrea (1983), *Right–wing Women: the Politics of Domesticated Females*, London: Women's Press.
Dworkin, Andrea (1988), *Letters From a War Zone: Writings, 1976–1987*, London: Lawrence Hill Books.
Dworkin, Andrea (1988), *Intercourse*, London: Free Press.
Faludi, Susan (1992), *Backlash: the Undeclared War Against Women*, London: Vintage.
Franzway, Suzanne, Court, Dianne, and Connell, Robert (1989), *Staking a Claim: Feminism, Bureaucracy and the State*, Cambridge: Polity Press.
Fukuyama, Francis (1992), *The End of History and the Last Man*, Harmondsworth: Penguin Books.
Grant, Linda (1993), *Sexing the Millennium: Women and the Sexual Revolution*, London: Grove Press.
Greer, Germaine (1971), *The Female Eunuch*, London: Granada.
Greer, Germaine (1999), *The Whole Woman*, London: Doubleday.
Guillaumin, Colette (1995), *Racism, Sexism, Power and Ideology*, London: Routledge.
Haug, Frigga (1992), *Beyond Female Masochism: Memory-work and Politics*, London: Verso.
Hagan, Kay Leigh (ed.) (1992), *Women Respond to the Men's Movement: a Feminist Collection*, London: Rivers Oram Press.
Heywood, Leslie, and Drake, Jennifer (1997), *Third Wave Agenda: Being Feminist, Doing Feminism*, Minneapolis, MA: University of Minnesota Press.
Kelly, Liz, Burton, Sheila, and Regan, Linda (1996), 'Beyond Victim or Survivor: Sexual Violence, Identity and Feminist Theory and Practice', in Adkins and Merchant (eds), *Sexualizing the Social: Power and the Organization of Sexuality*, Basingstoke: Macmillan, pp. 77–101.
King, Oona (1999), 'Why We Still Need Feminism', in Walter (ed.), *On the Move: Feminism for a New Generation*, London: Virago, pp. 48–61.

Lovenduski, Joni, and Randall, Vicky (1993), *Contemporary Feminist Politics: Women and Power in Britain*, Oxford: Oxford University Press.

Moscovici, Claudia (1997), *From Sex Objects to Sexual Subjects*, London: Routledge.

Paglia, Camille (1992), *Sexual Personae*, London: Penguin Books.

Paglia, Camille (1993), *Sex, Art and American Culture*, London: Penguin Books.

Roiphe, Katie (1994), *The Morning After: Sex, Fear and Feminism*, London: Hamish Hamilton.

Segal, Lynne (1994), *Straight Sex: the Politics of Pleasure*, London: Virago.

Segal, Lynne (1999), *Why Feminism?*, Cambridge: Polity Press.

Stacey, Margaret, and Price, Marion (1981), *Women, Power and Politics*, London: Tavistock Publications.

Walter, Natasha (1998), *The New Feminism*, London: Virago.

Walter, Natasha (ed.) (1999), *On the Move: Feminism for a New Generation*, London: Virago.

Wolf, Naomi (1994), *Fire with Fire: the New Female Power and How it Will Change the 21st Century*, London: Vintage.

Wolf, Naomi (1997), *Promiscuities: a Secret History of Female Desire*, London: Chatto and Windus.

Debates within lesbian, gay, bisexual and queer politics

Abelove, Henry, Barale, Michele A., and Halperin, David M. (eds) (1993), *The Lesbian and Gay Studies Reader*, London: Routledge.

Bamforth, Nicholas (1996), *Sexuality, Morals and Justice: A Theory of Lesbian and Gay Rights and the Law*, London: Cassell.

Blasius, Mark, and Phelan, Shane (1997), *We Are Everywhere: a Historical Sourcebook of Gay and Lesbian Politics*, London: Routledge.

Bristow, Joseph, and Wilson, Angelia (eds) (1993), *Activating Theory: Lesbian, Gay, Bisexual Politics*, London: Lawrence and Wishart.

Burston, Paul (1999), *Queen's Country*, London: Abacus.

Cooper, Davina (1992–3), 'Off the Banner and Into the Agenda: the Emergence of a New Municipal Lesbian and Gay Politics, 1979–86', *Critical Social Policy*, vol. 12, no. 36.

Cooper, Davina (1994), *Sexing the City: Lesbian and Gay Politics Within the Activist State*, London: Rivers Oram Press.

Cruikshank, Margaret (1992), *The Gay and Lesbian Liberation Movement*, London: Routledge.

Dunphy, Richard, and Clark, Ian (1995), 'The Effect of Parliamentary Lobbying on Scottish MPs in the Age of Consent Debate', *Scottish Affairs*, vol. 10, Winter.

Evans, David (1989–90), 'Section 28: Law, Myth and Paradox', *Critical Social Policy*, vol. 9, no. 27.

Evans, David (1993), *Sexual Citizenship: the Material Construction of Sexualities*, London: Routledge.

Jackson, Stevi (1996b), 'Feminist Politics, Gay Politics and the Problem of Heterosexuality', unpublished paper presented at the European Consortium for Political Research Joint Sessions, Oslo.

Jarman, Derek (1993), *At Your Own Risk*, London: Vintage Publishers.

Jeffery–Poulter, Stephen (1991), *Peers, Queers and Commons: the Struggle for Gay Law Reform from 1950 to the Present*, London: Routledge.

Jivani, Alkarim (1997), *It's Not Unusual: a History of Lesbian and Gay Britain in the Twentieth Century*, London: Michael O'Mara Books/BBC.

Lucas, Ian (1998), *Outrage! An Oral History*, London: Cassell.

Manning, Toby (1996), 'Gay Culture: Who Needs It?', in Simpson (ed.), *Anti-Gay*, London: Cassell, pp. 98–117.

Parnaby, Julia (1993), 'Queer Straits', *Trouble and Strife: the Radical Feminist Magazine*, No. 26, Summer.

Phelan, Shane (1996), *Playing with Fire: Queer Politics, Queer Theories*, London: Routledge.

Rahman, Momin (1996), 'Are Rights Essential?: Problematising Lesbian and Gay Politics', unpublished paper presented at the European Consortium for Political Research Joint Sessions, Oslo.

Schneider, Beth (1992), 'Lesbian Politics and AIDS Work', in Plummer, Ken (ed.), *Modern Homosexualities*, London: Routledge, pp. 160–74.

Shepherd, Simon, and Wallis, Mick (eds) (1989), *Coming On Strong: Gay Politics and Culture*, London: Unwin Hyman.

Signorile, Michelangelo (1994), *Queer in America: Sex, the Media and the Closets of Power*, London: Abacus.

Simpson, Mark (ed.) (1996), *Anti–Gay*, London: Cassell.

Smith, Anna Marie (1997), 'The Good Homosexual and the Dangerous Queer: Resisting the "New Homophobia"', in Segal (ed.), *New Sexual Agendas*, Basingstoke: Macmillan, pp. 214–31.

Smyth, Cherry (1993), *Lesbians Talk Queer Notions*, London: Scarlet Press.

Tatchell, Peter (1992), *Europe in the Pink: Lesbian and Gay Equality in the New Europe*, London: Gay Men's Press.

Watney, Simon (1994), *Practices of Freedom: Selected Writings on HIV/AIDS*, London: Rivers Oram Press.

Watney, Simon (1997), *Policing Desire*, third edition, London: Cassell.

Weeks, Jeffrey (1990), *Coming Out: Homosexual Politics in Britain from the Nineteenth Century to the Present*, (revised ed), London: Quartet Books.

Wilson, Angelia (ed.) (1995), *A Simple Matter of Justice? Theorizing Lesbian and Gay Politics*, London: Cassell.

Woods, Chris (1995), *State of the Queer Nation: a Critique of Gay and Lesbian Politics in 1990s Britain*, London: Cassell.

The emergence of men's politics

Baker, Peter (1994), 'Who's Afraid of the Big Bad Women?', *The Guardian*, 24 January.

Christian, Harry (1994), *The Making of Anti–Sexist Men*, London: Routledge.

Clatterbaugh, Kenneth (1990), *Contemporary Perspectives on Masculinity: Men, Women and Politics in Modern Society*, Boulder, CO: Westview Press.

Connell, Robert (1995), *Masculinities*, Cambridge: Polity Press.

Farrell, Warren (1993), *The Myth of Male Power: Why Men are the Disposable Sex*, New York, NY: Simon and Schuster.

Grant, Linda (1994), 'Troopers in the Sex War', *The Guardian*, 22 February.

Hearn, Jeff (1987), *The Gender of Oppression: Men, Masculinity and the Critique of Marxism*, Brighton: Wheatsheaf Books.

Hearn, Jeff, and Morgan, David (1990), *Men, Masculinities and Social Theory*, London: Unwin Hyman.

Hearn, Jeff, and Ford, David (1991), *Studying Men and Masculinity: a Sourcebook of Literature and Materials*, Bradford: University of Bradford.

Horrocks, Roger (1994), *Masculinity in Crisis: Myths, Fantasies and Realities*, Basingstoke: Macmillan.

Jackson, David (1990), *Unmasking Masculinity: A Critical Autobiography*, London: Unwin Hyman.

Kimmel, Michael (1988), *Changing Men: New Directions in Research on Men and Masculinity*, New York, NY: Sage Publications.

Kimmel, Michael, and Messner, Michael (eds) (1997), *Men's Lives*, third edition, London: Prentice Hall.

Kroker, Arthur, and Kroker, Marilouise (1991), *The Hysterical Male: New Feminist Theory*, Basingstoke: Macmillan.

Lyndon, Neil (1992), *No More Sex War: the Failures of Feminism*, London: Sinclair-Stevenson.

Lyndon, Neil (1993), *The Myth of Male Power: Why Men are the Disposable Sex*, London: Mandarin.

MacInnes, John (1998), *The End of Masculinity: the Collapse of Patriarchy in Modern Societies*, Buckingham: Open University Press.

Messner, Michael (1997), *Politics of Masculinities: Men in Movements*, London: Sage Publications.

Metcalf, Andy, and Humphries, Martin (1990), *Sexuality of Men*, London: Pluto Press.

Millar, Stuart (1997), 'Here Comes Trouble', *The Guardian*, 13 February.

Morgan, David (1990), *Discovering Men*, London: Routledge.

Porter, David (ed.) (1992), *Between Men and Feminism*, London: Routledge.

Roberts Yvonne (1992), *Mad About Women: Can There Ever be Fair Play Between the Sexes?*, London: Virago.

Segal, Lynne (1990), *Slow Motion: Changing Masculinities, Changing Men*, London: Virago.

Seidler, Victor (1989), *Rediscovering Masculinity: Reason, Language and Sexuality*, London: Routledge.

Seidler, Victor (1991), *Recreating Sexual Politics: Men, Feminism and Politics*, London: Routledge.

Chapter 5 Selling sex: the commercialisation of sex and sexuality

The media and commercial advertising

Baehr, Helen, and Gray, Ann (eds) (1996), *Turning it On: A Reader in Women and Media*, London: Edward Arnold.

Ballaster, Rosalind, et al. (1991), *Women's Worlds: Ideology, Femininity and Women's Magazines*, London: Macmillan.

Berger, John (1972), *Ways of Seeing*, Harmondsworth: Penguin Books.

Bonner, Frances, et al. (1992), *Imagining Women: Cultural Representation and Gender*, Cambridge: Open University Press/Polity Press.

Craig, Steve (1992), *Men, Masculinity and the Media*, London: Sage Publications.

Elliott, Judy, and Wootton, Tony (1997), 'Some Ritual Idioms of Gender in British Television Advertising', *Sociological Review*, vol. 45, no. 3.

Friedan, Betty (1963), *The Feminine Mystique*, New York, NY: W. W. Norton.

Gamson, Joshua (1998), 'Publicity Traps: Television Talk Shows and Lesbian, Gay, Bisexual and Transgender Visibility', *Sexualities*, vol. 1, no. 1, February.

Holmberg, Carl B. (1998), *Sexualities and Popular Culture*, London: Sage Publications.

Humm, Maggie (1997), *Feminism and Film*, Edinburgh: Edinburgh University Press.

Macdonald, Myra (1995), *Representing Women: Myths of Femininity in the Popular Media*, London: Edward Arnold.

Nixon, Sean (1996), *Hard Looks: Masculinities, Spectatorship and Contemporary Consumption*, London: UCL Press.

Signorile, Michelangelo (1994), *Queer in America: Sex, the Media and the Closets of Power*, London: Abacus.

Simpson, Mark (1994), *Male Impersonators: Men Performing Masculinity*, London: Cassell.

Simpson, Mark (1996), *It's a Queer World*, London: Radius.

Smith, Joan (1989), *Misogynies*, London: Faber and Faber.

Smith, Joan (1997), *Different For Girls: How Culture Creates Women*, London: Faber and Faber.

Tseelon, Efrat (1995), *The Masque of Femininity: the Presentation of Women in Everyday Life*, London: Sage Publications.

van Zoonen, Liesbet (1994), *Feminist Media Studies*, London: Sage Publications.

Waites, Bernard, et al. (1982), *Popular Culture: Past and Present*, London: Croom Helm/Open University Press.

Prostitution

Alexander, Priscilla (1996), 'Prostitution: a Difficult Issue for Feminists', in Jackson and Scott (eds), *Feminism and Sexuality: a Reader*, Edinburgh: Edinburgh University Press, pp. 342–57.

Delacoste, Frederique and Alexander, Priscilla (eds) (1988), *Sex Work: Writings By Women in the Sex Industry*, London: Cleis Press.

Gibson, Barbara (1995), *Male Order: Life Stories from Boys who Sell Sex*, London: Cassell.

Hoigard, Cecilie, and Finstad, Liv (1992), *Backstreets: Prostitution, Money and Love*, Cambridge: Polity Press.

Hoigard, Cecilie, and Finstad, Liv (1996), 'Prostitutes and Their Clients', in Jackson and Scott (eds), *Feminism and Sexuality: a Reader*, Edinburgh: Edinburgh University Press, pp. 358–66.

Kempadoo, Kemala, and Doezeme, Jo (1998), *Global Sex Workers: Rights, Resistance and Redefinition*, London: Routledge.

Lloyd, Robin (1979), *Playland: a Study of Human Exploitation*, London: Quartet.

McIntosh, Mary (1996), 'Feminist Debates on Prostitution', in Adkins and Merchant (eds), *Sexualizing the Social: Power and the Organization of Sexuality*, Basingstoke: Macmillan, pp. 191–203.

McKeganey Neil, and Barnard, Marina (1996), *Sex Work on the Streets: Prostitutes and their Clients*, London: Open University Press.

McLeod, Eileen (1982), *Women Working: Prostitution Now*, London: Croom Helm.

O'Connell Davidson, Julia (1996), 'Prostitution and the Contours of Control', in Weeks and Holland (eds), *Sexual Cultures: Communities, Values and Intimacy*, Basingstoke: Macmillan, pp. 180–98.

Sharpe, Karen (1998), *Red Light, Blue Light: Prostitutes, Punters and the Police*, Aldershot: Ashgate Publishing.

Walkowitz, Judith (1996), 'The Politics of Prostitution', in Jackson and Scott (eds), *Feminism and Sexuality: a Reader*, Edinburgh: Edinburgh University Press, pp. 288–96.

Pornography: the commodification of sex

Assiter, Alison (1989), *Pornography, Feminism and the Individual*, London: Pluto Press.

Assiter, Alison, and Avedon, Carol (eds) (1993), *Bad Girls and Dirty Pictures: the Challenge to Reclaim Feminism*, London: Pluto Press.

Cameron, Deborah, and Frazer, Elizabeth (1996), 'On the Question of Pornography and Sexual Violence: Moving Beyond Cause and Effect', in Jackson and Scott (eds), *Feminism and Sexuality: a Reader*, Edinburgh: Edinburgh University Press, pp. 321–32.

Dines, Gail, Jensen, Robert, and Russo, Ann (1998), *Pornography: the Production and Consumption of Inequality*, London: Pluto Press.

Dworkin, Andrea (1981), *Pornography: Men Possessing Women*, London: The Women's Press.

Easton, Susan (1994), *The Problem of Pornography*, London: Routledge.

Gubar, Susan, and Hoff, Joan (1989), *For Adult Users Only: the Dilemma of Violent Pornography*, Bloomington, IN: Indiana University Press.

Hunter, Ian, Saunders, David, and Williamson, Dugald (1992), *On Pornography*, London: Macmillan.

Itzin, Catharine (ed.) (1992), *Pornography: Women, Violence, and Civil Liberties*, Oxford: Oxford University Press.

Kimmel, Michael (ed.) (1991), *Men Confronting Pornography*, New York, NY: Meridian.

Lambevski, Sasho (1999), 'Suck My Nation – Masculinity, Ethnicity and the Politics of (Homo)Sex', *Sexualities*, vol. 2, no. 4.

Linz, Daniel, and Malamuth, Neil (1993), *Pornography*, London: Sage Publications.

MacKinnon, Catharine (1987), *Feminism Unmodified: Discourses on Life and Law*, London: Harvard University Press.

MacKinnon, Catharine (1993), *Only Words*, London: Harvard University Press.

McIntosh, Mary (1996), 'Liberalism and the Contradictions of Oppression', in Jackson and Scott (eds), *Feminism and Sexuality: a Reader*, Edinburgh: Edinburgh University Press, pp. 333–41.

O'Toole, Laurence (1998), *Pornocopia: Porn, Sex, Technology and Desire*, London: Serpent's Tail.

Rodgerson, Gillian and Wilson, Elizabeth (1991), *Pornography and Feminism: the Case Against Censorship*, London: Lawrence and Wishart.

Russell, Diana (ed.) (1993), *Making Violence Sexy: Feminist Views on Pornography*, Buckingham: Open University Press.

Russell, Diana (1998), *Dangerous Relationships: Pornography, Misogyny and Rape*, London: Sage Publications.

Segal, Lynne, and Wilson, Elizabeth (eds) (1992), *Sex Exposed: Sexuality and the Pornography Debate*, London: Virago.

Segal, Lynne (1998), 'Only the literal: the contradictions of anti–pornography feminism', *Sexualities*, vol. 1, no. 1, February.

Short, Clare (1991), *Dear Clare: This is what Women Feel about Page Three*, London: Radius.

Thompson, Bill (1994), *Soft Core: Moral Crusades Against Pornography in Britain and America*, London: Cassell.

Chapter 6 Regulating gender and sexuality: the state and the public policy agenda

General reading

Bridgeman, Jo, Millns, Susan and Moody, Susan (1995), *Law and Body Politics: Regulating the Female Body*, Aldershot: Dartmouth.

David, Miriam (1983), 'The New Right in the USA and Britain: a New Anti-feminist Moral Economy', *Critical Social Policy*, vol. 2, no. 3.

Durham, Martin (1991), *Sex and Politics: The Family and Morality in the Thatcher Years*, London: Macmillan.

Durham, Martin (1997), 'Conservative agendas and Government Policy', in Segal (ed.), *New Sexual Agendas*, Basingstoke: Macmillan. pp. 90–100.

Edwards, Susan (ed.) (1985), *Gender, Sex and the Law*, London: Croom Helm.

Foley, Conor (1995), *Human Rights, Human Wrongs: the Alternative Report to the UN*, London: Rivers Oram Press.
Gelsthorpe, Loraine, and Morris, Allison (eds) (1990), *Feminist Perspectives in Criminology*, Buckingham: Open University Press.
Randall, Vicky, and Waylen, Georgina (eds) (1998), *Gender, Politics and the State*, London: Routledge.
Smart, Carol (1995), *Law, Crime and Sexuality: Essays in Feminism*, London: Sage Publications.
Stychin, Carl (1995), *Law's Desire: Sexuality and the Limits of Justice*, London: Taylor and Francis.

Introduction

Durham, Martin (1991), *Sex and Politics: The Family and Morality in the Thatcher Years*, London: Macmillan.
Durham, Martin (1997), 'Conservative agendas and Government Policy', in Segal (ed.), *New Sexual Agendas*, Basingstoke: Macmillan. pp. 90–100.
Grant, Linda (1993), *Sexing the Millennium: Women and the Sexual Revolution*, London: Grove Press.

Promoting heterosexuality: the state and the enforcement of discrimination

National AIDS Trust (1998), *Aids 2000*, London: Millivres.
Coxon, Anthony (1996), *Between the Sheets: Sexual Diaries and Gay Men's Sex in the Era of AIDS*, London: Cassell.
Davenport-Hines, R. T. P. (1991), *Sex, Death and Punishment: Attitudes to Sex and Sexuality in Britain since the Renaissance*, London: Fontana.
Equality Network (1999), *Equality at Holyrood*, Edinburgh: Equality Network.
Garfield, Simon (1994), *The End of Innocence: Britain in the Time of AIDS*, London: Faber and Faber.
Holland, Janet, Ramazanoglu, Caroline, and Scott, Sue (1990), 'AIDS: from panic stations to power relations: sociological perspectives and problems', *Sociology*, vol. 24, no. 3.
King, Edward (1993), *Safety in Numbers: Safer Sex and Gay Men*, London: Cassell.
Richardson, Diane (1996), 'Contradictions in Discourse: Gender, Sexuality and HIV/AIDS', in Holland and Adkins (eds), *Sex, Sensibility and the Gendered Body*, Basingstoke: Macmillan, pp. 161–77.
Slater, Douglas and Mason, Angela (n.d.), *The Wrong Side of That Somewhere: Where Public Policy Stops and Private Morals Start for Homosexual Men and the Criminal Law*, London: Stonewall Publications.
Stonewall (1998), *Equality 2000*, London: Stonewall.
Waldby, Catherine (1996), *AIDS and the Body Politic*, London: Routledge.
Watney, Simon (1994), *Practices of Freedom: Selected Writings on HIV/AIDS*, London: Rivers Oram Press.

Weeks, Jeffrey (1992), 'The Body and Sexuality', in Bocock and Thompson (eds), *Social and Cultural Forms of Modernity*, Oxford: Polity Press, pp. 119.

Weeks, Jeffrey, Aggleton, Peter, McKevitt, Chris, Parkinson, Kay and Taylor-Laybourn, Austin (1996), 'Community Responses to HIV and AIDS: The "De-Gaying" and "Re-Gaying" of AIDS', in Weeks and Holland (eds), *Sexual Cultures: Communities, Values and Intimacy*, Basingstoke: Macmillan, pp. 161–79.

Wilton, Tamsin (1992), *Antibody Politic: AIDS and Society*, London: New Clarion Press.

Wilton, Tamsin, Doyall, Lesley, and Naidoo, Jennie (eds) (1994), *AIDS: Setting a Feminist Agenda*, London: Taylor and Francis.

Family policy and changing family realities

Abbott, Pamela, and Wallace, Claire (1992), *The Family and the New Right*, London: Pluto Press.

Ali, Turan, Robinson, Tom, and Hopper, Cathrine (1996), *We Are Family: Testimonies of Lesbian and Gay Parents*, London: Cassell.

Allan, Graham (1985), *Family Life*, Oxford: Blackwell.

Blaikie, Andrew (1996), 'From "Immorality" to "Underclass": the Current and Historical Context of Illegitimacy', in Weeks and Holland (eds), *Sexual Cultures: Communities, Values and Intimacy*, Basingstoke: Macmillan, pp. 115–36.

Chandler, Joan (1991), *Women Without Husbands: an Exploration of the Margins of Marriage*, Basingstoke: Macmillan.

Collier, Richard (1995), *Masculinity, Law and Family*, London: Routledge.

Collier, Richard (1998), *Family Law*, London: Longman.

Davies, Jon (ed.) (1993), *The Family: is it Just Another Lifestyle Choice?*, London: Institute of Economic Affairs.

Dennis, Norman (1993), *Rising Crime and the Dismembered Family*, London: Institute of Economic Affairs.

Dennis, Norman, and Erdos, George (1993), *Families Without Fatherhood*, second edition, London: Institute of Economic Affairs.

Ford, Reuben, and Millar, Jane (1998), *Private Lives and Public Responses: Lone Parenthood and Future Policy*, London: Policy Studies Institute.

Fraad, Harriet, Resnick, Stephen, and Wolff, Richard (1994), *Bringing it all Back Home: Class, Gender and the Modern Household*, London: Pluto Press.

Gelles, Richard (1994), *Contemporary Families: a Sociological View*, London: Sage Publications.

Gillis, John (1996), *A World of Their Own Making: a History of Myth and Ritual in Family Life*, Oxford: Oxford University Press.

Gittins, Diana (1993), *The Family in Question: Changing Households and Familiar Ideologies*, Basingstoke: Macmillan.

Harding, L. (1996), *Family, State and Social Policy*, Basingstoke: Macmillan.

Jackson, Gordon, and Stepney, Paul (1995), 'The Children Act 1989 – Protection or Persecution?: Family Support and Child Protection in the 1990s', *Critical Social Policy*, vol. 15, no. 43.

Jones, Helen and Millar, Jane (1996), *The Politics of the Family*, Aldershot: Avesbury.

Laws, Sophie (1996), 'The "Single Mothers" Debate: A Children's Rights Perspective', in Holland and Adkins (eds), *Sex, Sensibility and the Gendered Body*, Basingstoke: Macmillan, pp. 60–77.

Lewis, Jane, Kiernen, Kathleen, and Land, Hilary (1998), *Lone Motherhood in Twentieth Century Britain*, Oxford: Oxford University Press.

Morgan, Patricia (1995), *Farewell to the Family? Public Policy and Family Breakdown in Britain and the USA*, London: Institute of Economic Affairs.

Mount, Ferdinand (1982), *The Subversive Family*, London: Counterpoint.

O'Donovan, Katherine (1993), *Family Law Matters*, London: Pluto Press.

Parton, Nigel (1991), *Governing the Family: Child Care, Child Protection and the State*, Basingstoke: Macmillan.

Robertson Elliot, Faith (1995), *Gender, Family and Society*, Basingstoke: Macmillan.

Rodger, John (1996), *Family Life and Social Control: a Sociological Perspective*, Basingstoke: Macmillan.

Rowlingson, Karen, and McKay, Stephen (1998), *The Growth of Lone Parenthood: Diversity and Dynamics*, London: Policy Studies Institute.

Saffron, Lisa (1996), *What About the Children? Sons and Daughters of Lesbian and Gay Parents Speak About Their Lives*, London: Cassell.

Segal, Lynne (ed.) (1983), *What is to be Done About the Family?*, Harmondsworth: Penguin Books.

Smart, Carol (1984), *The Ties that Bind: Law, Marriage and the Reproduction of Patriarchal Relations*, London: Routledge and Kegan Paul.

Smart, Carol (1992), *Regulating Womanhood: Historical Essays on Marriage, Motherhood and Sexuality*, London: Routledge.

Smart, Carol, and Sevenhuijsen, Selma (1989), *Child Custody and the Politics of Gender*, London: Routledge.

VanEvery, Jo (1991–2) 'Who is "the Family"? The Assumptions of British Social Policy', *Critical Social Policy*, no. vol. no. 33.

Weeks, Jeffrey (1992), 'The Body and Sexuality', in Bocock and Thompson (eds), *Social and Cultural Forms of Modernity*, Cambridge: Polity Press.

State responses to sexual violence

Allison, Julie A., and Wrightman, Lawrence S. (1993), *Rape: the Misunderstood Crime*, London: Sage Publications.

Archer, John (ed.) (1994), *Male Violence*, London: Routledge.

Barnett, Ola, and LaViolette, Alyce (1993), *It Could Happen to Anyone: Why Battered Women Stay*, London: Sage Publications.

Bart, Pauline, and Moran, Eileen Geil (1993), *Violence Against Women: Gender and Society Reader*, London: Sage Publications.

Binney, Val (1988), *Leaving Violent Men*, London: Women's Aid Federation.

Bourlet, Alan (1990), *Police Intervention in Marital Violence*, Buckingham: Open University Press.

Brown, Beverley, Burman, Michele, and Jamieson, Lynn (eds) (1993), *Sex Crimes on Trial: the Use of Sexual Evidence in Scottish Courts*, Edinburgh: Edinburgh University Press.

Cameron, Deborah, and Frazer, Elizabeth (1987), *The Lust to Kill: a Feminist Investigation of Sexual Murder*, Cambridge: Polity Press/Blackwell.

Charles, Nickie (1995), 'Feminist Politics, Domestic Violence and the State', *Sociological Review*, vol. 43, no. 4.

Edwards, Susan (1989), *Policing 'Domestic' Violence: Women, the Law and the State*, London: Sage Publications.

Edwards, Anne (1996), 'Gender and Sexuality in the Social Construction of Rape and Consensual Sex: A Study of Process and Outcome in Six Recent Rape Trials', in Holland and Adkins (eds), *Sex, Sensibility and the Gendered Body*, Basingstoke: Macmillan, pp. 178–201.

Goldsack, Laura and Radford, Jill (1999), *Feminist Perspectives on Domestic Violence*, London: Longman.

Hague, Gill and Malos, Ellen (1994), *Domestic Violence: Action for Change*, London: New Clarion Press.

Hearn, Jeff (1998), *The Violences of Men: How men talk about and how agencies respond to men's violence to known women*, London: Sage Publications.

Hollway, Wendy and Jefferson, Tony (1998), '"A Kiss is Just a Kiss": Date Rape, Gender and Subjectivity', *Sexualities*, 1, 4, November.

Holmes, Ronald M. (1991), *Sex Crimes*, London: Sage Publications.

Hopkins, June (ed.) (1984), *Perspectives on Rape and Sexual Assault*, London: Harper and Row.

Jamieson, Lynn (1996), 'The Social Construction of Consent Revisited', in Adkins and Merchant (eds), *Sexualizing the Social: Power and the Organization of Sexuality*, Basingstoke: Macmillan, pp. 55–73.

Kelly, Liz (1989), *Surviving Sexual Violence*, Cambridge: Polity Press.

Kelly, Liz, and Radford, Jill (1990–1), '"Nothing Really Happened": the Invalidation of Women's Experience of Sexual Violence', *Critical Social Policy*, vol. 10, no. 30.

Kennedy Bergen, Raquel (1998), *Issues in Intimate Violence*, London: Sage Publications.

Lees, Sue (1996), *Carnal Knowledge: Rape on Trial*, London: Hamish Hamilton.

Lees, Sue (1997), *Ruling Passions: Sexual Violence, Reputation and the Law*, Buckingham: Open University Press.

Lees, Sue (1999), 'The Accused', in *The Guardian*, 1 March.

Maguire, Sara (1988), '"Sorry Love" – Violence Against Women in the Home and the State Response', *Critical Social Policy*, vol. 8, no. 23.

Matoesian, Gregory M. (1992), *Reproducing Rape: Domination Through Talk in the Courtroom*, Cambridge: Polity Press.

McColgan, Aileen (1996), *The Case for Taking the Date out of Rape*, London: Rivers Oram Press.

McMullen, Ritchie (1990), *Male Rape: Breaking the Silence on the Last Taboo*, London: Gay Men's Press.

Pizzey, Erin (1979), *Scream Quietly or the Neighbours Will Hear*, Harmondsworth: Penguin Books.

Russell, Diana (1990), *Rape in Marriage*, Bloomington, IN: Indiana University Press.

Scully, Diana (1990), *Understanding Sexual Violence*, London: Routledge.

Searles, Patricia, and Berger, Ronald (eds) (1995), *Rape and Society: Readings on the Problem of Sexual Assault*, Boulder, CO: Westview Press.

Stanko, Elizabeth (1990), *Everyday Violence; How Men and Women Experience Sexual and Physical Danger*, London: Rivers Oram Press.

Temkin, Jennifer (ed.) (1995), *Rape and the Criminal Justice System*, Aldershot: Dartmouth.

Thomas, Alison M., and Kitzinger, Celia (1997), *Sexual Harassment: Contemporary Feminist Perspectives*, Buckingham: Open University Press.

Tifft, Larry (1993), *Battering of Women: The Failure of Intervention and the Case for Prevention*, Boulder, CO: Westview Press.

Ward, Colleen (1995), *Attitudes Toward Rape*, London: Sage Publications.

Index

Index